Psychology and Biology of Language and Thought

ESSAYS IN HONOR OF ERIC LENNEBERG

Eric H. Lenneberg

1921–1975

Psychology and Biology
of Language and Thought
ESSAYS IN HONOR OF ERIC LENNEBERG

EDITED BY

George A. Miller
Elizabeth Lenneberg

ACADEMIC PRESS   New York   San Francisco   London   1978
A Subsidiary of Harcourt Brace Jovanovich, Publishers

ACADEMIC PRESS, INC.
111 Fifth Avenue, New York, New York 10003

United Kingdom Edition published by
ACADEMIC PRESS, INC. (LONDON) LTD.
24/28 Oval Road, London NW1 7DX

Library of Congress Cataloging in Publication Data
Main entry under title:

Psychology and biology of language and thought.

    "Bibliography of the writings of Eric H. Lenneberg" : p.
    Includes bibliographies.
     1.   Psycholinguistics––Addresses, essays, lectures.
2.   Thought and thinking––Addresses, essays, lectures.
3.   Psychobiology––Addresses, essays, lectures.
I.   Miller, George Armitage, Date   II.   Lenneberg,
Elizabeth.   III.   Lenneberg, Eric H.
BF455.P786   153   78–12788
ISBN 0–12–497750–2

This volume in tribute to Eric Lenneberg is dedicated by its editors to his son and daughter,
Roger A. Lenneberg and Miriam Lenneberg Alejandro

Contents

List of Contributors

Numbers in parentheses indicate the pages on which the authors' contributions begin.

Joseph Altman (87), Laboratory of Developmental Neurobiology, Department of Biological Sciences, Purdue University, West Lafayette, Indiana 47907

Roger Brown (151), Department of Psychology and Social Relations, Harvard University, Cambridge, Massachusetts 02138

Jack Catlin* (271), Department of Psychology, Cornell University, Ithaca, New York 14853

Noam Chomsky (199), Department of Linguistics and Philosophy, Massachusetts Institute of Technology, Cambridge, Massachusetts 02139

Nancy Kopell (65), Department of Mathematics, Northeastern University, Boston, Massachusetts 02115

Simeon Locke (111), Department of Neurology, Harvard Medical School, Boston, Massachusetts 02115

Humberto R. Maturana (27), Faculty of Sciences, University of Chile, Santiago, Chile

George A. Miller (1, 167), The Rockefeller University, New York, New York 10021

Hermine Sinclair (187), Ecole de Psychologie et des Sciences de l'Education, University of Geneva, CH-1211 Geneva 14, Switzerland

Aaron Smith (133), Department of Physical Medicine and Rehabilitation, Neuropsychological Laboratory, University of Michigan, Ann Arbor, Michigan 48109

Gabriel Stolzenberg (221), Department of Mathematics, Northeastern University, Boston, Massachusetts 02115

Paul A. Weiss (13), The Rockefeller University, New York, New York 10021

O. L. Zangwill (119), Department of Psychology, University of Cambridge, Cambridge CB2 3EB, England

* Deceased

Acknowledgments

The conference in honor of Eric Lenneberg, of which these essays are a reflection, was held at Cornell University in May 1976, approximately 1 year after his death. The group of people gathered in Ithaca on that occasion would have delighted Eric, so representative were they of his bewildering variety of intellectual interests. What would have delighted him still more was the spirit of the conference as a whole, the enthusiastic response of those participating to the very diversity of the papers presented.

The stature of the speakers at this meeting, and the importance of their contributions to it, are fitting testimony to Eric the man and the scientist. But the conference itself—that it happened at all and happened so well—was testimony to Eric the teacher, for it was his students, particularly Avis Cohen and Helen Neville, who were in large part responsible for devising a program that spoke to all his interests and for securing the participation of the speakers.

Good counsel and great encouragement were given them by Eric's colleagues at Cornell and elsewhere, particularly Harry Levin, Bruce Halpern, Roger Brown, and George Miller. But credit for the success of the conference (and it was an enormous success) is due mainly to Helen and Avis who, along with Barbara Susan Long, took many hours away from their own research to write the necessary letters, make innumerable phone calls, see that programs were printed and invitations issued, arrange for the accommodation and feeding of the multitude, and so forth and on and on. It was my privilege to be part of the planning, though not much a part of all the hard work. And it was my very great pleasure to be present during the wonderful weekend that climaxed all their months of effort.

We are all deeply indebted to Cornell University for hosting this event and, particularly, to the Grant Foundation and the National Science Foundation for the funds that made it possible.

Elizabeth Lenneberg

Introduction

GEORGE A. MILLER

Psychologists sometimes play a game of backward associations. Starting with one of those carefully tabulated lists of word associations that some psychologists are so fond of, the initiator of the game reads aloud one of the least frequent associations and the other players try to guess what test word could have elicited it. If all players fail, another association is read and the players try again. The game proceeds in this way, with the initiator giving ever more frequent associations, until someone guesses correctly and thereby is declared the winner.

The task of a reader of this volume is not totally unlike that of a player of the backward word-association game. The task is not, of course, to guess who all these contributors were honoring. That information was provided in advance by the initiators of the conference. The task, rather, is to guess what kind of man it could have been whose work, interests, and general frame of mind gained the respect of such a diverse group of scientists. Surely he must have had a large mind, if those who respected him could relate to so many facets of it. Large enough, at least, that these introductory remarks will not

1

PSYCHOLOGY AND BIOLOGY OF LANGUAGE AND THOUGHT
Essays in Honor of Eric Lenneberg

spoil the reader's fun by giving away the true answer, which tragedy has prematurely deprived us of. But the game is well worth playing, nonetheless.

Those willing to search for the character of Eric Lenneberg in this intersection of his friends should be warned, however, that many of the clues provided here are not what they may seem to be. This is not the fault of the initiators of the conference, who made every effort to construct a program of papers that Lenneberg would have enjoyed. But what interested Lenneberg and drew him into association with a particular contributor was not always what that contributor contributed to this volume. This spice was added for a variety of reasons. Some felt that what interested Lenneberg would be too technical for a general audience; some may have failed to grasp why their work interested Lenneberg or how it enriched his thought about apparently unrelated problems; some, perhaps sensing the man's ambition for a new intellectual synthesis, were inspired to attempt syntheses of their own. Consequently a determined player must enrich these clues, not only by studying Lenneberg's own writings, but also by delving deeper into the work of those he admired. It is not an easy game, but every player will be a winner—and the rewards are guaranteed to be proportional to a player's commitment to it.

The reader's task, therefore, is one of synthesis, and that is appropriate because synthesis was also Lenneberg's task. How he approached it can be gleaned from his 1967 book, *Biological Foundations of Language*. Even before 1967, the existence of biological foundations of language was clear enough from a variety of well-known facts:

1. Although other animals communicate, spoken language is uniquely human.
2. All human societies have languages that share certain general features.
3. Every normal member of the human species acquires language.
4. Language development in children unfolds in very regular ways.
5. Special evolutionary adaptations have fitted man for language.
6. Injuries to particular parts of the nervous system can result in abnormalities of language.

Each of these facts is important; each had stimulated a search for explanations in different scientific disciplines. It was Lenneberg, however, who saw most clearly that these facts were not unrelated, that how we explain one of them cannot be unrelated to how we explain the others. Pursuit of this realization was a task of synthesis; the product of this synthesis was a new scientific discipline, the biology of language, cutting across such older disciplines as psychology, linguistics, anthropology, neurology, physiology, and genetics. Those who come to this new discipline today must find it difficult to appreciate how it could ever have been otherwise, or what pain its synthesis could have caused its creator.

Synthesis is generally thought to be the converse of analysis, yet in the realms of intellectual activity the two are far from symmetric. Analysis is far easier. The basic lessons in almost every branch of science seem to be devoted to mastering analysis, whether it is the analysis of space into coordinates, the mathematical decomposition of complex functions into orthogonal components, the chemical analysis of a compound into elements, the biological analysis of organisms into organ systems or of tissues into cells, the psychological analysis of behavior into stimuli and responses, the linguistic analysis of sentences into phrases and words—the list goes on and on. Students of science are bombarded by rules of analysis. Given any interesting object or phenomenon, scientists typically proceed to analyze it into uninteresting parts. Synthesis, by comparison, is poorly understood, and where it is understood it is usually understood as the process of putting back together what analysis had previously taken apart.

A remarkable thing about this asymmetry in our understanding is that the closer we approach the study of man the worse it gets. Microbiologists can now synthesize complex organic molecules and even parts of cells; their achievements have been so spectacular that no one would think of criticizing them for not yet synthesizing a cow. At more abstract levels, we have some ideas how particular kinds of behavior or symbolic communication might be analyzed, but how they are synthesized by the behaving, communicating organism is still a mystery.

Fortunately, the prospects for understanding such syntheses are no longer as dark as they once were. In this century, scientists have begun to study a concept that is widely known as "the system." Their ideas were foreshadowed in the nineteenth century by the invention of governors for steam engines and by the discovery of internal self-regulation in organisms, but the real work on systems has only just begun. It is characteristic of systems that they exhibit properties that would not be suspected from a study of their parts in isolation, properties that tend to be lost under analysis. As we have come to understand better what these properties are and how to characterize them, we have opened new ways of thinking about synthesis.

It is no accident that progress in understanding the properties of complex systems has proceeded on two fronts: on the one hand, in the engineering of ever more complex machines and, on the other hand, in the understanding of biological systems. The parallel between these two intellectual adventures was recognized by Norbert Wiener, who joined them together in the new science that he dubbed *cybernetics*. Although their affinities are obvious, however, workers on both sides of the fence have frequently expressed doubts as to whether it is yet time to take the fence down. Many of those who are most knowledgeable about the properties of complex modern machines run by computers are embarrassed by biological or psychological analogies; many of those most knowledgeable about biological and psychological systems still refuse to accept the computer analogy. Good fences, both seem to say, make good neighbors.

Those biologists who are most reluctant to model biological systems in terms of computers or computer programs are, by and large, those who are most interested in the processes of growth—which is, after all, the paradigm of biological synthesis. As long as a theorist is content to stay at a level of abstraction where the functional properties of a system do not depend critically on the material properties of its components, engineers and biologists can think profitably together. When details of the manufacture or the growth of a system are at issue, however, the material properties of its components cannot be ignored. Then the analogies usually become too strained or too abstract to be a serious interest.

Growth, of course, was one of Lenneberg's passionate interests. It is not surprising, therefore, that he turned to the biological rather than the engineering approach to systems. Nor is it surprising that this turn brought him into contact with Paul Weiss, whose brilliant studies of growth in living systems are rivaled in importance only by his pioneering recognition of the need for a theory of systems in understanding all biological processes, large and small.

Weiss (Chapter 1) sees system thinking as allowing a reconciliation between holism and reductionism, and offers an objective criterion for recognizing a system when we see one: A system is much less variable than would be predicted by summing the variabilities of its component parts. Living systems, moreover, are hierarchically organized; systems can be recognized as component parts of larger systems. Weiss's contribution to the symposium was originally intended to be a discussion of the papers by Altman, Kopell, and Maturana, but his remarks were too cogent and important for such a secondary role. They appear here, therefore, as a separate chapter, one that expresses the mature wisdom of a senior scientist on basic issues that Lenneberg struggled with and fought over. Weiss's remarks, probably more than any others, capture the common spirit of all the contributors who were trying to find a larger system of invariants within which to view the variant phenomena of growth, behavior, and language.

Both Maturana and Altman, like Weiss, took a philosophical approach to their subjects. Although Lenneberg was perhaps more interested in their experimental findings than in their philosophical opinions, these speculations are so bold that it is difficult to believe they would not have elicited his full attention and respect.

Since Maturana (Chapter 2) also took system thinking as basic to his argument, its conjunction here with Weiss's views is particularly revealing. For Maturana the central problem is to characterize the observer as a biological system that is both isolated from and coupled to other observers. Whereas Weiss is concerned to define systems in terms of limitations on their degrees of freedom, Maturana defines them in terms of the human observer's capacity to distinguish and specify an entity, a system, from its background. The observer's capacity to describe what he distinguishes, however, depends on his structural coupling to other observers in a consensual domain—which extends system thinking into the realm of social phenomena.

Maturana begins with organisms as closed biological systems and, step by step, builds a language and a point of view adequate to describe how such isolated organisms can operate effectively in a socially valid and seemingly objective physical world. Along the way he develops his views on such challenging questions as the nature of science, materialistic explanation, organization and structure, homeostasis and adaptation, learning and instinct, social consensus, language and communication, reality and prediction, creativity and freedom. Maturana and Weiss illustrate the richness of this approach by their different emphases; together, they offer a hopeful contradiction to the view that science is necessarily analytic and reductionistic, and man the helpless pawn of deterministic nature.

Kopell's (Chapter 3) discussion of various chemical and biological mechanisms that can lead to the formation of regular physical structures can be viewed as providing test cases for systems theorists. Similar structures can result from very different mechanisms. Geometrical descriptions of their form are too superficial, but molecular dissection is too analytic—the mechanisms of pattern formation are lost in the molecular details. What is needed is a systems analysis. It is obvious that the similarity of the patterns must have something to do with how the observer distinguishes systematic entities from their backgrounds. And it is obvious that the variance of the whole is less than the sum of the variances of the parts. But when systems philosophy is confronted by such a variety of theoretical possibilities, it also becomes obvious that a program for formulating answers is very different from a set of well-formulated answers. Philosophy may rationalize science, but it cannot replace it.

Altman's (Chapter 4) philosophy begins from a more traditional concern with the nature of the relation between the mind and the brain. Whereas Maturana makes no attempt to include consciousness in his system thinking about cognition, Altman takes it as a fundamental phenomenon requiring biological explanation. Whereas Altman sees mentation as required for the operation of choice, Maturana denies that organisms make choices—they only seem to because the observer is ignorant of what the system is actually doing. Yet Altman, too, talks about systems, about the structure and organization of hierarchically related neuropsychic systems. It is obvious that system thinking imposes no monolithic dogma on its proponents.

Although Altman's theory of mentation is conventional, his speculations on the neural systems that support pathic, iconic, and noetic mental processing are not. A special system, the anthropocephalon, restricted to the dominant cerebral hemisphere, is said to account for man's capacity for language and the symbolic, noetic mentation that language supports. Routine, unconscious processes, processes requiring no decisions, are mediated by the spinal cord, cerebellum, and basal ganglia; motivational, emotional, pathic processes are mediated by the paleocephalon; iconic percepts, projected into the external world, are mediated by the neencephalon. But the anthropocephalon is uniquely human. Much remains to be learned about the lateralization of functions in the cerebral hemispheres of the human brain; Altman's formulation is not likely to be the final word on this complex matter. But a species-specific neural system to account for a species-specific form of thought and behavior has an intrinsic plausibility that is very attractive.

Psychologists sometimes wonder (and so did Lenneberg) why their neurological colleagues place so much store by the localization of functions in different parts of the brain, since it is not obvious that knowing where something happens tells us much about what is going on there. But localization is merely one aspect of the traditional neurological approach to brain science; a more comprehensive view of the neurological approach would have to include the general assumptions that:

1. Complex brain functions can be decomposed into simpler, more general processes.
2. These component processes can be localized anatomically and studied in relative isolation.
3. Complex behavior can also be decomposed into simpler, more general processes.
4. The simpler brain processes can be correlated directly with the simpler behavioral processes.

This set of assumptions dictates a strategy of research that has been successful often enough in the past to justify its application to the relation between brain and language.

Suppose, for example, that the complex brain functions involved in the use of language were decomposed into sensory processes initiated by acoustic stimuli, motor processes leading to vocalization, and associative processes connecting the sensory and motor systems. The sensory processes can be localized in the auditory system and its projection areas in the cortex; the motor system can be localized as beginning in the cortex and extending through fiber tracts to the articulatory and respiratory musculature; the associative system can be localized in particular regions of the left cerebral hemisphere. Moreover, the use of language can be analyzed into listening, speaking, and comprehending, which are presumably correlated with processes in the sensory, motor, and association systems, respectively. As a first approximation, therefore, the neurological approach seems quite plausible.

As soon as we try to go beyond this gross anatomy, however, we come face to face with the complexity of both human brains and human languages. The critical problems seem to reside in the association system where, presumably, the syntactic, semantic, and pragmatic aspects of language must be accounted for. Since the neurological approach would not be judged successful unless it could at least approximate these distinctions, which are so fundamental for any decomposition of language behavior, much theoretical speculation has been devoted to these central processes. Indeed, some theorists have become so preoccupied with the mysterious role of the cerebral cortex that they write as if they had forgotten the contributions of the more peripheral systems.

Although the highest centers controlling human thought and language may be located in the left cerebral hemisphere, Locke (Chapter 5) reminds us forcefully that speech is a motor skill involving all levels of the hierarchy of neural systems—a reminder that Lenneberg would surely have welcomed. Unfortunately, the medium of print makes it impossible to reproduce here Locke's recordings of the speech of patients with Alzheimer's disease, but in Ithaca they provided a dramatic demonstration of the importance of all levels in the hierarchy. Not all language functioning is a consequence of activity in the cerebral cortex; not all disorders of language functioning are a consequence of cortical lesions.

It would seem, therefore, that much about the motor systems of speech is still not understood. A serious discussion of sensory systems for speech perception would reveal comparable mysteries in the operation of that component, which also involves all levels of the hierarchy of neural systems. When these enigmas are coupled with the enormous complexity of the central brain processes that are supposed to relate speech perception and speech production, the problems seem very challenging indeed.

The uniquely human character of language and the ethics of experimentation on human subjects make it impossible to perform decisive experiments to discover the neurological correlates of human language functions. It has been necessary, therefore, to rely on such natural experiments as misfortune has provided for clinical observation. Zangwill (Chapter 6) reviews more than a century of such evidence, and the kinds of conclusions that have been drawn from it, and argues that it does not support any circumscribed localization of component functions in particular brain centers. He does not conclude, however, that the traditional approach of neurology should be abandoned, but merely that the assumption that component processes can be localized anatomically and studied in isolation is probably inappropriate in the case of language.

Of the four assumptions listed above, however, it is the fourth that seems in greatest need of justification and defense. Even if it should prove to be the case that complex brain processes can be analyzed neurologically and that complex behavioral functions can be analyzed psychologically or linguistically, there is at present little more than optimism to support the faith that neurologically interesting analyses will be psychologically or linguistically interesting, or vice versa. To make the point more obvious, we might imagine an elaborate theory of the economics of communication in industrialized societies; surely no one would expect a successful neurological analysis of language to yield generalizations of any relevance to such an economic analysis, or vice versa. Nor would such a failure be construed as casting doubt on the validity of either neurology or economics. The difference in the levels of explanation accepted in neurology and in psychology or linguistics is, of course, less extreme than the difference between neurology and economics, but the difference is real and deserves critical attention—especially in these days when many psychological and linguistic functions can be performed by machines that have no neurology at all. A basic test of the validity of Lenneberg's synthesis, therefore, will be whether psychologists and linguists are led to general principles that can be correlated with general principles of neural organization and function. This question was the major focus of Lenneberg's research toward the end of his life.

Smith's (Chapter 7) comments on the chapters of Locke and Zangwill relate them not only to Lenneberg's work but also to his own. When compared with the relative uniformity of intact linguistic functioning, the variability of aphasic symptomatology is a clear indication of the need for systems analysis. Zangwill and Smith know as much about the clinical aspects of aphasia as anyone; both recognize the need to rise above the traditional concern with the assignment of specific functions to localizable neural centers. But they are unable to meet the need for a systemic characterization.

This observation sounds harsh, and must be qualified. Many students of language too easily come to regard aphasics as experimental subjects, and are interested in them only insofar as their symptoms reveal something about the neurological mechanisms of speech and language. A physician's immediate responsibility, however, is to his patient and to the amelioration of that patient's affliction. His work is not to be evaluated solely in terms of his contributions to linguistic theory. Smith's optimistic concern with the prospects for retraining and remediation reminds us that the aphasiologist serves two masters.

History will probably remember Lenneberg best for his synthesis of the biological issues that must be faced by any serious student of the human capacity for language. But that was only one aspect of his work. Before he became engrossed in the biological foundations of language, he was a psychologist. Some of his earliest papers, written as a psychologist, were critical discussions of claims by Benjamin Lee Whorf (1956) and others that the language a society speaks places strong constraints on the ways people in that society habitually think about themselves and the world they live in.

It was his desire to test Whorf's hypothesis that led Lenneberg, in the early 1950s, to conduct experiments in color naming. At that time color seemed an ideal domain for such tests. By physical description, in terms of energy and wave length, color formed a seamless continuum that, presumably, man could divide and name however he pleased. It was known that different languages divide the continuum differently; it was believed that the particular way speakers of English divide it is arbitrary—it could be divided differently if all speakers would agree to it. Therefore, if differences in the recognition and memorability of colors could be associated with the names assigned arbitrarily by the conventions of English, that should count as evidence in favor of Whorf's hypothesis.

In retrospect, the choice of color seems ironic. It was subsequently discovered that the focal colors—the best instances of any color named in some language—are much the same everywhere, and depend on the neurophysiology of the human visual system, not on arbitrary conventions of particular societies. Since different languages have different numbers of basic color terms, the *boundaries* between color categories do vary from one language to another, but the names of *focal* instances of whatever colors are named in one language are translatable to other languages. From this research on color naming came most of the ingredients for what Brown calls the new paradigm of reference: variable category boundaries, focal or prototypical instances, a level of basic names. As Brown points out, however, Lenneberg was aware of these ingredients 10 years before the new paradigm began to crystallize. What would probably have interested Lenneberg most, however, is the relation Brown describes between this new paradigm of reference and the order of lexical acquisition in children.

Both Brown and I (Chapters 8 and 9, respectively) write about reference, although we consider very different referents: Brown is concerned principally with concrete objects, I with temporal relations. The lack of any tangible referent for time words is a major source of interest in this aspect of language. When a child learns to call a lemon "lemon," it is reasonably clear what he is learning to refer to, but when he learns to call a past happening "happened," what he has learned is much more obscure. Adults respect a reference time that young children do not; a logical argument is offered that this reference time must be distinguished both from the time of speech and the time of the episode that the utterance identifies. But much remains to be settled in this area—about adult as well as child time language.

Sinclair (Chapter 10) also speaks to Lenneberg's interest in growth and development. She sees a parallel between Lenneberg's views of maturation and those of Jean Piaget, a parallel that would escape those who have not bothered to look behind the fact that Lenneberg studied language and Piaget did not. Both men were concerned with the development of hierarchically related, self-regulating, neural systems. In order to bring out this parallel, Sinclair compares the successive substages in the development of conservation of length (a typical Piagetian study) with those in the development of the ability to express temporal orders of events (a typical psycholinguistic study). In both cases, the child advances by discovering a conflict between two patterns of thought, then finding a more mature pattern of thought that resolves the conflict—by moving through disequilibria to a new equilibrium. Once again, the need for system thinking is obvious; once again, the critical details are still unknown. But the regular unfolding of cognitive and linguistic capacities is clear evidence that there are systematic principles worth searching for.

Lenneberg's concern to put the study of cognitive and linguistic development on a firm biological foundation is treated most sympathetically by Chomsky (Chapter 11), who takes Lenneberg's view of innate mechanisms as his starting point. Chomsky has repeatedly insisted that the study of grammar, not the study of language use, is most likely to provide valid insights into the limits that man's genetic endowment imposes on the languages that it is possible for children to master. It is not that he considers semantic theories of meaning or pragmatic theories of language use to be either hopeless or trivial, but rather that meaning and use reflect to a far greater extent the effects of environmental influences. If psychology is, as Chomsky believes it should be, primarily interested in aspects of mental life that are common to all mankind, psychologists should investigate the principles of grammar that are common to all languages. This advice is based on the assumption (which Catlin questions in Chapter 13) that universal grammar is a theory of innate human mechanisms. To those who complain that studying principles common to all known languages is a task for linguists, not for psychologists, Chomsky replies that, at least in this aspect of their work, linguists *are* psychologists. And to those who protest that the theory of universal grammar is too abstract to support genetic experiments (even if they were ethically feasible), Chomsky replies that he is advancing a scientific hypothesis that, like any other, will be tested, and possibly revised, as better techniques of observation provide better evidence.

Catlin's discussion of the chapters by Chomsky and Stolzenberg concentrates almost exclusively on Chomsky's ideas. Although their shared interest in the biological foundations of language formed a lifelong bond between Lenneberg and Chomsky, Catlin finds Chomsky's claims more extreme than Lenneberg's; Catlin prefers the more cautious view that he attributes to Lenneberg. In particular, he doubts that valid judgments about what is innate and what is learned can be based on the analysis of idealized grammars, independent of detailed information about the conditions under which language actually emerges during the course of development. If Catlin is right, much more research on child language will be required before any claims about innateness can be substantiated.

Catlin, however, would not have contested the claim that deeper understanding of the neurobiology of language will require deeper understanding of language. Where else could serious hypotheses about the neural mechanisms subserving language come from? As Lenneberg was well aware, however, the responsibilities of a neurobiologist are broader than those of a neurolinguist. The human organism is capable not only of learning language, but of such other accomplishments as science, art, and mathematics. Who knows what further untapped capacities it may yet reveal?

There must be biological foundations for conceptual thought as well as for language. Because we are able to understand one another, we must share some minimal capacities for logic. Lenneberg was intrigued by such prospects, but frustrated in his efforts to formulate the issues clearly. It was this interest that attracted him to Stolzenberg, whose views on what the foundations of mathematics can tell us about the human mind fascinated him. Unlike Chomsky, Stolzenberg (Chapter 12) makes no claims about genetic bases for mathematics. His concern is more with the effects of social consensus on what is judged to be true, on what will be accepted as really so—an interesting echo of Maturana's speculations in a very different context. Stolzenberg's analysis of mistakes that result from habits of thought based on uncritical use of language should be of especial interest to both the supporters and the critics of Whorf's principle of linguistic relativity.

These are some of the clues to the thought and character of Eric Lenneberg that readers will find in the following pages. One final hint, however, written by Eric R. Brown (1975):

> Eric Lenneberg's conception of human behavior was different from that held by most research psychologists. Though sometimes called a "nativist," he believed the continuing debate over innate versus environmental factors in human behavior was irrelevant. Behavior for him was "but the outward manifestation of

physiological and anatomical interactions under the impact of environmental stimulation." This is a point of view more congenial to biology than to psychology, but one certainly destined to become increasingly important in the study of human behavior. His conception of the brain was that of a highly integrated organ constantly changing over time according to certain epigenetic trajectories. . . . He believed that man's functional activity cannot be separated from structural changes in the human brain [p. vi].

All contributors to this volume join Eric Brown in mourning the loss of "this courageous and profound thinker" at a time when leadership in developing his new scientific discipline is most needed.

REFERENCES

Brown, Eric. R. Eric H. Lenneberg. In Eric Lenneberg & Elizabeth Lenneberg (Eds.), *Foundations of language development: A multidisciplinary approach.* New York: Academic Press, 1975.
Lenneberg, Eric. *Biological foundations of language.* New York: Wiley, 1967.
Whorf, Benjamin Lee. *Language, thought, and reality.* New York: Wiley, 1956.

chapter 1

Causality: Linear or Systemic?

PAUL A. WEISS

INTRODUCTION

The first three chapters of this volume, although diverse, are all concerned, in spirit and in pertinence, with the principle of the basic conformance of all our biological systems. I think that what emerges here is a consolidated effort to introduce a new and necessary way of thinking, not only in science, but in all human activity. I want to add a few summarizing remarks to this theme (of necessity condensed and hence rather apodictic). The core is the necessity for conciliation between "holism" and "reductionism," which can be achieved by adopting the *system* view of the network causality of nature, rather than relying on the currently dominant linear cause–effect chain reaction concepts (Weiss, 1969, 1973).

I should, perhaps, have given this chapter the title, "Nature discredits all 'isms, and 'isms distort nature." For I will take issue, as I have in my late writings, with the incessant ideological warfare between the addicts of reductionism and those of holism. This is the upshot of my past 59 years in

13

PSYCHOLOGY AND BIOLOGY OF LANGUAGE AND THOUGHT
Essays in Honor of Eric Lenneberg

scientific research, principally laboratory research of a strictly analytical kind. I have learned that we cannot continue to adhere to those traditions inherited from the Greeks. Democritus gave us "atomism." This has retained its prevalence for millennia, up to our own day. Yet it was controverted almost immediately by Heraclitus, in his doctrine of *panta'reih* (all is in flux). However, these views are not strictly antithetic nor mutually exclusive, as is implied by the "either–or" terms in which the issue is commonly presented. Contrary to that concept of fundamental incompatibility, new, sober, practical experience in the life sciences has merged these two one-sided views into a broad and unified perspective.

Reductionism and holism are simply alternative approaches—either from near or from far—to viewing, assessing, and coming to understand nature. And the farther our distance from our subject—that is, the wider the domain we encompass—the less dispensable becomes holistic complementation. *Pari passu,* as the monopoly of *linear causality* as the unique and comprehensive road, not just to knowledge but to understanding, dwindles, the theory of *network causality* (the recognition of systemic cohesiveness) becomes increasingly indispensable. In fact, the verbal expression of causality as a "chain reaction"—that is, an event called "cause" entails a change called "event," which then itself becomes a "cause" yielding a further "event," and so forth—must be regarded as either a colloquialism or a conscious abstraction for the sake of simplicity. Almost all our textbook drawings, by leaving the space between two "related" objects on white paper white, practice that trick, either for *emphasis* on what is momentarily the essential point, or because of actual *ignorance* of what happens between the two objects. Note in this sentence the alternative of two "causes" (emphasis and ignorance, one positive, the other negative). This exemplifies the more restricted definition I have suggested earlier (Weiss, 1973, pp. 101–105) for the term "cause," according to which all so-called causes refer to negative observations; a cause is a phenomenon *without* which an expected correlated change in nature would *not* take place. This should give man some food for thought and care in his choice of language—which leads me to our next question.

WHEN DO WE GIVE A THING A NAME?

This is a question that is frequently discussed with regard to language. But even speechless animals can perfectly well "tell" an edible plant from a poisonous one and can recognize and "identify" a particular *kind* of plant. Cells have the same kind of ability, in that they "recognize" one another and behave accordingly as either affinitive or disaffinitive. In cell biology, this is called "molecular recognition." But cells can also identify each other according to their specific tissue types.

How does man get to calling things and acts by name? Evidently, by his selective awareness of particular items or circumstances in an otherwise undisrupted, unfragmented, and undisruptable universal continuum, which he, in his observing mind, breaks up for his human comprehension into so-called things, parts, entities, attributes, phases, and what not. And from this primary abstraction he then proceeds as if the pieces thus conceived of as "isolated" were actually, in reality, of isolated autonomic "existence" (albeit perhaps "related to" or "interacting with" or "dependent upon," etc., other equally "autonomous" items within or without).

In other words, man extrapolates the subjective range of his limited cerebral recognition of reality, which is to *him* physically perceptible, into a *universal* criterion of corresponding definition.

Now, space is lacking here to dwell further on this shortcoming of human perception and its impotence ever to yield, whether through scientific technology, or mathematical transcription, or verbal circumscription, a truly complete replica or realistic effigy of the world in its totality and wholeness. Yet, two fundamental blocks, at least, should be listed.

In the first place, we give a name to a phenomenon of nature, either observed or deduced, only if in our experience or logical derivation it manifests a certain measure of relative *durability* of properties and pattern (as in "things") or, although its state appears to be more variable than permanent (as in "processes"), it exhibits a definable *regularity* in the mode and timing of its changes. In either case, the time criteria involved in different "natural phenomena" may differ on a scale from the infinitely short (note the ever more shrinking life expectancy of the "elementary particles" of modern physics) to the infinitely long (e.g., in the aeonic periods of astronomy). Thus the nomenclatural schism between the two Greek philosophical generalizations mentioned earlier, of "atomism" at one end and *panta'rhei* at the other, turns out to be merely an expression of the human monomania for endowing antithetical personal viewpoints with the validity of universal pertinence. In fact, both views are equally "true"; it all depends on whether one is looking from the top down or from the bottom up.

The second major misconception inherent in man's attempts to generalize the picture of the world that he has assembled in his own self-contented mind and disseminated profusely as the genuine model of the universe stems from the *primitivity* of that procedure. This primitivity, incidentally, finds no fundamental mitigation in its sophisticated refinements through science or terminological obscuration. The underlying error is em-

bedded in a vicious circle. On the one hand, man realizes (or should) that all
the personal information about "reality" accessible to him by experience or
language is but a filtered emanation of the action of his own brain; on the
other hand, he persists in pretending that that very action must be amenable
to explanatory resolution in terms of solely those filtered cerebral products.
Obviously man, including many a man of science, has inadvertently overlooked this circularity of reasoning. So, should we not explore, for once,
whether that brain machine of ours can "really" give us a "realistic" copy of
the universe?

DEVELOPMENT OF THE BRAIN

The network of lines in Figure 1.1 represents some of the known
interactive processes in the embryonic development of an amphibian brain,
progressing from the egg stage to the finished, mature central nervous
system. These interdependencies have been tracked down by extensive
work in experimental embryology, which has also revealed the high degree
of their individual *variance* prerequisite to the attainment of a steady terminal result—a further evidence for the systemic properties of development.
They thus confirm the general experience that essentially typical end products result adaptively even though the tributary dynamic processes are not

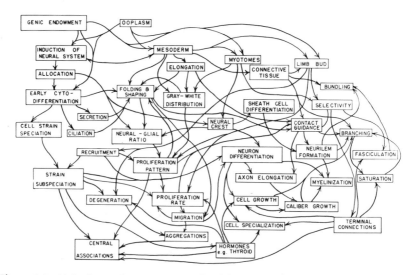

Figure 1.1 Major interactive processes in the elaboration of the nervous system in amphi-
bians, from its early stages to maturity.

stereotyped in the details of their individual component courses. True though this is, the conception of entirely fortuitous ways in the establishment of the eventual traffic lines between the brain and the peripheral organs would be erroneous. In fact, extremists who maintain that the appropriateness of primary cerebral patterns of behavior is molded mainly by trial and error learning have simply been unaware of, or have ignored, the fact that brainy animals, hatched or born without access to sensory information because they lack (or early in development were deprived of) all informative access roads to the brain, perform quite normally when they emerge to the outer world.

The study of nature requires a sober and broad perspective, not a simplistic exploitation of one-sided views. I ought, therefore, to justify our dictum that the brain attains its terminal, fully developed stage with a high degree of structural and functional orderliness, notwithstanding the wide range of freedom of details given to the tributary developmental processes involved in its formation (see Figure 1.1). Most of our difficulty in understanding this apparent incongruity stems from the analytical practice of trying to derive by some sort of backward projection the observable shape or order of a given *final* product from a correspondingly rigid dynamic pattern of its *formative* past. The correct interpretation rests on two facts, one self-evident, the second empirically established.

In the first place, one must keep in mind that the processes of interaction symbolized in Figure 1.1 are by no means so stereotyped as are the rigid lines in the picture. On the contrary, the processes enter into action at different times, their rate of progress is unsteady, and their degree of effectiveness is varied; hence there is a fluctuating hierarchical competition throughout the whole system. Furthermore, the earliest nerve fibers sprouting from the groups of primordial central nerve cells have only very short spans of territory to pass to reach and connect with their prospective internal or peripheral destinations; whether or not such pioneering connections are executed seems to depend on mutually selective contact affinities between senders and receivers.

A second set of factors relevant to the eventual orderliness of the whole then supervenes. The end organs (e.g., muscles or groups of shifting and growing clusters of central nerve cells) take independent courses along surrounding prepatterned tracks, thereby dragging along the strings of pioneering nerve fibers already attached to them with their distal ends. This results in a network of more and more meandering and interlacing cords of primary nerve connections. These pioneering units then become guidelines for the younger fibers that continue to grow out from the still proliferating nerve cell bodies. These younger fibers, which have longer distances to span before they reach their destinations, tend to apply themselves to the surfaces of those of their pioneer precursors that are of matching type-specificity. This principle of "contact guidance" now keeps the aggregate mass from straggling, which ensures some degree of "order in the gross"—that is, lengthwise orientation—although with "arbitrariness" among the additional accessories in their detailed distribution (e.g., the route that single fibers within a bundle take at branching points of the whole mass).

CHARACTERIZING A SYSTEM OBJECTIVELY

This very simple combination of processes is a primitive example of how to characterize a *system* objectively: Its stability, as a whole, is greater than could be calculated simply by summarizing the freer behavior of its componentry; in short, "order in the gross with freedom in the small [Weiss, 1971, p. v]." The objectivity of a system is authenticated by its accessibility to measurement and representation in mathematical terms, as follows: If we record measurements of a set of parameters of one given object (or phenomenon) S over a time T and find them to vary in size or other characters, we can define their average deviation from the mean as *Variance* (V_S). Measuring similarly the relevant parameters of all componental parts (objects or phenomena) of S ($a, b, c, d, \ldots, n$) over the same length of time and under the same conditions as the whole of which they are parts, we establish the individual variances of those parts ($= v_a, v_b, v_c, v_d, \ldots, v_n$). If we then compare V_S with the sum of the variances of the component parts and find the latter sum to be significantly larger than the Variance of the whole complex V_S:

$$V_S << (v_a + v_b + v_c + v_d + \cdots + v_n),$$

the whole thus being revealed as much more *invariable* than the sum of its parts, we have identified S as having the mark of a system. In other words, contrary to the platitudinous statement that "the whole *is* more than the sum of its parts" (the words "*is* more" implying a *numerical* addition of something), systemic wholeness refers solely to *our* recognition of a critical *difference* in the recorded behavior of a given set of partial items, depending on whether *we* study them separately in what appears to us as "random isolation" (in nature or by experimental dispersion) or whether *we* record them in toto on a larger scale in functionally and temporally more invariant states of group interdependence. Again, the sharpness of the differences between such states is likewise a matter of the object of *our* observation and the orbit *we* have chosen to encompass. The relation of the problems of reversibility and irreversibility of "random" and "systems" states to the principle of entropy is too obvious to be taken up here. But for living systems, the variance of ups and downs in energy production and consumption, although admitting reversibility in *parts* (e.g., in regenerative processes), still negates it empirically (i.e., within the range of scientific conceptualization over extended periods of time).

A further key point to be stressed in dealing with the systemic, rather than the mechanical, nature and behavior of "living systems" is their *hierarchical* character; the more variable parts of a higher system of greater invariance can be subsystems of greater stability and invariance than their own subcomponents, and so on, up and down through the universe. A primitive but realistic model of such hierarchical configurations of "systems within systems," like boxes within boxes, is given in Figure 1.2. It indicates the hierarchical encapsulation of a living organism and its componentry within its environment and, similarly, of the components within one another. If we take the genes in the center as the most invariant of the encircled domains (disregarding mutational aberrations), all the more outward shells owe their measure of relatively conservative properties to their own systemic character. The potential interdependence among relations, which accounts for the degree of orderliness in subordinated and superordinated shells despite their own degrees of inner freedom (in the small), is indicated by symbolic outer → inner and inner → outer arrows, all of which

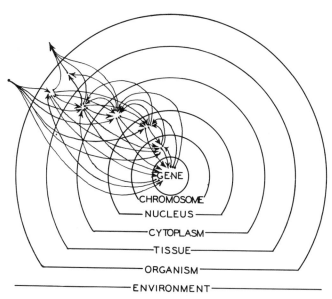

Figure 1.2 Structural suborganization of the components of a living organism.

must be given cognizance in such factual network processes as those symbolized by the arrow nets of brain development in Figure 1.1.

MISREPRESENTING THE BRAIN AS A MECHANICAL MACHINE

This brings us back to our main subject, the brain, and, in particular, its misrepresentation as some sort of mechanical machine operating according to a linear cause–effect program. That misconcept can perhaps be attributed to residues of the original idea that coordinated functions of the nervous system in general are nothing but combinations of rigidly premechanized "reflexes." Let me state, therefore, from the start and without going into further evidence, that true linear reflexes must be considered as terminal specializations within systemic nervous operations, rather than as component rows of the bricks of which neural performances are thought to be composed. And if the preceding comments about the systemic character of all living nature seem incomprehensible or enigmatic, the following factual data about the brain itself may resolve the controversy about whether or not the brain can be viewed as a micromechanically operating gadget. These data stem from the enormous variance and instability of the neural elements that we have come to view as the carriers of cerebral function. That variance is infinitely greater than the one already ascribed to brain development in connection with Figure 1.1. It is based on the following set of numerical data.

The human brain contains about 10^{11} nerve cells (i.e., about 100 billion neurons, not counting glia cells). Each cell has, on an average, about 10^4 (10,000) connections with other cells; so there, already, we have 10^{15} variances of individual and multiply paired cells. Macromolecules per cell, assessed very conservatively at 10^7, raise the total variance to 10^{22}. And finally, my discovery of the "axonal *flow*" has added another factor of variance, amounting to 10^4 in a lifespan of 30 years; this figure is based on the approximate turnover rate of protein in the nerve cell body, but if one were to include the more general macromolecular renewal in the cell that occurs in the up to 100 times faster "intra-axonal *transport*," the variance rate would be still higher. Now, in lumping together all these numbers of the incidence of unstable states on the microlevel of the individual brain function, we arrive at a total sum of probabilities of detailed variations of the order of 10^{26}. This is an astronomically high figure, considering that physicists have estimated the total number of protons in the whole universe to be only about 10^{78}. In interpreting our data, two major points must be kept in mind. On the one hand, the total degree of possible variance is greatly reduced by what was described above as the "hierarchical structure" of the organism (Figure 1.2), which step-by-step maintains the *holistic conformity* of the various subunits. On the other hand, the individual behavior of the subunits is too variable to be ever constrained to interindividually and temporally rigorously standardized, mechanically stereotyped performances. Point one is valid and fully acknowledged; point two, however, in its confirmation of brain function as "systemic" (that is, abiding by the rule of "order in the gross with greater freedom in the small") is the one of greatest importance in the present context.

The antiquated habit of conceiving of the products of our brain activity—our thinking, our decision making, our language, our judgments and prejudices, etc.—as being *mechanistic* performances, comparable to the performance of a wired telephone, must definitely be discarded. Yet, what shall we then substitute as an alternative "explanation"?

The more rigorously we study the dynamics of living systems (indeed, of nature in general), the less satisfactory will be our search for "explanation," in the sense of *understanding*, if it derives solely from the analytical study of isolated fragments of systemic entities (see Weiss, 1975).

In many branches of physics this is, in fact, a commonplace. The thermal uniformity of a huge volume of gas in a container could never be derived from the most meticulous determination of the motile behavior of the component gas molecules individually, followed by simple summation of the data. Actually, the exercise would be an outright waste of time—no single constellation thus recorded would ever repeat itself, and in its hunt for firm rules and laws, science has little interest in nonrecurrent episodes.

Similarly, there would be little scientific sense in cracking walnuts unceasingly to obtain a complete record of the individual configurations of their surface architecture. All this exercise would yield would be an impressive lesson that all walnuts are not "created equal."

The difference between the mere amassing of data (save for statistical needs) on the one hand, and concentration on sets of data that promise to lead to some unifying generalizations, on the other, lies in the scientific purpose of the undertaking. In the latter case, the aim is to deduce a rule of a higher order of the whole as compared to indeterminacy of the individual parts.

Obviously, this is as valid for walnuts as it is for men; as valid, but not of equal relevance. The mere number of tests is no measure of their significance. While we could rightly belittle interminable record taking of the contorted physiognomies of walnuts, the study of the convolutions (sulci) of the brains of animals and man belongs in a totally different class. Why? Because in any species of vertebrates, for example, all the brains of all its members are essentially rather consistently identical in patterns of shape, proportions, and functional specificity. This relative invariance of the macropattern of the sulci of our developed brain reemphasizes the "systemic" dynamics of the processes of its development; for one could scarcely ascribe that resultant standard configuration of a crowd of 10^{11} nerve cells (plus uncounted glia cells, extraneous nerve fibers, and vascular networks) to have emerged from initially more erratic states through a subsequent militaristic, ultraminiaturely preformed, blueprint-guided "information" chart.

THE AMBIGUITY OF
SCIENTIFIC LANGUAGE

This reference to "information" may serve as a link to a brief scrutiny of the use (or futility) of that term as explanation of incompletely understood phenomena in living systems, most commonly in the science of genetics. As I have indicated before, human language, being a brain product, can never be entirely unambiguous. This fact is necessarily reflected in the verbal description of natural phenomena and often leads to meaningless or wrong conceptions. Consider, for instance, the usage of purely anthropomorphous terminology for referring scientifically to the functional operations of genes: to "explain" their functions, genes are endowed with the human powers of "commanding, controlling, regulating, dictating, informing, etc." All those terms are basically denominative of *human* actions, thus implying the functions of the brain, which *itself* has contrived those very terms for specific application to human behavior. Now, how much elucidation could one expect to gain from such a vicious circle, which backtracks from the accomplished brain to the presumption of wholly unidentified machinists equipped with tools that are no less than offsprings of that finished product itself, the constellation and faculties of which they were to have revealed?

While on this topic of genetic nomenclature, we might also briefly touch on another usually disregarded, but potentially ambiguous, interpretation of "genetic determinism." Linguistically, the common references to a "genetic *character*" or a "gene-determined *feature*" or the like are completely unequivocal, as they denote *properties* or *attributes* of *wholes*, that is, of organized entities. They never refer to the subject or object or substance or universality of those entities. This is fundamentally relevant to human thinking, and hence deserves a few factual examples. These refer to the general experience that all genetic differences between species, strains, individuals, mutations, etc., are expressed in terms of *differentials* between observed features—never in absolutes. They apply to *differences* between comparable subjects, but not to subjects themselves. In discussing eye color, we speak of "genes for blue" or "for brown." In the study of the structure or color of hair, we establish genetic distinctions between whether the specimen is straight or curly, black or blond. Yet we never speak of "genes for the eye" or "genes for the hair." This proper kind of verbal restraint ought to be taken seriously as an expression of current evidence that "genic information" (for those who want to operate mentally with that term) should be held within that frame of "differentials." It should not be arbitrarily expanded to a universal formula of *all* organisms on the globe having emerged through the same singular principle.

The preceding cautions about the occurrence of some vagueness in scientific language has been instigated only by its potential sociological effects on the thinking and acting of individual people in our day. When it was predicated, 200 years ago, that "All men are created equal," the words meant that all newborns have equal rights to strive for successful *self-development* in accordance with their capacities. There was no reference to racial or other "genetic" predestinations of those capacities. Unfortunately, the statement has frequently been reinterpreted to mean that, according to modern science, "the life of the individual is preordained (or predetermined) by its genes." Acceptance of this formulation instigates the radically unsocial attitude of fatalism: "If my type and fate and potential are already unalterably prepatterned by my genetic constitution, why should I be concerned about my actions and whether they are good or bad?"

To counteract that primitive deduction, let me stress the postgenetic history of development, properly termed *epigenetic*, which, after the earliest appearance of the fertilized egg, continues to express itself throughout life. Genetically, the embryo of an individual possesses a permanent frame for the course of subsequent steps, whose *diversity* becomes increasingly manifest as time goes on. This results from the freedom of internal interactions (see Figure 1.2) and the unpredictable variance of the environment. Consequently, even identical genomes cannot be expected to yield strictly identical results. Figure 1.3 gives an illustration. It represents the two back sides of a bivalve conch. At first glance, the black-striped patterns of both sides seem to mirror each other. Yet closer comparison shows no sign of correspondence of patterns (save for identical distances between all stripes, due to a uniform growth rhythm). But taking "genetic determinism" literally, would not the two sides of the same animal, both containing the same genome, have been expected to reveal bilateral symmetry?

Let me expand this example. Many eggs, invertebrate and vertebrate, when cut in half can develop into twins, each half forming a whole animal. But, significantly, the structure of the right partner of each pair is usually a mirror image of the structure of the left, with all unilateral organs shifted to

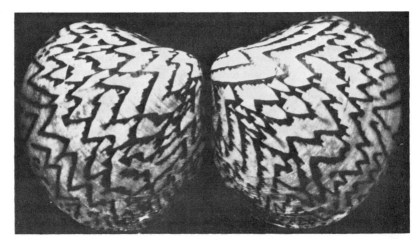

Figure 1.3 Bivalve conch shell: gross conformity of overall design with evident diversity in detailed execution.

the opposite side. Single-egged ("identical") twins in man likewise show inversions (situs inversus) to various degrees (heart to the right, liver to the left, etc.), all of which discounts all primitive dogmas of the "predestination" of the total aspects of an organism by a "genetic code." And this confronts us once more with the practical necessity of blending holism and reductionism by "system-thinking."

CONCLUSIONS

My presentation has had a dual purpose: to keep the empirical knowledge of nature through analytical science free from excessive verbal pollution and unjustified vulgarisation, and, at the same time, to confess that behind our knowledge is the still enormous range of our ignorance—not to exempt my own, after 59 years of experimental research. What I did not emphasize, but to be honest should add at the end, is that my true knowledge of the brain is not a domain that analytical science will ever fully command in terms of what it has at hand. This is the reason why I entitled one of my later books *Within the Gates of Science and Beyond* (1971a).

Many outstanding scientists indulge in the secure satisfaction that analytical science will eventually provide man with a complete, and not just a verbal, explanation of the dynamics of human life and thinking. I must, however, withhold from myself the enviable comfort of that attitude exactly *because* of the long time I have spent working and cogitating on the interconnecting of all the little that we do know. I have come to three conclusions:

1. There is, thus far, no evidence other than counterevidence that the coordinated functions of our brain, let alone its mental performances, are reducible in their wholeness to sheer mosaic programs—the brain is not a jigsaw puzzle. The study of developmental dynamics fully corroborates that conclusion.

2. My understanding of the dynamics of what we can observe, explore, test, and express in terms that are communicable and understandable to others has convinced me that whatever evidence for an explanation man will ever be able to validate as "realistic" is strictly limited to the potentialities of the rational functions of his brain. That is as far as "science" (English version) can go.

3. "Wissenschaft" (science, German version) goes "beyond the gates of science" in that it does *not* confine itself to that part of human experience that can be universally affirmed by its proof of "objectivity"; it encompasses all sorts of personal opinion, dreams, and fancies, appropriately described as "subjective."

Admittedly, the border between (2) and (3) is somewhat blurred and vacillating, but that which lies beyond it is unquestionably mankind's outstanding distinction from other creatures. Roughly, I would equate it with Polanyi's "Private Knowledge," and would advocate respect for that transscientific endowment of man as a true "systemic" manifestation of the character of "wholeness" of his brain functions.

A Personal Statement

As a personal privileged addition to (3), stemming from my own "private knowledge," I wish to supplement the commonly cited "suprascientific" spiritual experiences of personal uniqueness, such as dreams, conceptions, premonitions, poems, musical creations, etc., by adding the variety of religious contentions that exist either in communal convergence or in sectarian dispersion. To my mind there exists, beyond all the diversity of specific differentials of human discordance, and among all human beings, some common fundamental unity (though not uniformity) of sensing a superordinated universality of the Universe. Regardless of whether left nameless or labeled "religious spirit," its manifestations in the form of morality, humanity, love, and creative urge seem to be unfractionably universal. Thus, as I respect both holism and reductionism as merely antidirectional orientations of our human view of the same indivisible world unit, so I believe that human society would stand to gain by acknowledging likewise that the ascending *analytical* perspectives of science and the *unitarian* vision in our mind of the Universe as a coherent entity are just two splintered views of one and the same world.

This closing section, aimed at proving the inseparability or mental indissociability of science (2) and language (2 and 3), a major task of this volume, seemed to me an appropriate tribute to Eric Lenneberg; to me he was a rare model of scholarship, a man who never permitted his brain to become sidetracked solely into natural science, or philosophy, or linguistics, or human relations, or what not. Rather, he cultivated the faculty of the brain to preserve and expand its *multidimensionality*—combining the verticality of ever deeper penetration into factual knowledge with an ever wider horizontal intertwining of data, forming a cohesive network; actually a native gift we call "perspective"—the bridge that leads "from knowledge to understanding." I hope that scholars and students, whether in science, the arts, or with broadly human interests, whether in practice or in theory or, better still, in both in individually appropriate proportions, will earn the benefits of following such a model.

REFERENCES

Weiss, P. A. The living system: Determinism stratified. In A. Koestler & J. R. Smythies (Eds.), *Beyond reductionism—New perspectives in the life sciences.* The Alpbach Symposium 1968. London: Hutchinson, 1969.

Weiss, P. A. *Within the gates of science and beyond: Science in its cultural commitments.* New York: Hafner, 1971. (a)

Weiss, P. A. *Hierarchically organized systems in theory and practice.* New York: Hafner, 1971. (b)

Weiss, P. A. *The science of life: The living system—A system for living.* Mount Kisco, New York: Futura, 1973.

Weiss, P. A. (Ed.) *Knowledge in search of understanding: The Frensham papers.* New York: Futura, 1975.

chapter 2

Biology of Language: The Epistemology of Reality

HUMBERTO R. MATURANA

I am not a linguist, I am a biologist. Therefore, I shall speak about language as a biologist, and address myself to two basic biological questions, namely:

1. What processes must take place in an organism for it to establish a linguistic domain with another organism?
2. What processes take place in a linguistic interaction that permit an organism (us) to describe and to predict events that it may experience?

This is my way of honoring the memory of Eric H. Lenneberg, if one honors the memory of another scientist by speaking about one's own work. Whatever the case, I wish to honor his memory not only because of his great accomplishments, but also because he was capable of inspiring his students, as the symposium on which this book is based revealed. The only way I can do this is to accept the honor of presenting my views about biology, language, and reality.

I shall, accordingly, speak about language as a biologist. In doing so, I

27

shall use language, notwithstanding that this use of language to speak about language is within the core of the problem I wish to consider.

EPISTEMOLOGY

Since I am writing about language as a scientist attempting to address myself to the biological phenomena involved in its generation and use, I shall make the following epistemological assumptions in order to characterize the language I shall use.

Science

We as scientists make scientific statements. These statements are validated by the procedure we use to generate them: the scientific method. This method can be described as involving the following operations: (a) observation of a phenomenon that, henceforth, is taken as a problem to be explained; (b) proposition of an explanatory hypothesis in the form of a deterministic system that can generate a phenomenon isomorphic with the one observed; (c) proposition of a computed state or process in the system specified by the hypothesis as a predicted phenomenon to be observed; and (d) observation of the predicted phenomenon.

In the first operation, the observer specifies a procedure of observation that, in turn, specifies the phenomenon that he or she will attempt to explain. In the second, the observer proposes a conceptual or concrete system as a model of the system that he or she assumes generates the observed phenomenon. In the third, the observer uses the proposed model to compute a state or a process that he or she proposes as a predicted phenomenon to be observed in the modeled system. Finally, in the fourth operation he or she attempts to observe the predicted phenomenon as a case in the modeled system. If the observer succeeds in making this second observation, he or she then maintains that *the model* has been validated and that the system under study is in that respect isomorphic to it and operates accordingly. Granted all the necessary constraints for the specification of the model, and all the necessary attempts to deny the second observations as controls, this is all that the scientific method permits.

This we all know. Yet we are seldom aware that an observation is the realization of a series of operations that entail an observer as a system with properties that allow him or her to perform these operations, and, hence, that the properties of the observer, by specifying the operations that he or she can perform determine the observer's domain of possible observations. Nor are we usually aware that, because only those statements that we generate as observers through the use of the scientific method are scientific statements, science is necessarily a domain of socially accepted operational statements validated by a procedure that specifies the observer who generates them as the standard observer who can perform the operations required for their generation. In other words, we are not usually aware that science is a closed cognitive domain in which all statements are, of necessity, subject dependent, valid only in the domain of interactions in which the standard observer exists and operates. As observers we generally take the observer for granted and, by accepting his universality by implication, ascribe many of the invariant features of our descriptions that depend on the standard observer to a reality that is ontologically objective and independent of us. Yet the power of science rests exactly on its subject dependent nature, which allows us to deal with the operative domain in which we exist. It is only when we want to consider the observer as the object of our scientific inquiry, and we want to understand both what he does when he makes scientific statements and how these statements are operationally effective, that we encounter a problem if we do not recognize the subject dependent nature of science. Therefore, since I want to give a scientific description of the observer as a system capable of descriptions (language), I must take the subject dependent nature of science as my starting point.

Explanation

As scientists, we want to provide explanations for the phenomena we observe. That is, we want to propose conceptual or concrete systems that can be deemed to be intentionally isomorphic to (models of) the systems that generate the observed phenomena. In fact, an explanation is always an intended reproduction or reformulation of a system or phenomenon, addressed by one observer to another, who must accept it or reject it by admitting or denying that it is a model of the system or phenomenon to be explained. Accordingly, we say that a system or a phenomenon has been scientifically explained if a standard observer accepts that the relations or processes that define it as a system or phenomenon of a particular class have been intentionally reproduced, conceptually or concretely.

Two basic operations must be performed by an observer in any explanation: (a) the specification (and distinction thereof) of the system (composite unity) or phenomenon to be explained; and (b) the identification and distinction of the components and the relations between components that permit the conceptual or concrete reproduction of the system or phenomenon to be explained. Since these two operations are not independent, when the ob-

server specifies a system or phenomenon to be explained he or she defines
the domain in which it exists and determines the domain of its possible
components and their relations; conversely, when the observer specifies the
actual components and relations that he or she intends to use in the explanation, he or she determines the domain in which this will be given and in
which the reproduced system will exist. Yet the kind of explanation that an
observer accepts depends on his or her a priori criteria for the validation of
his or her statements. Thus the observer may accept either a *mechanistic* or a
vitalistic explanation.

In a mechanistic explanation, the observer explicitly or implicitly accepts that the properties of the system to be explained are generated by
relations of the components of the system and are not to be found among the
properties of those components. The same applies to the mechanistic explanation of a phenomenon, in which case the observer explicitly or implicitly
accepts that the characteristics of the phenomenon to be explained result
from the relations of its constitutive processes, and are not to be found
among the characteristics of these processes. Contrariwise, in a vitalistic
explanation, the observer explicitly or implicitly assumes that the properties
of the system, or the characteristics of the phenomenon to be explained, are
to be found among the properties or among the characteristics of at least one
of the components or processes that constitute the system or phenomenon.
In a mechanistic explanation the relations between components are necessary; in a vitalistic explanation they are superfluous. An example of a
mechanistic explanation is: The weight of a body is the sum of the weight of
its components. The relation *sum,* applied to the components as defined by
their property weight, determines the property weight of the body. Example
of a vitalistic explanation: Jacques Monod said in *Le Hasard et la Nécessité*
(1970) "L'*ultima ratio* de toutes les structures et performances téléo-
nomiques des être vivants est donc enfermée dans les sequences de
radicaux des fibres polipeptidiques, 'embryons' de ces démons de Maxwell
biologiques que sont le protéines globulaires. En un sense très réel c'est à ce
niveau d'organization chimique que gît, s'il y a en a un, le secre de la vie
[p. 110]." [The *ultima ratio* of all telenomic structures and functions of living
systems is, then, embeded in the amino acidic sequence of the polypeptide
chains that truly constitute embryos of Maxwell's biological demons that are
the globular proteins. It is at this level of chemical organization that in a very
real sense lies, if there is any, the secret of life.] This statement answers the
question—What kinds of systems are living systems?—by reference to the
properties of one of their components.

In a mechanistic explanation the observer explicitly or implicitly distinguishes between a system and its components, treating the system and the
components as operationally different kinds of unities that belong to disjoint

sets that generate nonintersecting phenomenic domains. The relation of correspondence between the phenomenal domain generated by a system and the phenomenal domain generated by its components, which an observer may assert after enuciating a mechanistic explanation, is, therefore, established by the observer through his or her independent interactions with the system and with its components and does not indicate a phenomenal reduction of one domain to another. If it appears as if there were a phenomenal reduction, it is because in the description all phenomena are represented in the same domain, and, unless care is taken to preserve it, the relation established through the observer is lost. The reality described through mechanistic explanations, then, implies the possibility of an endless generation of nonintersecting phenomenal domains as a result of the recursive constitution (organization) of new classes of unities through the recursive novel combinations of unities already defined. For epistemological reasons, then, mechanistic explanations are intrinsically nonreductionist.

With vitalistic explanations, the situation is the contrary: They do not distinguish between the phenomenal domain generated by a unity and the phenomenal domain generated by its components. The reality described through vitalistic explanations is, necessarily, a reality of a finite number of phenomenal domains. For epistemological reasons, then, vitalistic explanations are intrinsically reductionist.

Operational Characteristics of a Mechanistic Explanation

Observer

An observer is a human being, a person, a living system who can make distinctions and specify that which he or she distinguishes as a unity, as an entity different from himself or herself that can be used for manipulations or descriptions in interactions with other observers. An observer can make distinctions in actions and thoughts, recursively, and is able to operate as if he or she were external to (distinct from) the circumstances in which the observer finds himself or herself. Everything said is said by an observer to another observer, who can be himself or herself.

Unity

A unity is an entity, concrete or conceptual, dynamic or static, specified by operations of distinction that delimit it from a background and characterized by the properties that the operations of distinction assign to it. A unity may be defined by an observer either as being simple or as composite. If defined as simple, the properties assigned to the unity by the operations of distinction that specify it are supposed to be constitutive, and no question about their origin arises. If the unity is defined as composite, it is assumed that it has components that may be specified through additional operations of distinction, and that it is realized as a unity by an organization that determines its properties through determining those relations between its components that specify the domain in which it can be treated as simple.

Organization

This word comes from the Greek term *organon*, which means "instrument"; by making reference to the instrumental participation of the components in the constitution of a composite unity, it refers to the relations between components that define and specify a system as a composite unity of a particular class, and determine its properties as such a unity. Hence, the organization of a composite unity specifies the class of entities to which it belongs. It follows that the concept or generic name that we use to refer to a class of entities points to the organization of the composite unities that are members of the class. From the cognitive point of view, then, it also follows that, in order to define or identify a system as a composite unity of a particular class, it is necessary and sufficient to state (or to point to) its organization; a mechanistic explanation is an explicit or implicit subject dependent statement that entails, or describes, the organization of a system.

Structure

This word comes from the Latin verb *struere*, which means to build; by making reference to the processes of construction, as well as to the components of a composite unity, it refers to the actual components and to the actual relations that these must satisfy in their participation in the constitution of a given composite unity. An observer may recognize a known system by identifying some of its components, but he or she cannot define or characterize an unknown system merely by pointing to its structure—the observer must state its organization.

Organization and structure, therefore, are not synonyms. The organization of a system defines it as a composite unity and determines its properties as such a unity by specifying a domain in which it can interact (and, hence, be observed) as an unanalyzable whole endowed with constitutive properties. The properties of a composite unity as an unanalyzable whole establish a space in which it operates as a simple unity. In contrast, the structure of a system determines the space in which it exists as a composite unity that can be perturbed through the interactions of its components, but the structure does not determine its properties as an unity. An unanalyzable unity can be designated by a name and identified by a concept that refers to the constellation of properties that define it, but it has no organization or structure. A simple unity has only a constellation of properties; it is a fundamental entity that exists in the space that these properties establish. It follows that spatially separated composite unities (systems) may have the same organization but different structures, and that a composite unity remains the same only as long as its organization remains invariant. Whenever the structure of an entity changes so that its organization as a composite unity changes, the identity of the entity changes and it becomes a different composite unity—a unity of a different class to which we apply a different name. Whenever the structure of a composite unity changes and its organization remains invariant, the identity of the entity remains the same and the unity stays unchanged as a member of its original class; we do not change its name. It follows that whenever a system is to be explained, it is necessary and sufficient to reproduce its organization. Yet when a particular system is to be reproduced, both its organization and its structure must be reproduced.

Property

A property is a characteristic of a unity specified and defined by an operation of distinction. Pointing to a property, therefore, always implies an observer.

Space

Space is the domain of all the possible interactions of a collection of unities (simple, or composite that interact as unities) that the properties of these unities establish by specifying its dimensions. It can be said, of a composite unity on the one hand, that it exists in the space that its components specify as unities because it interacts through the properties of its components, and, on the other hand, that it is realized as a unity in the space that its properties as a simple unity specify. Once a unity is defined, a space is specified.

Interaction

Whenever two or more unities, through the interplay of their properties, modify their relative position in the space that they specify, there is an interaction. Whenever two or more composite unities are treated as simple, they are seen to be realized and to interact in the space that they specify as simple unities; however, if they are treated as composites unities, then they are seen to interact through the properties of their components and to exist in the space that these specify.

Structure-Determined Systems[1]

These systems undergo only changes determined by their organization and structure that are either changes of state (defined as changes of structure without loss of identity) or disintegration (defined as changes of structure with loss of identity). For these systems it is necessarily the case that: (a) they may undergo only interactions that either perturb them by triggering in them structural changes that lead to changes of state or disintegrate them by triggering in them structural changes that lead to their loss of identity; (b) the changes of state they undergo as a result of perturbing interactions are not specified by the properties of the perturbing entities, which only trigger them; (c) the structural changes they undergo as a result of disintegrating interactions are not specified by the properties of the disintegrating entity, which only trigger them; and (d) their structure, by specifying which relations must arise between their components as a result of their interactions in order to initiate their triggered changes of state, specifies the configuration of properties that an entity must have in order to interact with them and operate either as a perturbing or as a disintegrating agent.

The organization and structure of a structure-determined system, therefore, continuously determine: (a) the domain of states of the system, by specifying the states that it may adopt in the course of its internal dynamics or as a result of its interactions; (b) its domain of perturbations, by specifying the matching configurations of properties of the medium that may perturb it; and (c) its domain of disintegration, by specifying all the configurations of properties of the medium that may trigger its disintegration.

If the state a system adopts as a result of an interaction were specified by the properties of the entity with which it interacts, then the interaction would be an instructive interaction. Systems that undergo instructive interactions cannot be analyzed by a scientific procedure. In fact, all instructable systems would adopt the same state under the same perturbations and would necessarily be indistinguishable to a standard observer. If two systems can be distinguished by a standard observer, it is because they adopt different states under what he or she would otherwise consider identical perturbations and are not instructable systems. The scientific method allows us to deal only with systems whose structural changes can be described as determined by the relations and interactions of their components, and which, therefore, operate as structure-determined systems. Structure-determined systems do not undergo instructive interactions. In these circumstances, any description of an interaction in terms of instructions (or of information transfer) is, at best, metaphorical; it does not reflect the actual operation of the systems

---

[1] I (1975) have called these "state-determined systems."

involved as objects of scientific description and study. Consequently, every scientific assertion is a statement that necessarily implies a structure-determined system proposed by the standard observer as a model of the structure-determined system that he or she assumes to be responsible for his or her observations. For epistemological reasons, then, scientific predictions are computations of state trajectories in structure determined systems, and chance or indeterminism enter in scientific assertions only as computational artifices used in models that assume object systems that cannot be observed in detail, not as a reflection of an ontological necessity.

Structural coupling

For an observer, the organization and structure of a structure-determined system determine both its domain of states and its domain of perturbations as collections of realizable possibilities. This is so because an observer can imagine, for any structure-determined system that he or she conceives or describes, different state trajectories arising from correspondingly different sequences of perturbations by imagining the system under different circumstances of interactions. Yet what in fact occurs during the ontogeny (individual history) of any particular structure-determined system is that the structure of the medium in which it interacts and, hence, exists, and which, in this respect, operates as an independent dynamic system even while changing as a result of the interactions, provides the actual historical sequence of perturbations that, in fact, selects which of the imaginable possible state trajectories of the system indeed takes place. If the structure of the medium that matches the domain of perturbations of the structure-determined system is redundant or recurrent, then the structure-determined system undergoes recurrent perturbations; if the structure of the medium is in continuous change, then the structure-determined system undergoes continuously changing perturbations; finally, if the matching structure of the medium changes as a result of the operation of the structure-determined system, then this system undergoes changing perturbations that are coupled to its own state trajectory. Now, if a structure-determined system, as a result of its interactions, undergoes changes of state that involve structural changes in its components (and not only in their relations), then I say that the system has a second-order plastic structure, and that it undergoes plastic interactions. When this is the case, the plastic interactions that such a system undergoes select in it trajectories of second-order structural changes that result in the transformation of both its domain of states and its domain of perturbations. The outcome of the continued interactions of a structurally plastic system in a medium with redundant or recurrent structure, therefore, may be the continued selection in the system of a structure that determines in it a domain of states and a domain of perturbations that allow it to operate recurrently in its medium without disintegration. I call this process "structural coupling." If the medium is also a structurally plastic system, then the two plastic systems may become reciprocally structurally coupled through their reciprocal selection of plastic structural changes during their history of interactions. In such a case, the structurally plastic changes of state of one system become perturbations for the other, and vice versa, in a manner that establishes an interlocked, mutually selecting, mutually triggering domain of state trajectories.

LIVING AND NERVOUS SYSTEMS

Living System: Autopoiesis[2]

Living systems are autonomous entities, even though they depend on a medium for their concrete existence and material interchange; all the phenomena related to them depend on the way their autonomy is realized. A perusal of present-day biochemical knowledge reveals that this autonomy is the result of their organization as systems in continuous self-production. This organization in terms of self-production can be characterized as follows.

There is a class of dynamic systems that are realized, as unities, as networks of productions (and disintegrations) of components that: (a) recursively participate through their interactions in the realization of the network of productions (and disintegrations) of components that produce them; and (b) by realizing its boundaries, constitute this network of productions (and disintegrations) of components as a unity in the space they specify and in which they exist. Francisco Varela and I called such systems *autopoietic systems,* and *autopoietic organization* their organization (Maturana & Varela, 1973). An autopoietic system that exists in physical space is a living system (or, more correctly, the physical space is the space that the components of living systems specify and in which they exist) (Maturana, 1975).

In this characterization of the organization of living systems, nothing is stipulated about their structure, which can be any form that satisfies it. Also, nothing is said about the medium in which an autopietic system may exist, or about its interactions or material interchanges with the medium, which can be any that satisfy the constraints imposed by the actual structure through which the autopoiesis is realized. In fact, to the extent that an

[2] Autopoiesis is a word composed of the Greek words for 'self' and 'to produce.'

autopoietic system is defined as a unity by its autopoiesis, the only constitutive constraint that it must satisfy is that all its state trajectories lead to autopoiesis; otherwise it disintegrates. Therefore, an autopoietic system, while autopietic, is a closed dynamic system in which all phenomena are subordinated to its autopoiesis and all its states are states in autopoiesis. This conclusion has several fundamental consequences.

Autonomy

Autopoietic closure is the condition for autonomy in autopoietic systems in general. In living systems in particular, autopoietic closure is realized through a continuous structural change under conditions of continuous material interchange with the medium. Accordingly, since thermodynamics describes the constraints that the entitites that specify the physical space impose on any system they may compose, autopoietic closure in living systems does not imply the violation of these constraints, but constitutes a particular mode of realization of autopoiesis in a space in which thermodynamic constraints are valid. As a result, a structurally plastic living system either operates as a structurally determined homeostatic system that maintains invariant its organization under conditions of continuous structural change, or it disintegrates.

Phenomenal Distinctions

As I stated when discussing the notion of explanation, a scientist must distinguish two phenomenal domains when observing a composite unity (a) the phenomenal domain proper to the components of the unity, which is the domain in which all the interactions of the components take place; and (b) the phenomenal domain proper to the unity, which is the domain specified by the interactions of the composite unity as a simple unity. If the composite unity is a living system, the first phenomenal domain, in which the interactions of the components are described with respect to the living system that they constitute, is the domain of physiological phenomena; the second phenomenal domain, in which a living system is seen as if it were a simple unity that interacts with the components of the environment in which its autopoiesis is realized, is the domain of behavioral phenomena. Accordingly, from the point of view of the description of behavior, a living system interacts as a simple unity in the space it specifies through its interactions as a unity and changes its relations with the components of its environment as a result of these interactions; from the point of view of physiology, the components of the living system interact with each other and or with elements of the medium in their space, and as a result, their structure and or reciprocal relations change. For the observer who beholds simultaneously both phenomenal domains, however, the changes in the relations of the components appear as changes in state in the living system that modify its properties and, hence, its interactions in its environment—all of which he or she describes by saying that the physiology of the organism generates its behavior. Yet, since these two phenomenal domains do not intersect, the relations that an observer may establish between the phenomena of one and the phenomena of the other do not constitute a phenomenal reduction, and the generative operational dependency of behavior on physiology that the observer asserts in this manner does not imply a necessary correspondence between them. Accordingly, in no particular case can the phenomena of one domain be deduced from the phenomena of the other prior to the observation of their actual generative dependency. The implicative relation that an observer can use a posteriori to describe an observed generative dependency existing between a particular behavior and a particular physiological phenomenon is necessarily contingent on the particular structure of the living system which, at the moment of observation, determines the changes of state that the observer sees as behavior. Therefore, the implicative relation used by the observer in his description is not a logical implication as would be the case if behavioral and physiological phenomena belonged to the same phenomenal domain. The result is that, in order to explain a given behavior of a living system, the observer must explain the generation and establishment of the particular structures of the organism and of the environment that make such behavior possible at the moment it occurs.

Adaptation

The history of structural change without loss of identity in an autopoietic unity is its ontogeny. The coupling of the changing structure of a structurally plastic autopoietic unity to the changing structure of the medium is called ontogenic adaptation. The history of successively produced, historically connected unities generated through sequential reproductive steps is evolution. The coupling of the changing structures of the sequentially generated unities to a changing medium is called evolutionary adaptation.

Ontogenic and evolutionary adaptations in living systems arise through the selection of the structures that permit the autopoiesis of the living system in the medium in which it exists. In both cases, selection takes place as a differential structural realization that results from the operational confrontation of systems endowed with independently determined domains of structural diversity and plasticity. In the case of the evolution all the structural diversity of living systems, available for selection is produced in them in parallel, through each reproductive step, as a result of their genetic properties, and the selection takes place as differential survival or differential reproductive success. In the case of ontogenic changes, the structural diversity of living systems available for selection is present, at any instant, in the domain of perturbations of each living system, and selection takes place during the history of each individual according to the sequence of perturbations provided by the medium. No example of evolutionary selection is needed. As examples of ontogenic selection the following two are presently adequate:

1. In vertebrates, specific immunity responses result from the differential multiplication of cells capable of producing antibodies when the organism is confronted with antigens that select, through differential triggering, which cells multiply (Edelman, 1975).
2. The consolidation of bone lamelli following the lines of stress is a result of the preferential reabsorption of lamelli that are not under stress from a domain of lamelli otherwise in continuous turnover and initially deposited with no preferential relation to stress (J. Y. Lettvin, personal communication, 1976).

Adaptation, then, is always a trival expression of the structural coupling of a structurally plastic system to a medium. Adaptation always results from sequences of interactions of a plastic system in its medium that trigger in the plastic system structural changes or changes of state that, at any instant, select in it a structure that either matches (is homomorphic to) the structure of the medium in which it operates (interacts or behaves) as such a system, or disintegrate it. It follows that, in the operation of living systems as autopoietic unities in a medium, the coincidence between a given structure of the medium (place in the medium) and a given structure in the living system is always the result of the history of their mutual interactions, while both operate as independent, structurally determined systems. Furthermore, as a result of the structural coupling that takes place during such a history, history becomes embodied both in the structure of the living system and in the structure of the medium, even though both systems necessarily, as structure-determined systems, always operate in the present through locally determined processes. Therefore, although from the cognitive point of view adequate behavior as a case of adaptation cannot be understood without reference to history and context, from the operational point of view adequate behavior is only an expression of a structural matching in the present between organism and medium, in which history does not participate as an operative component. History is necessary to explain how a given system or phenomenon came to be, but it does not participate in the explanation of the operation of the system or phenomenon in the present.

Selection

Although the result of selection, whether through evolution or ontogeny, is structural coupling (because what is selected is always a structure), selection takes place through the operational confrontations of a
composite system in the medium in which it interacts as a simple unity
through the properties of its components. Thus, it is the differential effectiveness of the actual operation of different structures of different organisms of
the same kind in parallel existence, or of the same organism in different
instances of its individual history, that constitutes the process of selection in
living systems. Accordingly, selection always takes place in a domain orthogonal to (different from) the domain of existence of that which is selected. It is
this feature of the process of selection that enables an observer to claim that
selection takes place through the functional value of the structures selected,
giving with this judgment, a posteriori, the misleading impression that what
takes place in selection is a semantic coupling that allows for an infinity of
structural realizations. In other words, although the metaphorical description in functional (semantic) terms is useful for referring to the orthogonal
relation between the domains in which the selective interactions take place
and in which the selected structures exist, the result is structural coupling,
because the operational effectiveness of the selected system depends exclusively on the unique correspondence thus obtained between its structure
and the structure of its medium. Furthermore, it is also this feature of the
process of selection that allows for the diversity of sequential or simultaneous structural couplings that may take place during evolutionary or
ontogenic adaptation. If the organization of a system is homeostatically maintained invariant, as occurs in autopoietic systems, adaptation is the homeostatic clamping through behavior (the actual operation of the autopoietic
system in its medium) of the structural coupling of a system (ontogeny) or of
a succession of systems (evolution) to their static or changing medium.

Nervous System: Neuronal Network

The nervous system is a network of interacting neurons that generates a
phenomenology of neuronal interactions subservient to the autopoiesis of
the organism in which it is embedded and of which it is a component.
Therefore, in order to explain the nervous system as a system, it is necessary
and sufficient to point to the organization that defines a neuronal network
that generates its phenomenology of neuronal interactions as a constitutive
component of an autopoietic system, such as a metazoan.

Such organization can be described as follows. The nervous system is
defined as a system (a unity) by relations that constitute it as a closed

network of interacting neurons such that any change in the state of relative activity of a collection of its component neurons always leads to a change in the state of relative activity of other (or the same collection of) neurons: All changes in relative neuronal activity in the nervous system always lead to other changes in relative neuronal activity in it. With respect to its dynamics of states, the nervous system is a closed system.

A closed neuronal network does not have input or output surfaces as features of its organization, and, although it can be perturbed through the interactions of its components, for it, in its operation as a system, there are only states or changes of states of relative neuronal activity, regardless of what the observer may say about their origin. Given a closed system, inside and outside exist only for the observer who beholds it, not for the system. The sensory and effector surfaces that an observer can describe in an actual organism do not make the nervous system an open neuronal network, because the environment where the observer stands acts only as an intervening element through which the effector and sensory neurons interact, completing the closure of the network. This organization of the nervous system has several fundamental consequences.

Closure

If an observer of a nervous system, either experimentally or conceptually, were to stand in a synaptic cleft, and if while observing the pre- and post-synaptic surfaces he were to describe the transfer properties of the system thus obtained in terms of input and output relations, he would describe an open network, not a nervous system. This is what, in fact, happens when an observer describes the organism as a system that has independent sensory and effector surfaces for its interactions with the environment. By doing this, the observer opens the nervous system and destroys its organization, leaving another system organized as an open network that one can describe in terms of hierarchical transfer functions that are relevant only for the system of references that the observer introduces when he or she describes the changes of state of the nervous system by mapping them on the changes of state of the environment (observable medium). As a closed neuronal network, however, the nervous system operates only by generating relations of relative neuronal activity determined by its structure, not by the environmental circumstances that may trigger changes of state in it.

Behavior

The observer sees as behavior, or conduct, the changing relations and interactions of an organism with its environment, which appear to him or her to be determined by sequences of changes of state generated in the organism by sequences of changes of state in its nervous system. Furthermore, the observer can, with no difficulty, describe any given behavior or conduct in purposeful (functional or semantic) terms that reflect the value or role that the observer ascribes to it in reference to the realization of the autopoiesis of the organism. Yet it is also apparent to the observer that, since the nervous system is a structure-determined system, the sequence of changing relations of relative neuronal activity that appears to him or her as determining a given behavior is not determined by any functional or semantic value that he or she may ascribe to such a behavior, but that, on the contrary, it is necessarily determined by the structure of the nervous system at the moment at which the behavior is enacted.

An example may clarify this situation. Let us consider what happens in instrumental flight. The pilot is isolated from the outside world; all he can do is manipulate the instruments of the plane according to a certain path of change in their readings. When the pilot comes out of the plane, however, his wife and friends embrace him with joy and tell him: "What a wonderful landing you made; we were afraid, because of the heavy fog." But the pilot answers in surprise: "Flight? Landing? What do you mean? I did not fly or land; I only manipulated certain internal relations of the plane in order to obtain a particular sequence of readings in a set of instruments." All that took place in the plane was determined by the structure of the plane and the pilot, and was independent of the nature of the medium that produced the perturbations compensated for by the dynamics of states of the plane: flight and landing are irrelevant for the internal dynamics of the plane. However, from the point of view of the observer, the internal dynamics of the plane results in a flight only if in that respect the structure of the plane matches the structure of the medium; otherwise it does not, even if in the nonmatching medium the internal dynamics of states of the plane is indistinguishable from the internal dynamics of states the plane under observed flight. It follows that since the dynamics of states of an organism, or of a nervous system, or of any dynamic system, is always determined by the structure of the system, adequate behavior is necessarily only the result of a structural matching between organism (dynamic system) and medium.

Coupling

The presence of a nervous system in a living system does not entail a change in the nature of the operation of the living system as a structure-determined autopoietic unity; it implies only an enlargement of the domain of possible states of the living system through the inclusion of structure-determined relations of relative neuronal activity in the autopoietic network. The observable effectiveness that the relations of relative neuronal activity have for the realization of the autopoiesis of a given organism in its medium is the result of the structural coupling existing between the nervous system and the organism, and between these and the medium.

The argument for structural coupling of autopoietic systems can be summarized as follows. Given that the interactions of a composite unity in the space of its components are interactions through its components (that is, are structural interactions), if, as a result of a structural interaction, the components of a unity or their relations change, the structure of the unity changes and, if this structural change occurs without a change in the organization of the composite unity, the identity of the unity remains invariant. A composite unity whose structure can change while its organization remains invariant is a plastic unity, and the structural interactions under which this invariance can be sustained are perturbations. Since it is a constitutive feature of an autopoietic system to maintain homeostatically invariant its organization under conditions of structural change, the realization of the autopoiesis of a plastic living system under conditions of perturbations generated by a changing medium must result in the selection of a structure in the living system that incorporates, in its autopoietic network, specific processes (changes of state) that can be triggered by specific changes of state of the medium; otherwise, the system disintegrates. The result of establishing this dynamic structural correspondence, or structural coupling, is the effective spatiotemporal correspondence of the changes of state of the organism to the recurrent changes of state of the medium, while the organism remains autopoietic.

The same general argument can be applied to the nervous system in particular. The organization of the nervous system as a closed network of interacting neurons must remain invariant, but its structure may change if it is coupled to the structural change of other systems in which it is embedded, such as the organism, and through this, the medium in which the organism exists as an autopoietic unity, or, recursively, itself. If the structure of the nervous system changes, the domain of possible states of relative neuronal activity of the nervous system changes, and, hence, the domain of possible behavioral states of the organism itself changes, too. Therefore, if as a result of the structural changes of the nervous system the organism can go on in autopoiesis, the nervous system's changed structure may constitute the basis for a new structural change, which may again permit it to go on in autopoiesis. In principle, this process may be recursively repeated endlessly throughout the life of an organism.

That the ontogenic structural coupling of the nervous system to the organism, to the medium, and to itself should occur through recursive selective interactions is an epistemological necessity. Which interactions select which structural change in a particular nervous system depends on the particular case under consideration. There are well-documented examples that I will not describe, but I will add that to the extent that the nervous system operates as a closed neuronal network its actual operation in the domain of relations of relative neuronal activities could not lead in it to second-order structural changes. However, since, in addition to their participation in the closed neuronal network that the nervous system is, neurons exhibit properties common to all other cells, neurons can be perturbed chemically or physically by the products of other cells of the organism, whether or not they are members of the nervous system, or of the medium. These perturbations, which are operationally orthogonal to the domain of relations of neuronal activities in which the nervous system operates, may trigger structural changes in the neurons that result in second-order structural changes in the nervous system that result in changes in its domain of states that result (for the observer) in changes in behavior. Since these orthogonal perturbations constitute selective interactions, structural selection must take place through them in the domain of potential structural diversity constituted by the domain of perturbations of the organism, and it must take place through the spatial and temporal concomitances of chemical and physical neuronal perturbations determined by the structure of the media in which the nervous system is embedded. At this point it should be apparent that the only structure of the nervous system that allows for this sort of structural change is that in which the nervous system operates as an homeostatic closed neuronal network that generates and maintains invariant relations of relative neuronal activity that are selected, through interactions orthogonal to this domain of operation, by the actual realization of the autopoiesis of the organism that it integrates.

While autopoiesis lasts, (a) continued ontogenic structural coupling of the nervous system selects the neuronal network structure that generates the relations of relative neuronal activity that participate in the continued autopoiesis of the organism in the medium to which it is coupled; and (b) the structural coupling of the nervous system to the organism, to its medium, or to itself that adequate behavior (interactions without disintegration) reveals may appear to an observer as a semantic coupling, because he or she can ascribe functional significance or meaning to any behavior, and can describe the underlying physiology as if caused by these semantic relations.

Learning and Instinct

If the structural coupling of an organism to its medium takes place during evolution, the structure that the organism exhibits at a particular moment as a result of such evolution would have arisen in it through a developmental process and not as a result of the history of its interactions as an individual. Any behavior that an observer may detect in an organism determined by a dynamics of states dependent on structures acquired by the species during evolution will be called instinctive behavior by the observer. If the structural coupling of the organism to its medium takes place during its ontogeny, and if this structural coupling involves the nervous system, an observer may claim that learning has taken place because he or she observes adequate behavior generated through the dynamics of states of a nervous system whose structure has been specified (selected) through experience. If, in these circumstances, the observer wants to discriminate between learned and instinctive behavior, he or she will discover that in their actual realization, both modes of behavior are equally determined in the present by the structures of the nervous system and organism, and that, in this respect, they are indeed indistinguishable. The distinction between learned and instinctive behaviors lies exclusively in the history of the establishment of the structures responsible for them.

Any description of learning in terms of the acquisition of a representation of the environment is, therefore, merely metaphorical and carries no explanatory value. Furthermore, such a description is necessarily misleading, because it implies a system in which instructive interactions would take place, and such a system is, epistemologically, out of the question. In fact, if no notion of instruction is used, the problem becomes simplified because learning, then, appears as the continuous ontogenic structural coupling of an organism to its medium through a process which follows a direction determined by the selection exerted on its changes of structure by the implementation of the behavior that it generates through the structure already selected in it by its previous plastic interactions. Accordingly, the significance that an observer may see a posteriori in a given behavior acquired through learning plays no part in the specification of the structure through which it becomes implemented. Also, although it is possible for us as human beings to stipulate from a metadomain of descriptions an aim in learning, this aim only determines a bias, a direction, in a domain of selection, not a structure to be acquired. This latter can only become specified during the actual history of learning (ontogenic structural coupling), because it is contingent on this history. A learning system has no trivial experiences (interactions) because all interactions result in a structural change, even when the selected structure leads to the stabilization of a given behavior.

Finally, to the extent that the nervous system operates as a closed neuronal network, the performance of learned or instinctive behavior as an expression of a structural coupling is always the action of a spatiotemporal network of relations of relative neuronal activities that appear to an observer as a network of sensori-motor correlations. If the observed behavior is instinctive and is realized in an inadequate environment, the observer claims that it is instinctive behavior in a vacuum. If the observed behavior is learned and is realized in an inadequate environment, the observer calls it a mistake. In both cases, however, the situation is the same: circumstantial structural uncoupling due to operational independence between the dynamics of states of the organism and the dynamics of states of the medium, under circumstances in which their time courses for structural change do not allow structural coupling.

Perception

When an observer sees an organism interacting in its medium, he observes that its conduct appears to be adequate to compensate for the perturbations that the environment exerts on it in each interaction. The observer describes this adequacy of conduct as if it were the result of the acquisition by the organism of some feature of the environment, such as information, on which it computes the adequate changes of state that permit it to remain in autopoiesis, and calls such a process *perception*. Since instructive interactions do not take place, this description is both operationally inappropriate and metaphorically misleading. Similarly, if the observer beholds a conduct that he or she usually sees under conditions of what he or she calls perception to be enacted in the absence of the adequate environmental perturbations, the observer claims that the observed conduct is the result of an illusion or hallucination. Yet, for the operation of the nervous system (and organism), there cannot be a distinction between illusions, hallucinations, or perceptions, because a closed neuronal network cannot discriminate between internally and externally triggered changes in relative neuronal activity. This distinction pertains exclusively to the domain of descriptions in which the observer defines an inside and an outside for the nervous system and the organism. In fact, for any given animal, the structure of its nervous system and its structure as a whole organism, not the structure of the medium, determine what structural configuration of the medium may constitute its sensory perturbations and what path of internal changes of states it undergoes as a result of a particular interaction. Furthermore, since these structures are the result of the structural coupling of the organism to its medium, closure in the organization of the nervous system and the organism make perception an expression of the structural coupling of an organism to its medium that is distinguishable from illusion or hallucination only in the social domain.

LANGUAGE AND
CONSENSUAL DOMAINS

Consensual Domains

When two or more organisms interact recursively as structurally plastic systems, each becoming a medium for the realization of the autopoiesis of the other, the result is mutual ontogenic structural coupling. From the point of view of the observer, it is apparent that the operational effectiveness that the various modes of conduct of the structurally coupled organisms have for the realization of their autopoiesis under their reciprocal interactions is established during the history of their interactions and through their interactions. Furthermore, for an observer, the domain of interactions specified through such ontogenic structural coupling appears as a network of sequences of mutually triggering interlocked conducts that is indistinguishable from what he or she would call a consensual domain. In fact, the various conducts or behaviors involved are both arbitrary and contextual. The behaviors are arbitarary because they can have any form as long as they operate as triggering perturbations in the interactions; they are contextual because their participation in the interlocked interactions of the domain is defined only with respect to the interactions that constitute the domain. Accordingly, I shall call the domain of interlocked conducts that results from ontogenic reciprocal structural coupling between structurally plastic organisms a *consensual domain* (Maturana, 1975).

Once a consensual domain is established, in the same manner as occurs generally whenever there is structural coupling between several systems, any member of the coupling can be replaced by a novel system that, with respect to the structural features involved in the coupling, has the same structure. Thus, a consensual domain is closed with respect to the interlocking conducts that constitute it, but is open with respect to the organisms or systems that realize it.

Descriptions

What is significant for an observer in a consensual domain is that the observed organisms can be described as simultaneously existing as composite and simple unities, and, thus, as defining two nonintersecting phenomenic domains. In the first domain, the observer can describe the organisms as interacting through the properties of their components; in the second domain, he or she can describe them as interacting through their properties as unities. In both cases, the interaction of the organisms can be described in strictly operational terms, without recourse to such semantic notions as function or meaning. Yet, when an observer communicates with another observer, he or she defines a metadomain from the perspective of which a consensual domain appears as an interlocked domain of distinctions, indications, or descriptions, according to how the observer refers to the observed behavior.

If the observer considers every distinguishable behavior as a representation of the environmental circumstances that trigger it, he or she considers the behavior as a description, and the consensual domain in which this behavior takes place as a domain of interlocked descriptions of actual environmental states that are defined through the behaviors that represent them. In this manner a description always implies an interaction. What we do as observers when we make descriptions is exactly that: We behave in an interlocked manner with other observers in a consensual domain ontogenically generated through our direct (mother–child relation) or indirect (membership in the same society) structural coupling. But if the observer forgets that the interlocked adequacy of the mutual triggering changes of state of the mutually perturbing systems in the consensual domain is the result of their ontogenic structural coupling, he or she may describe the consensual domain as if it constituted an intrinsic descriptive system in which the descriptive interactions give information to the organisms to compute the ad hoc states needed to handle the described environment. To do this is both to assume instructive interactions that for epistemological reasons are out of the question and to lose the domain of descriptions as a metadomain that exists only in a consensual domain in reference to another domain. The following considerations should make this clear.

1. If the organisms that operate in a consensual domain can be recursively perturbed by the internal states generated in them through their consensual interactions and can include the conducts generated through these recursive interactions as behavioral components in their consensual domain, a second-order consensuality is established from the perspective of which the first-order consensual behavior is operationally a description of the circumstances that trigger it. Yet, for the establishment of this second-order consensuality and, hence, for the occurrence of the recursive operation of consensus on consensus that leads to the recursive application of descriptions to descriptions, it is necessary that all perturbing processes, including the descriptions, should take place in the same domain.

2. The presence of a structurally plastic nervous system in animals makes possible this recursive mapping of all the interactions of the

organism and its nervous system, as well as of most (if not all) of its internal processes, in a single phenomenic domain. In fact, since the nervous system operates as a closed neuronal network in which all states of activity are relations of relative neuronal activity, all the interactions and all the changes of state of the organism (including its nervous system) that perturb the nervous system, regardless of how they arise, necessarily map in the same domain of relations of relative neuronal activities. As has been said, the result of this is the ontogenic recursive structural coupling of the structurally plastic nervous system to its own changing structure through a process in which the sequence of structural changes is determined by the sequence of structural perturbations generated either by these same structural changes, or by the interactions of the organism in its medium.

3. The magnitude of this recursive ontogenic structural coupling in any particular organism depends both on the degree of structural plasticity of its nervous system and on the degree to which the actual structure of its nervous system at any instant permits the occurrence of distinct relations of relative neuronal activity that operate as internal structural perturbations. When this takes place, even in the slightest manner, within the confines of a consensual domain, so that the relations of neuronal activity generated under consensual behavior become perturbations and components for further consensual behavior, an observer is operationally generated. In other words, if as a result of the mapping of all the states of the organism onto the states of activity of its nervous system, an organism can be perturbed by the relations of neuronal activity generated in its nervous system by relations between relations of neuronal activity triggered in it through different interactions, consensually distinguishing them as components of a second-order consensual domain, the behavior of the organism becomes indistinguishable from the behavior of an observer; the second-order consensual domain that it establishes with other organisms becomes indistinguishable from a semantic domain. In still other words, if an organism is observed in its operation within a second-order consensual domain, it appears to the observer as if its nervous system interacted with internal representations of the circumstances of its interactions, and as if the changes of state of the organism were determined by the semantic value of these representations. Yet all that takes place in the operation of the nervous system is the structure-determined dynamics of changing relations of relative neuronal activity proper to a closed neuronal network.

4. Representation, meaning, and description are notions that apply only and exclusively to the operation of living systems in a consensual domain, and are defined by an observer to refer to second-order consensual behavior. For this reason, these notions have no explanatory value for the characterization of the actual operation of living systems as autopoietic systems, even though they arise through structural coupling. Because a description always implies an interaction by a member of a domain of consensus, the domain of descriptions is necessarily bounded by the ultimate possible interactions of a living system through the properties of its components.

Language

The word *language* comes from the Latin noun *lingua,* which means "tongue," and, in prior usage referred mainly to speech. By extension, however, language is now used to refer to any conventional system of symbols used in communication. A language, whether in its restricted or in its generalized form, is currently considered to be a denotative system of symbolic communication, composed of words that denote entities regardless of the domain in which these entities may exist. Denotation, however, is not a primitive operation. It requires agreement—consensus for the specification of the denotant and the denoted. If denotation, therefore, is not a primitive operation, it cannot be a primitive linguistic operation, either. Language must arise as a result of something else that does not require denotation for its establishment, but that gives rise to language with all its implications as a trivial necessary result. This fundamental process is ontogenic structural coupling, which results in the establishment of a consensual domain.

Within a consensual domain the various components of a consensual interaction do not operate as denotants; at most, an observer could say that they connote the states of the participants as they trigger each other in interlocked sequences of changes of state. Denotation arises only in a metadomain as an a posteriori commentary made by the observer about the consequences of operation of the interacting systems. If the primary operation for the establishment of a linguistic domain is ontogenic structural coupling, then the primary conditions for the development of language are, in principle, common to all autopoietic systems to the extent that they are structurally plastic and can undergo recursive interactions.

Linguistic behavior is behavior in a consensual domain. When linguistic behavior takes place recursively, in a second-order consensual domain, in such a manner that the components of the consensual behavior are recursively combined in the generation of new components of the consensual domain, a language is established. The richness attained by a language throughout its history, therefore, depends necessarily both on the diversity of behaviors that can be generated and distinguished by the organisms that participate in the consensual domain, and on the actual historical realization of such behaviors and distinctions. The various failures and successes attained in the attempts to generate a linguistic domain of interactions with chimpanzees illustrate this point (Linden, 1978). In fact, whenever an attempt has been made to couple a sufficiently diversified domain of arbitrary distinctions that both the chimpanzee and the observer could make (such as visual or manual distinctions) to an at least commensurable domain of nonarbitrary distinctions (biologically significant) again common to both, an expanding linguistic domain could indeed be developed. Conversely, when the attempt was to couple two domains of distinctions whose varieties did not match in the chimpanzee and the observer, no expanding linguistic domain could be developed. The sign language of the deaf is another illustration of these points.

Linguistic Regularities

Since I have not mentioned grammar or syntax in this characterization of language, the following comments are necessary.

1. The behavior of an organism is defined in a domain of interactions under the conditions in which the organism realizes its autopoiesis. The result, if the organism is structurally plastic, is its ontogenic structural coupling to its medium through selective interactions determined by its behavior. Which structure, which physiology, is selected in a particular history of interactions in a particular organism, however, is determined by the original structure of the organism at each interaction, and not by the nature of the selecting behavior. As a result, as is well known to biologists, different physiologies can be selected through which the same behavior is enacted in different organisms, or in the same organism at different moments of its ontogeny. Accordingly, the regularities or rules that an observer can describe in the performance of any particular behavior, whether it is courtship, hunting, or speaking by the different organisms that enact it, do not reveal homorphisms in the underlying physiologies. The regularities in the performance of the behavior pertain to the domain in which the behavior is described by the observer, not to the underlying physiology. Therefore, the describable regularities of the linguistic behavior of the members of a consensual domain do not necessarily reflect an identity of the underlying physiologies that generate the linguistic behavior of the different members. Only if the original structures of the consenting organisms had been isomor-

phic could some isomorphism be expected in the physiology of similarly behaving organisms that participate in a consensual domain. Such a coincidence, however, would be a matter of historical contingency, not of structural necessity.

2. Every kind of behavior is realized through operations that may or may not be applied recursively. If recursion is possible in a particular kind of behavior and if it leads to cases of behavior of the same kind, then a closed generative domain of behavior is produced. There are many examples: Human dance is one; human language, another. What is peculiar about a language, however, is that this recursion takes place through the behavior of organisms in a consensual domain. In this context, the superficial syntactic structure or grammar of a given natural language can only be a description of the regularities in the concatenation of the elements of the consensual behavior. In principle, this superficial syntax can be any, because its determination is contingent on the history of consensual coupling, and is not a necessary result of any necessary physiology. Conversely, the "universal grammar" of which linguists speak as the necessary set of underlying rules common to all human natural languages can refer only to the universality of the process of recursive structural coupling that takes place in humans through the recursive application of the components of a consensual domain without the consensual domain. The determination of this capacity for recursive structural coupling is not consensual; it is structural and depends entirely on the operation of the nervous system as a closed neuronal network. Furthermore, this capacity for recursive structural coupling is at work both in spoken and in sign languages of human beings and in the sign and token linguistic domains established with chimpanzees (Gardner & Gardner, 1974; Premack, 1974). Thus, the structure required for a universal grammar understood as a capacity for recursive structural coupling in the operation of the nervous system is not exclusively human. The contingencies of evolution that led in man to the establishment of spoken language, however, are peculiarly human.

3. For an observer, linguistic interactions appear as semantic and contextual interactions. Yet what takes place in the interactions within a consensual domain is strictly structure-determined, interlocked concatenations of behavior. In fact, each element of the behavior of one organism operating in a consensual domain acts as a triggering perturbation for another. Thus, the behavior of organism A perturbs organism B, triggering in it an internal change of state that establishes in it a new structural background for its further interactions and generates a behavior that, in turn, perturbs organism A, which . . . perturbs organism B, which . . . , and so on in a recursive manner until the process stops—either because, as a result of the structural changes of A and B some behavior is triggered that does not belong to the

consensual domain, or because some independent intercurrent interaction occurs that leads them out of the consensual domain.

What happens in a linguistic interaction, therefore, depends strictly on the structural state of the organism undergoing the interaction. For an observer who does not know the structural states of the linguistically in-teracting organisms, the outcome of a particular linguistic interaction may seem ambiguous, as if the actual syntactic value of a particular linguistic conduct were determined by some internal, not apparent, rule. Yet for each of the actual linguistically interacting organisms there is no such ambiguity. Their internal structure, as the structural background on which their linguis-tic interactions operate as triggering perturbations, is at any moment deter-mined by their previous interactions and by their previous independent structural dynamics in a nonambiguous manner. Therefore, the context on which the outcome of a linguistic interaction depends is completely deter-mined in the structure of the interacting organisms, even if this is unknown to the observer. The overheard sentence, "They are flying planes," is am-biguous only for the observer who wants to predict the outcome of the interaction with insufficient knowledge of the structural state of the speaking organism. The question in the mind of an observing linguist would be: "How can I determine the superficial syntactic value of the components of the sentence if I do not know its deep structure that determines its effective surface structure, or if I do not know the semantic value of the sentence that, by determining its deep structure, determines its surface syntax?" In fact, this question is irrelevant; it does not refer to the processes that take place in the linguistic interactions and that determine their outcome in the consensual domain. Superficial and deep syntactic structures are features of one descrip-tions of linguistic utterances, not of the processes of their generation.

4. To understand the evolutionary origin of natural language requires the recognition of a basic biological process that could generate it. So far, this understanding has been impossible, because language has been viewed as a denotative system of symbolic communication. If that were, in fact, the way language operates in a linguistic interaction, then its evolutionary origin would demand the preexistence of denotation for agreement on the sym-bolic values of the arbitrary components of the system of communication. Yet denotation is the very function whose evolutionary origin should be explained. If we recognize that language is a system of generative consen-sual interactions, and that denotation, as merely a recursive consensual operation, operates only in a domain of consensus and not in the processes through which linguistic interactions take place, then it becomes obvious that language is the necessary evolutionary outcome, in the recursive in-teractions of organisms having closed, structurally plastic nervous systems, of a selection realized through the behavior generated on the interacting

organisms through their structural coupling in a domain of expanding ambient diversity.

Communication

The task of an observer who faces a problem in communication is either to design a system with emitter and receiver components connected via a conducting element, such that for every distinguishable state produced in the emitter a single distinguishable state is generated in the receiver, or to treat a preexisting system as if it operated like this. Since instructive interactions do not take place in the operational domains that we are considering, the emitter and receiver must be operationally congruent for the phenomenon of communication to occur. In other words, the domain of possible states of the emitter and the domain of possible states of the receiver must be homomorphic, so that each state of the emitter triggers a unique state in the receiver. If the communication system is designed by the observer, this homomorphism is obtained by construction; if a preexisting system is described as a communication system by the observer, he or she assumes this homomorphism in his or her description. In fact, every interaction can be trivially described as a communication. Therefore, it must be understood that the current view of communication as a situation in which the interacting systems specify each other's states through the transmission of information is either erroneous or misleading. If this view assumes that instructive interactions take place, it is erroneous; if this view is only meant as a metaphor, it is misleading because it suggests models that imply instructive interactions. Such errors frequently occur in attempts to explain the semantic role of language.

From all these considerations, it is apparent that an established linguistic domain is a system of communication that reflects a behavioral homomorphism resulting from structural coupling. In other words, linguistic communication always takes place after the establishment of an ontogenic structural coupling, and in that sense is trivial because it shows only that the engineer's situation has been established. What is not trivial, however, is what takes place in the process of attaining communication through the establishment of ontogenic structural coupling and the shaping of the consensual domain. During this process there is no behavioral homomorphism between the interacting organisms and, although individually they operate strictly as structure-determined systems, everything that takes place through their interactions is novel, anticommunicative, in the system that they then constitute together, even if they otherwise participate in other consensual domains. If this process leads to a consensual domain, it is, in the strict sense, a conversation, a turning around together in such a manner that all participants undergo nontrivial structural changes until a behavioral homomorphism is established and communication takes place. These precommunicative or anticommunicative interactions that take place during a conversation, then, are creative interactions that lead to novel behavior. The conditions under which a conversation takes place (common interest, spatial confinement, friendship, love, or whatever keeps the organisms together), and which determine that the organisms should continue to interact until a consensual domain is established, constitute the domain in which selection for the ontogenic structural coupling takes place. Without them, a consensual domain could never be established, and communication, as the coordination of noncreative ontogenically acquired modes of behavior, would never take place.

REALITY

The word *reality* comes from the Latin noun *res,* meaning "thing." The fundamental operation that an observer can perform is an operation of distinction, the specification of an entity by operationally cleaving it from a background. Furthermore, that which results from an operation of distinction and can thus be distinguished, is a thing with the properties that the operation of distinction specifies, and which exists in the space that these properties establish. Reality, therefore, is the domain of things, and, in this sense, that which can be distinguished is real. Thus stated, there is no question about what reality is: It is a domain specified by the operations of the observer. The question that remains is a question in the domain of cognition: It is a question about objectivity. In other words, to paraphrase the questions presented at the beginning, "How is it that we, human beings, can talk about things, describe things, and predict events in terms of things to be observed?"

After all that I have said throughout this chapter, the answer to this question should be unambiguous. Yet let me recapitulate, as an observer, the essence of what I have said.

First, the epistemological analysis of our operation as scientists showed that all scientific statements are necessarily subject-dependent, even these that I am making now as a scientist writing about the problem of objectivity.

Second, the analysis of the organization of the living and the nervous systems showed: (a) both are closed systems and, accordingly, do not offer means for the description of an objective reality; and (b) that the effective operation of a living system (nervous system included) in the medium in which it is realized (as an autopoietic unity) is the result of its structural coupling to that medium.

Third, the analysis of language showed: (a) that language exists in a consensual domain generated by the interactions of closed systems and not in the domain of states of each individual system; and (b) that a description always implies an interaction of the system that describes.

Let us now, as author and reader, adopt the roles of superobservers and answer two questions, which again are reformulations of the questions presented at the beginning:

1. How is it that human beings, being closed autopoietic systems, can talk about things and make descriptions of them?
2. How is it that, if language is behavior in a consensual domain, human beings can use language to predict events to be individually experienced?

Superobserver's Answer to the First Question

Human beings can talk about things because they generate the things they talk about by talking about them. That is, human beings can talk about things because they generate them by making distinctions that specify them in a consensual domain, and because, operationally, talking takes place in the same phenomenic domain in which things are defined as relations of relative neuronal activities in a closed neuronal network. In other words, for us as superobservers, it is apparent that human beings can talk about only that which they can specify through their operations of distinction, and that as structure-determined systems, they can only make distinctions that their structural coupling to their medium (other organisms included) permits. Accordingly, the changes of state that human beings or their instruments undergo in their interactions constitute the specification and description of the things entered as elements in their consensual domains, and this occurs under conditions in which their changes of state are determined by their structures and their structures are the result of their structural couplings. Obviously, this result is possible because, although every internal or external interaction of an organism is mapped in the relations of relative neuronal activities of its nervous system, where they cannot be distinguished as individual experiences, they can be distinguished socially in terms of behavior within a consensual domain. As a consequence, although descriptions ultimately always imply interactions of the organism through its components, language permits descriptions of entities in as many different domains as can be defined consensually, however removed from actual interactions they may seem to an observer, because linguistic descriptions always take place as consensual distinctions of relations of relative neuronal activities in the talking organisms, and consensual distinctions always imply interactions between organisms through their components. Thus, talking human beings dwell in two nonintersecting phenomenal domains: the domain of their internal states and the domain of their interactions in the consensual domain. Since these two domains are nonintersecting, neither can be reduced to the other, even though an observer can establish a homomorphism between them. This is obvious for me as a superobserver because I am external to both. For the human being talking, however, all that exists is his or her domain of experiences (internal states) on which everything is mapped, and the human being operates through experiences as if a phenomenal reduction had taken place. Yet, if he or she could be led to become a superobserver, he or she would accept the legitimacy of these multiple, nonintersecting phenomenal domains in which he or she can operate without demanding reductionist explanations.

In synthesis, although many spaces can be described through language, no space can be described that cannot be mapped onto the changes of state of the linguistically interacting organisms through the interactions of their components. Therefore, the ultimate and basic space that a composite unity can describe in a consensual domain is the space in which its components exist; the space in which its components exist determines the ultimate domain of interactions through which a composite unity can participate in the generation of a consensual domain. Thus, the human domain of descriptions is both bounded and unlimited. It is bounded, because every description that a human being makes necessarily implies an interaction through his components; it is unlimited, because through the operation of the nervous system the person can always recursively refine new phenomenic domains through the consensual specification of new unities composed through the coupling of old ones. In general, then, the ultimate space that the components of a composite system define is for such a system its ground space. Men, in particular, specify their ground space, the space which they define as composite unities by describing their components through their interactions through their components, as *the physical space*. As a consequence, the human cognitive domain, the human domain of descriptions, is necessarily closed: every human assertion implies an interaction. That about which man cannot talk he cannot speak.

Superobserver's Answer to the
Second Question

First, it is apparant that if, for the organisms that possess a natural language, to enact it is to realize their autopoiesis through their behavior in a consensual domain, then effective linguistic interactions between organisms (linguistic interactions that lead to their continued operation within the consensual domain without loss of autopoiesis) are necessarily an expression of (a) their reciprocal structural coupling; and (b) the changes in relations of relative neuronal activities in their respective nervous systems as determined by their structures and selected by their interactions.

Second, from the perspective of an observer, it is apparent that the relations of relative neuronal activities that take place in the nervous system of an organism that participates in a consensual domain result either from its structural coupling to the other members of the consensual domain, and represent (for the observer) external interactions, or from the recursive structural coupling of the nervous system to its own structure, and represent (for the observer) internal interactions. Relations of the first kind correspond to things distinguished in a consensual, social, domain; whereas relations of the second kind correspond to things distinguished in a private, personal domain that may or may not intersect with the social domain. The first correspond to experiences that pertain to a consensual reality, the second to experiences that pertain to a private, individual reality. In these circumstances, since a prediction is the realization in a consensual domain of a state in a model, and since the operation within a consensual domain as well as all the external and internal interactions of an organism involving its nervous system are equally realized as configurations of changing relations of relative neuronal activities in its nervous system, a prediction cannot but correspond to a configuration of relations of relative neuronal activities to be obtained if certain operations (other relations of relative neuronal activities) are realized. If the operations to be realized arise from relations of relative neuronal activities that correspond to external interactions, then the prediction belongs to the domain of consensual reality; if the operations to be realized arise from relations of relative neuronal activities that correspond to internal interactions, then the prediction belongs to the domain of private reality. In either case, however, predictions are realized as actual experiences, that is, as actual states of the organisms obtained through the realization of the operations that constitute the predictions if the organisms operate within the domains of structural couplings in which the predictions are made. In other words, the realization of a prediction in a consensual domain is a necessary result of the structural coupling that constitutes the consensual domain. Only if it implies operations outside the consensual domain in which it is made is a prediction not fulfilled. The operation of a structure-determined system is necessarily perfect; that is, it follows a course determined only by neighborhood relations in its structure and by nothing else. It is only in a referential domain, such as the domain of behavior, that an observer can claim that an error has occurred when his or her expectations are not fulfilled because, contrary to them, the operation of the organism reveals that it is not structurally coupled to the medium in which he or she observes it and in which he or she predicts its behavior.

Observer's Reduction to Actual Agent

These answers made by a human observer in the role of superobserver also apply to his or her own operation as an observer, because the operation of an observer is an operation in a second-order consensual domain. Accordingly, although we have played the role of superobservers in order to reveal the manner of operation of linguistic interactions, no human being can effectively operate as an absolute superobserver, because of the closure of his domain of descriptions. This, however, does not weaken the argument, which remains fully valid after collapsing the superobserver into the observer, because it is based only on relations proper to a second-order consensual domain that permit an observer to play such a role: the role of a second-order observer, the observer of the observer in its medium.

We live in a domain of subject-dependent realities, and this condition is the necessary result of our being structure-determined, closed, autopoietic systems. Yet we are not like the chained men in the cave of Plato's *Republic* who saw only the shadows of objective entities that could, at least in principle, be conceived as having an absolute reality. We are more like pharmacologists describing biologically active substances by means of the changes of state of their biological probes. There is no similarity between the changes of state that a female rabbit undergoes and the hormone that brings them about; nobody claims that there is. However, strictly, for a long time and in the absence of other methods, many substances have been characterized by the changes of state of the biological probes that revealed them. Furthermore, other methods are not effectively different from the pharmacological one. This is not a novelty. Yet it is not frequently realized, and it is less frequently taken seriously in the domain of science, that we human beings operate in our cognitive domain like the pharmacologist and that we can only operate in this way by using ourselves as biological probes with which we specify and describe the domains of reality in which we live. That we should be living systems is obviously not a necessary condition, but it is an existential condition that determines how our domains of reality are generated; because in us, as in all living systems, all operations are subordinated to the invariance of our autopoiesis.

CONCLUSION

The extent of what an organism can do is determined by its organization and structure, and all that an organism can do constitutes its cognitive domain. The way we (human beings) determine knowledge shows that implicitly or explicitly we accept this to be the case: We ask a question in a given domain and, as an answer, we expect an action, or the description of an action, in the same domain. The fact that we usually demand that human beings should be aware of their knowledge—that is, that they should be observers—does not change the matter. Our cognitive domain is bounded and unlimited in the same manner in which our domain of reality is bounded and unlimited. Knowledge implies interactions, and we cannot step out of our domain of interactions, which is closed. We live, therefore, in a domain of subject-dependent knowledge and subject-dependent reality. This means that if the questions, "What is the object of knowledge?" or "What is the objective reality of an object?" are meant to be answered by an absolute observer, then they are meaningless, because such an absolute observer is intrinsically impossible in our cognitive domain. In fact, any knowledge of a transcendental absolute reality is intrinsically impossible; if a supposed transcendental reality were to become accessible to description then it would not be transcendental, because a description always implies interactions and, hence, reveals only a subject-dependent reality. The most we can say, therefore, is that the observer generates a description of the domain of reality through his or her interactions (including interactions with instruments and through instruments), and that the observer can describe a system of systems (a system of consensus) that leads to the emergence of systems that can describe: observers. As a consequence, because the domain of descriptions is closed, the observer can make the following ontological statement: The logic of the description is isomorphic to the logic of the operation of the describing system.

Apparently all that remains is the observer. Yet the observer does not exist alone, because his existence necessarily entails at least an other being as a necessary condition for the establishment of the consensual domain in which he exists as an observer. However, what is unique to each observer and makes each observer stand alone, is, on the one hand, his or her experiences, which remain necessarily secluded in his or her operational closure, and, on the other hand, the observer's ability through second-order consensuality to operate as external to the situation in which he or she is, and thus be observer of his or hers circumstance as an observer.

Postscript: Creativity and Freedom

Much of what I have said has been intuitively accepted by philosophers since antiquity, but until now no one had proposed an explanation that could show the biological nature of the phenomena of cognition and reality. This chapter is such an explicit attempt (see also Maturana, 1970, 1974). Furthermore, until now, it had not been shown that there is no contradiction between the subject-dependent nature of our reality and our effective operation in a socially valid and seemingly objective physical world. Since a description always implies an interaction, and since the describing systems describe their components via their interactions through their components, there is a constitutive homomorphism between descriptions, and behavior in general, and the operation of the systems that describe. Therefore, we literally create the world in which we live by living it. If a distinction is not performed, the entity that this distinction would specify does not exist; when a distinction is performed, the created entity exists in the domain of the distinction only, regardless of how the distinction is performed. There is no other kind of existence for such an entity.

In this context, then, what are creativity and freedom?

Answers to these questions have been entangled in a frequent confusion of determinisms with predictability, and in the belief in the objective occurrence of the phenomenon of choice. That a system is structure determined means that it is deterministic and that in its operation choice is out of the question, but it does not mean that it is necessarily predictable. Determinism is a feature of the operation of a system, while predictability and choice are expressions that reflect the state of knowledge of the observer. If the system observed and the medium in which it is observed are known, then the system does not appear to encounter alternatives in its interactions, because it and its medium form for the observer a single predictable system; if the system or the medium are unknown, then the system appears to encounter alternatives in its interactions, because system and medium constitute operationally independent systems for the observer who cannot predict their course: in such a case the observer projects his or her own uncertainty on the system by claiming that it must make a choice. An unknown system is, for the ignorant observer, a chaos, however deterministic it may appear to the knowing observer who sees it as a structure-determined system. Once this is understood, it becomes apparent that a novelty, the new, is always an event viewed in a frame of reference from which it could not have been predicted by an observer.

When an organism enters into an interaction that arises from a contingency, that is, from an encounter with an operationally independent system (which could be part of the organism itself), the ensuing triggered changes of state of the organism could not have been predicted by an observer of the operation of the organism alone. For the observer, the organism performs a novel distinction and specifies a new reality. This is creativity: the generation by an organism of distinctions (unexpected for an observer) through its interactions with systems to which it is not structurally coupled (operationally independent systems), and to which it may become structurally coupled as a result of the interactions. Since the structure of an organism (its nervous system included) is under continuous change as a result of its autopoiesis in an operationally independent medium, organisms are, at least potentially, in the position of undergoing a continuous change in their structural couplings and, hence, of continuously encountering independent systems and thus of undergoing continuous changes of state unpredictable from their perspective alone. Creativity, then, is a necessarily widespread feature in living systems.

If an organism exists in a domain that does not determine all its interactions, so that it can undergo interactions with independent systems, there is freedom in the domain of existence of the organism. The organism is free even if its operation is deterministic, and if it can generate second-order consensual domains, it can, as an observer, recursively generate operationally independent consensual entities as a recursive observer of its circumstance. This has been well understood throughout the history of mankind. If a human being can observe the social system that he creates with his behavior, he may dislike it and reject it, and thus become a source of change; but if he can only undergo interactions specified by the social system that he integrates, he cannot be an observer of it and his behavior can only confirm it. Accordingly, all coercive political systems aim, explicitly or implicitly, at reducing creativity and freedom by specifying all social interactions as the best means of suppressing human beings as observers and thus attaining political permanence. To obtain this ultimate goal, however, the typically human mode of creativity must be completely suppressed, and this, as long as there is any capacity to establish such second-order consensual domains as the use of language requires, is impossible.

Every human being, as an autopoietic system, stands alone. Yet let us not lament that we must exist in a subject-dependent reality. Life is more interesting like this, because the only transcendence of our individual loneliness that we can experience arises through the consensual reality that we create with others, that is, through love.

ACKNOWLEDGMENT

I wish to acknowledge my indebtedness to Gloria Guiloff D., my close collaborator, to whom I owe the most fundamental insight here given, namely, the understanding of the consensual domains.

REFERENCES

Edelman, G. M. Molecular recognition in the inmune and nervous systems. In F. G. Worden, J. P. Swazey, & G. Adelman (Eds.), *The neurosciences: paths of discovery*. Cambridge: MIT Press, 1975.

Gardner, A. R., & Gardner, B. T. L'ensegnement du langage de souds-muet a Washoe. In E. Edgard-Morin & M. Piatteli-Palmarini (Eds.), *L'unite de l'homme*. Paris: Editions du Seuil, 1974.

Linden, E. *Apes, men and language*. Reino Unido: Pinguin Books, 1976.

Maturana, H. R. *Biology of cognition* (B. C. L. Report 9.0). Urbana: University of Illinois, 1970.

Maturana, H. R. Strategies cognitives. In E. Edgrad-Morin & M. Piattelli-Palmarini (Eds.), *L'unite de l'homme*. Paris: Editions du Seuil, 1974.

Maturana, H. R. The organization of the living: a theory of the living organization. *The International Journal of Man–Machine Studies*, 1975, 7, 313–332.

Maturana, H. R., & Varela, F. *De maquinas y seres vivos*. Santiago: Editorial Universitaria Santiago, 1973.

Monod, Jacques. *Le hasard et la necessite*. Paris: Editions du Seuil, 1970.

Premack, D. Le langage et sa construction logique chez l'homme et chez le chimpanze. In E. Edgard-Morin & M. Piattelli-Palmarini (Eds.), *L'unite de l'homme*. Paris: Editions du Seuil, 1974.

Varela, F., Maturana, H. R., & Uribe, R. Autopoiesis. *Biosystems*, 1974, 5, 187.

chapter 3

Pattern Formation in Chemistry and Biology: A Mini-Survey of Mechanisms

NANCY KOPELL

INTRODUCTION

For the purposes of this chapter I am tempted to rename this volume: *Language and Thought and Other Interests of Eric Lenneberg.* Eric was interested in how structures in language develop in time. Although his attention was focused mainly on language and thought, he was also interested in the formation of other kinds of structures. He was acquainted with my own work with L. N. Howard on pattern formation in chemical systems, and he raised with me the general question of whether there could be a common way of talking about pattern formation in physical systems and structure in language and thought. What I am going to discuss bears on this question and contains a word of caution. I will try to argue that, even among chemical systems, if any such language for describing the origin of structures is to be insightful, it must go beyond surface analogy and take into account some of the mechanisms that lead to the formation of the structure.

I am going to do this by examining a collection of phenomena that

65

PSYCHOLOGY AND BIOLOGY OF LANGUAGE AND THOUGHT
Essays in Honor of Eric Lenneberg

appear to be very similar. All are patterns of parallel bands or concentric circles (which are locally like parallel bands). We may ask: What do these phenomena have in common with each other besides their geometry? As we will see, although the detailed mechanisms for most of these are still controversial, enough is known to realize that, when one looks harder, the surface analogies break down badly. I will not be arguing against the use of analogy per se, only that the analogies must be deeper ones in order to be useful; in this case, geometry is not enough. I'll give some examples below of what I mean by deeper analogies.

PATTERNS INDUCED BY
EXTERNAL PERIODICITIES

The easiest types of patterns to understand are those that are induced by external periodicities. The most well-known example of this is the growth of tree rings (see Figure 3.1). It is well accepted that the growth is seasonal and that one can see the separation between periods of growth because the latewood of the summer has different characteristics from the earlywood of the spring. (The cells of the latewood are flatter and more densely packed together than those of the earlywood.)

This is not to say that the growth of wood is completely understood. Indeed, there is still controversy about how the periodicities of the environment are translated into periodicity of growth in the tree. (See Zimmerman & Brown, 1971.) One theory, popular for a long time, associated the rings with different levels of the water supply; the earlywood is formed in the spring, when it is wetter than it is in the summer. It was also known that other factors, such as length of daylight and changing temperatures, could affect the growth. More recently, there has been growing evidence that the ring formation is controlled by the seasonal levels of various types of growth promoters, including auxins and gibberellins; thus the environment can make itself felt indirectly, by stimulating the production of hormones and inhibitors that directly affect the growth.) However, at least for most trees of the temperate region, the growth rings are directly connected with the periodicities of the seasons.

Actually, the preceding statement does not adequately reflect the complexities of tree ring formation. There are some trees, particularly in tropical regions, which live in environments that are more or less constant, but which nevertheless have cycles in growth. (These cycles are not necessarily annual.) For some of these, the periodicities seem to be correlated with small changes in the environment (such as amount of rainfall); in others, they remain quite mysterious, possibly the manifestation of internal biological

Figure 3.1. Cross section of a branch of an oak tree. (Photograph by J. Schrader.)

rhythms that may also play a role in ring formation in trees of the temperate zone.

A variation on this theme involves bands in the otoliths and scales of some fish. As in tree rings, the number of these is believed to tell the age of the fish. According to Thompson (1942) however, such patterns sometimes exist in fish that live so deep that their environment appears to be unseasonal. Again there is the question: Is the microenvironment periodic, or do the rings reflect an internal rhythm?

PATTERNS PRODUCED BY
FREQUENCY GRADIENTS

The second set of phenomena I will discuss is much less known. It also involves an oscillation, one that is a little more mysterious. There is an oscillating chemical reaction, discovered by Belousov (1959), but better known as the Zhabotinskii reaction. If the appropriate oxidation-reduction indicator (ferroin) is added to the reaction mixture, the color of the fluid turns back and forth between bright blue and reddish purple several times a minute at regular intervals. Busse (1969) noticed that if this fluid is placed in a test tube and allowed to sit, it often happens that red and blue bands form in the fluid (see Figure 3.2). He thought that the bands were related to diffusion.

Later research revealed that these bands have almost nothing to do with diffusion (Kopell & Howard, 1973a). The crucial fact is that the period of the oscillation is quite sensitive to many things, including the initial concentrations of the reactants, temperature, and exposure to oxygen and other gases. If the fluid in the test tube is not very thoroughly mixed up and protected against temperature gradients, a frequency gradient can form in the tube. For example, if the sulfuric acid is added last and not mixed well, it tends to sink to the bottom since it is heavier. But higher concentrations of sulfuric acid lead to higher frequencies. Thus the oscillation frequency will be higher at the bottom than at the top. This means that any particular phase (for example, the blue phase) occurs more frequently at the bottom than at the top; what one sees is the blue phase arising at the bottom of the tube and moving upward.

It is easy to tell from simple mathematics that whenever there is a frequency gradient, if one plots in space and time points that have a particular phase, one gets a plot similar to the one in Figure 3.3, in which the spacing (period in t) at any given height is constant, but varies with height z. Indeed, this gives a way of telling whether there is a frequency gradient at work producing a given pattern; one makes a space–time picture of any given phase and looks to see if there is a constant period in time for each fixed z. Such a picture was made for the "Busse bands". As one can see from Figure 3.4, the periods are constant.

Patterns produced by a frequency gradient do not have a characteristic spatial wavelength. As time goes on, the spacing between the bands (the

Figure 3.2. Horizontal bands in the Belousov reagent. (The vertical line is a reflection of light.) (Photograph by J. Schrader.)

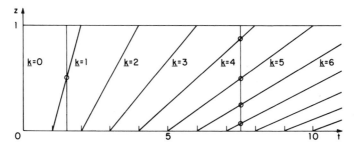

Figure 3.3 Space-time graph of points having phase $\phi = 2\pi k$, where the variation of period P with height z is $P(z) = 1 + z$, and the initial phase is zero. Note that at $t = 1.5$ there is just one point having phase $2\pi k$ for some k; at $t = 7.5$ there are four. (From N. Kopell & L..N. Howard, Horizontal bands in the Belousov reaction, *Science*, 1973, *180*, 1171–1173. Copyright 1973 by the American Association for the Advancement of Science. Reprinted by permission.)

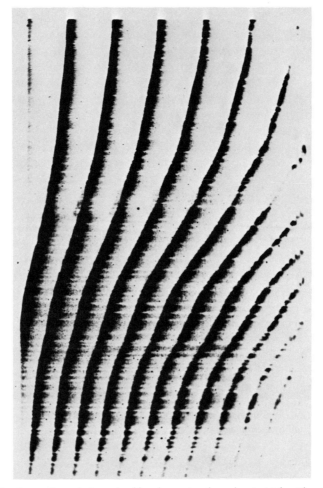

Figure 3.4. Space–time photograph of bands moving through a test tube. The picture was taken by blocking the light from all but a thin vertical strip of the tube. A camera focussed on the slit was then moved slowly so that the image of the slit swept across the film. The proportion of the horizontal axis shown represents approximately 7 minutes and the vertical range is about 20 cm. (Photograph by L. N. Howard and N. Kopell.)

blue phase) gets progressively smaller, and the bands propagate progressively more slowly. Of course, when the bands become very close to one another, diffusion must begin to play some role.

An important point to make about these patterns is that there need be no coupling of the local oscillations in order to produce the waves; the waves are so-called "kinematic waves" in which there is only the appearance of cooperative action. In fact, one can reproduce all the phenomena of the

Busse bands using a row of uncoupled pendulums of increasing frequency (see Figure 3.5). Again, if the pendulums are started together, one will see waves propagating from the point of highest frequency to the point of lowest frequency, with a constantly decreasing spatial wavelength. Here it is clear that there is no cooperative action; each pendulum acts separately.

Before I go on, I would like to use the previously cited examples to make some general points. First of all, although I am stressing the need to know something about mechanisms, I am not arguing for a reductionist approach. In the case of the moving bands in the chemical fluid, it is not necessary to know why the fluid oscillates in order to understand the formation of the bands. Why the fluid oscillates is an interesting question, and some people have worked quite hard to understand the mechanism of the oscillation (Noyes, Field, & Koros, 1972). But the mechanism of the banding is separate from the mechanism of the oscillation; the banding mechanism involves the existence of a frequency gradient which can be established independently of understanding how the frequency gradient comes about.

The second general point is about analogy. The analogy between the Busse bands and the waves in the row of pendulums is a very good one. Although the two phenomena superficially appear to be quite different (for example, one is chemical and the other is physical), the underlying mechanism for the pattern formation is exactly the same. This is an example of what I mean by an analogy deeper than geometry.

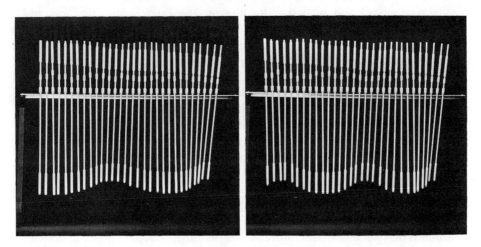

Figure 3.5. A set of compound pendulums with frequency increasing from one side to the other. The pendulums are started at the same time with the same amplitude and they develop waves such as these. If a specific phase (say zero amplitude) is illuminated in a different way, one would see bands propagating from the side of higher frequency. (Photograph by J. Schrader.)

LIESEGANG RINGS: PERIODIC
PRECIPITATION PATTERNS

It may seem by now that all spatial "periodicity" involves some kind of oscillation in time, but this is not the case. For example, there are the well-studied Liesegang rings of periodic precipitation (Stern, 1954, 1967). After more than three-quarters of a century of study there is still controversy over the formation of these rings, but nobody has yet suggested that it involves an oscillating chemical reaction. This precipitation phenomenon occurs for an enormously wide variety of reactions, possibly, in the appropriate circumstances, for almost any slightly soluble material. For definiteness, I choose a particular example: Consider a test tube filled partly with a gel that contains a small amount of potassium iodate (KIO_3). Suppose a more concentrated solution of silver nitrate ($AgNo_3$) is placed on top and allowed to diffuse downward. The silver reacts with the iodate to produce insoluble $AgIO_3$. If the concentrations are in the right ranges, the precipitate appears, not continuously, but in bands (see Figure 3.6). When the reaction is carried out in a watchglass, concentric rings appear.

In many of the reactions, these bands have a predictable spacing. At the top there is a thickish band of continuous precipitation, and then a sequence of bands obeying the following law: If D is the distance from the interface to the first band, then the distance from the interface to the $(n+1)^{st}$ band is Dk^n, where k is a constant greater than 1 that depends on initial concentrations, the type of gel and other factors; that is, the ratio of the distances of successive bands to the interface is constant. This "law" is far from universal. Recently, investigators have discovered that some systems give precipitation bands for which the spacing decreases with distance to the interface. These are the so-called "revert" structures (Mather & Ghosh, 1958), which remain a major mystery of the Liesegang literature. There are also secondary structures, which fill in between the bands of the first structure. (See Thompson, 1942, for a picture of such secondary structures.)

The Liesegang rings were first explained as a supersaturation phenomenon by Ostwald (1897), and the most quantitative discussion available is a model by Prager (1956) based on that idea. Using the previous example, very roughly the argument is this: It is assumed that precipitation will occur only when the concentration product $[Ag^+][IO_3^-]$ reaches some critical level K_c which is above the equilibrium level. ($[Ag^+]$ and $[IO_3^-]$ denote the concentrations of silver and iodate ions.) It is also assumed that after precipitation at some height, the concentration of iodate remains zero at that place (an assumption which is plausible since $[IO_3^-]$ starts out quite low). The argument is a little hazy right at the interface, so we go to a band that has just

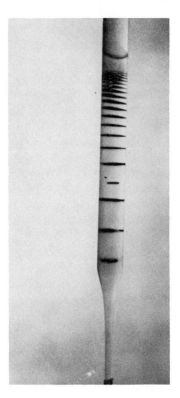

Figure 3.6. Liesegang bands. (Photograph courtesy of J. Ross and M. Flicker.)

precipitated to see why there is a spacing before the next band. The main point is that the silver continues to diffuse downward and the iodate just below the band diffuses upward toward the band. Thus, for fixed times, the concentrations of silver and iodate are as in Figure 3.7a with x measured downward from the band of precipitation. The product $[Ag^+]$ $[IO_3^-]$ has the form given in Figure 3.7b. The maximum of the product occurs for increasing x as time increases; this maximum first decreases and then increases until it reaches the critical value K_c. At that time, and at that point in space, a new band emerges.

The supersaturation explanation has been controversial from the beginning, but it has never been fully superseded. In any case, it is clear that it is not the whole story, which involves the details of the precipitation. In most cases, the precipitate appears first as a colloid; its formation depends on such things as the nature of the gel and the concentrations of all the electrolytes in the solution, some of which tend to coagulate the colloid and some of which stabilize it. The colloid adsorbs some of the electrolytes, and

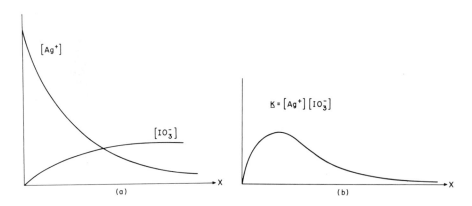

Figure 3.7 (a) Schematic diagram of concentration of silver and iodate ions at some fixed time as a function of distance from the last band. (b) Schematic diagram of the solubility product $[Ag^+] [IO_3^-]$ at some fixed time as a function of distance from the last band. (After Prager, 1956.)

this seems to be an important feature in ring formation. Competing theories of Liesegang rings emphasize either adsorption or coagulation (see Stern, 1954). It seems safe to say that for each theory there is an experiment that is unexplainable.

It seems possible that much of the data may be rationalized by using a model similar to Prager's, in which all the names are changed (see Hedges, 1932). For example, instead of a critical solubility product, one may speak of critical levels of concentration needed for coagulation. If this turns out to be true, then the family of phenomena lumped together as Liesegang rings would at least be mathematically alike, if not physically the same. None of the above theories can yet adequately explain the revert structures.

Some naturally occurring minerals (e.g., some forms of agate and jasper) are thought to form patterns for such reasons (see Figure 3.8). But it is very difficult to sort out the effects of the Liesegang phenomena from other factors that also produce rings. For example, agates form in the hollows of other rocks that fill in with silica gel; other minerals flow in through small passages in the outer rock, react with ions in the spaces of the gel, and form insoluble precipitates, often iron oxides. (Later, the gel and the precipitates crystallize.) These are the circumstances appropriate for the formation of Liesegang rings (C. Frondel, personal communication. See also Dana, 1944–1962; Liesegang, 1915). However, rings also appear in agate because the factors affecting the precipitation, such as the composition of the mineral solution flowing in, the temperature, and the pressure, change over time. Thus the rings can be seen partially as a history of the agate. Similarly, the bands in malachite (Figure 3.9) form when conditions change as the material is being deposited out of solution onto rough surfaces.

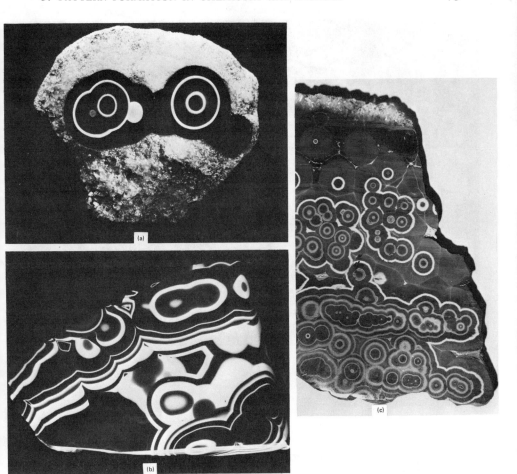

Figure 3.8. (a) Agate. (b) Agate. (c) Jasper. (Photographs courtesy of D. Cook. Specimens from the Harvard University Mineralogical Museum.)

HYDRODYNAMICAL PATTERNS: DOUBLE DIFFUSION

So far, all the examples have been chemical; the next set shows that bands can occur for reasons that are purely hydrodynamical, without any chemical reactions. There is a variety of related phenomena in fluid mechanics in which pairs of gradients interact to produce spatial bands. These phenomena appear to be important in understanding ocean currents,

Figure 3.9. Malachite. (Photograph courtesy of D. Cook. Specimen from the Harvard University Mineralogical Museum.)

but can also be reproduced in the laboratory. A typical one is as follows (Turner 1974): A tank of water is filled in such a way that there is a gradient in salt concentration, with the saltier water on bottom. Since salty water is denser than fresh water, this creates a density gradient, which tends to prevent convective motion. Now the tank is heated from below, so there is also a heat gradient. The hot water is less dense than the cold water, so this tends to destabilize the fluids, but the rise of the warm fluid is opposed by the other gradient. The following compromise happens: The bottom layer begins to convect, becoming reasonably uniform in salt and temperature, and this layer keeps growing in depth up to a certain size. The heat diffuses across the interface faster than the salt, and starts a new convective layer; in this way successive layers are formed (see Figure 3.10). This process is known in hydrodynamics as a double diffusion phenomenon and occurs for pairs of substances like salt and heat, or sugar and salt, which have different diffusion coefficients and which affect the density of a fluid.

Figure 3.10. Layers formed in a 25 cm wide tank of smoothly stratified salt solution by heating from below. The layers are marked with fluorescein dye and aluminum powder. (From Turner, 1974. Reproduced, with permission, from the *Annual Review of Fluid Mechanics*, Volume 6, © 1974 by Annual Reviews Inc.)

PATTERNS FORMED BY CHEMICAL
REACTION AND DIFFUSION

We have already seen in the case of agates that the same system is capable of producing bands for quite different reasons. The next phenomenon is a more spectacular example of this. It involves the oscillating chemical reaction mentioned earlier. This time, the fluid is thoroughly mixed and placed in a thin (approximately 2 mm) layer; there are no long distance gradients involved. One sees the following: Bright blue spots appear in the darker background and grow in size, moving outward. The centers of these spots then turn dark, and the dark centers grow. This keeps repeating, and

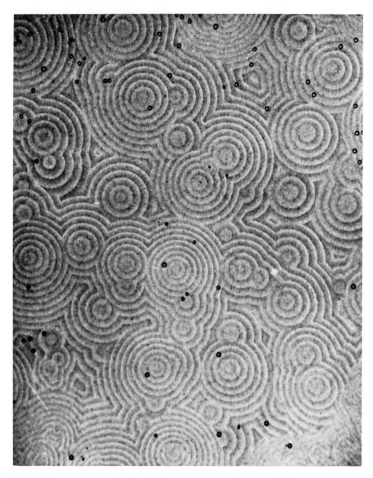

Figure 3.11. Target patterns in the Belousov reagent. (Photograph by L. N. Howard and N. Kopell.)

after 5 to 10 min the entire sheet of fluid is covered with sets of concentric rings or "target patterns (see Figure 3.11). In detail, the pattern is never the same, but certain features of the pattern are always the same. For example, within any given target pattern the spacing of the rings is almost constant, though this constant varies from one target pattern to another; similarly each target pattern has its own characteristic frequency of oscillation and speed of propagation of its rings. Where the target patterns touch each other, there are "shocks" across which the spacing, frequency, and propagation speed change abruptly. This was essentially described by Zaiken and Zhabotinskii (1970).

For these phenomena diffusion is important. If one analyzes the equations describing the interaction of the chemical reaction with diffusion, many of the repeatable features of the patterns can be rationalized (Howard & Kopell, 1977; Kopell & Howard, 1973b). Furthermore, one need not know very much about the oscillation itself in order to understand the pattern formation. That is, the mathematics says roughly that if there is an oscillation in the chemical reaction, and some other checkable conditions hold, the patterns can form. Thus, as in the case of the Busse bands, the pattern formation problem is quite independent of the question: Why does the system oscillate? I use this point to emphasize once more that when I discuss the need to look at mechanisms for pattern formation, I am not advocating a completely reductionist approach; the chief mechanism here involves the interaction between a chemical oscillation and diffusion, regardless of how that oscillation comes into being.

BIOLOGICAL EXAMPLES OF PATTERN FORMATION

Dictyostelium Discoideum

Finally, we shall get to some biological examples where it becomes much harder, but no less important, to spell out the mechanisms. The first example involves waves of aggregation in the slime mold amoebae *Dictyostelium discoideum*. These social amoebae live as separate one-celled creatures until the food supply runs out; then they begin a complex series of events that culminate in the erection of a multicelled fruiting body (Bonner, 1967). The first stage of this is aggregation. In some species, the amoebae migrate to a central spot in pulsating waves (see Figure 3.12). Some investigators have postulated that the central amoebae send out periodic pulses of a chemical called an acrasin (probably cyclic AMP) that triggers each wave, and the pulses are relayed by the rings of amoebae. (See Cohen & Robinson 1971a, b; Gerisch, 1968 for further references.)

The waves of aggregation are sometimes compared with the target patterns in the Zhabotinskii reaction (Gerisch, Malchow, & Hess, 1974; Winfree, 1972). It is unclear whether this comparison captures the essential reasons for the waves in *Dictyostelium*. In the chemical reagent, each point in the fluid is undergoing spontaneous oscillations; in the case of the amoebae, most of the creatures appear to be quiescent until triggered. However, there is a modification of the Zhabotinskii reagent which is not oscillatory, but is capable of sustaining propagating waves (Winfree, 1972). (This is less understood mathematically.) Furthermore, in a modified environment, the *Dictyostelium* amoebae do sometimes oscillate; spontaneous

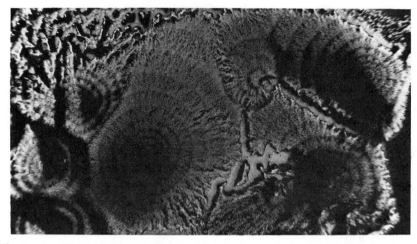

Figure 3.12. Rings of different densities of *D. discoideum* during aggregation. (Photograph courtesy of G. Gerisch.)

periodic activity in the level of cAMP has been observed in stirred cell suspensions (Gerisch *et al.,* 1974). The real question about the analogy is whether the other processes involved in the aggregation, notably the movement of the amoebae in response to the gradients of acrasin, are a crucial part of the production of the waves or merely a consequence that can be uncoupled in an analysis (if not in fact).

The aggregation in *Dictyostelium* is an interesting case, since it highlights a difficulty in the scientific formulation of a problem: What does one assume as given, and what does one try to explain from there? The description of aggregation given by Cohen and Robertson (1971 a, 1971b) assumes that the central amoebae have differentiated to be able to produce pulses of acrasin. Why that happens is a different question; the aggregation problem is to understand how the rest of the colony reacts to the acrasin by producing pulsing waves of movement. This point of view is not necessarily applicable to aggregation in the other species of slime mold which do not appear to have autonomous oscillations. Keller and Segel (1970) think that the start of aggregation could be due to instabilities in the concentration of acrasin produced by the sheet of amoebae spread out uniformly on the agar. The amoebae that are to become centers for the aggregation are different only in their location (relative to small differences in acrasin concentration). The central amoebae eventually do have different properties, but this differentiation is treated as a consequence of the instabilities that initiate the aggregation, and not as an event prior to it. Indeed, this point of view may be useful for analyzing an early phase of aggregation in *D. discoideum.* Before forming dense rings of amoebae, the creatures first organize themselves into streams of cells that then curl around some points. The amoebae at these points become aggregation centers; but there are no functional differences which can be observed prior to the curling stage (Gerisch, 1968). (Even in the Zhabotinskii reagent, it is controversial whether or not a foreign body at the center of each target pattern is needed.)

Nectria Cinnabarina

The next example involves the fungus *Nectria cinnabarina* (see Figure 3.13). There are various fungi that produce banded patterns as the hyphae of

Figure 3.13. *Nectria cinnabarina.* (From Winfree, 1973. Reprinted by permission.)

a colony grow radially outward from a point innoculation; the bands are rings of dense and less dense growth of hyphae. Some of these, such as the "clock" mutant of Neurospora (Pittendrigh, Bruce, & Rosensweig, 1959) produce bands in response to diurnal light cycles. In contrast, the banding in Nectria does not seem to be due to a circadian rhythm. The bands form in cultures maintained in continuous light, and the time it takes to produce a new ring ranges from 6 to 16 hr depending on temperature (Bourret, Lincoln, & Carpenter, 1969).

The mechanism of the ring formation is unknown. However, the experiments of Bourret, Lincoln, and Carpenter (1971) seem to implicate diffusion. These experiments showed that the periodicity is unaffected by food levels, as long as the organism is not starved. But various manipulations that affect the diffusion in the agar do affect the spacing of the bands; this includes using heavy water or a more concentrated agar, or growing the fungus on dialysis membrane. It is possible that the colony produces an inhibitor which diffuses outward into the gel.

In this case, as in the Liesegang rings, there is no reason to believe that spatial patterns are due to an underlying temporal oscillation. One possibility is suggested by the models of Meinhardt and Gierer (1974). These authors model the interaction of an "activator" and an "inhibitor" with diffusion, the inhibitor having a much larger diffusion coefficient. Their computer simulations indicate that if growth is modeled by infrequently lengthening the spatial field, the equations have solutions similar to patterns of the fungi; new regions of high activation concentration appear periodically in space as the length of the field grows. Unlike the reaction–diffusion equations used to model the target patterns in the Zhabotinskii reagent, there is no temporal oscillation in the reaction between the chemicals; without diffusion, the reaction tends to a stable steady state, which the diffusion acts to destabilize. (Turing [1952] was the first person to suggest this idea in a biological context.) This model requires at least two chemicals to be reacting and diffusing at different rates. So far, there is not enough evidence to know if this model, or some modification of it, is applicable (see also Winfree, 1973).

As Bourret et al. (1971) point out, even if a mechanism involving diffusion in the substrate turns out to be correct for Nectria, it probably does not provide a general explanation for zonation patterns in other fungi. The circadian rhythms of Neurospora behave quite differently. Furthermore, there are noncircadian hyphal growth rhythms, for example, in Ascobolus immersis (Chevaugon & van Huong, 1969), which seem to use internal control mechanisms rather than diffusion in the substrate.

There is another, more complicate phenomenon in which diffusion of an inhibitor is thought to play a part. This is banding of the feathers in the appropriately named Barred Plymouth Rock Fowl (Ursprung, 1966; see his bibliography for further references on this topic).

CONCLUSION

What are we to make of these examples? It seems clear to me that one has to be careful about classifying patterns by their geometry, without taking a hard look at the specifics of each pattern. Indeed, if I were to be faced with still another unexplored example of banding (see Figure 3.14), I would not immediately assume it resembles any of the examples I have discussed. We have seen various examples of mechanisms for producing a banding pattern; these include externally imposed oscillations, internal oscillations interacting with diffusion, frequency gradients, chemical gradients with diffusion, chemotaxis, instabilities, and growth. This is hardly and inclusive list. In biological situations, in addition to the chemistry and transport processes,

Figure 3.14. Convict cichlid (*Nigrofascium*). (Photograph by J. Schrader.)

there are electrical effects, pressure, crystal properties, and many other candidates for mechanisms.

I have tried to make a distinction between surface analogies, derived from the geometry of the forms, and deeper analogies based on underlying mechanisms. Such deeper analogies need not be in the physics, but could be in the similarity of the mathematical description; for example, the kinematic waves in the row of pendulums are essentially the same as those in Busse bands of the oscillating chemical reaction and quite different from the Liesegang rings or the target patterns.

I have also tried to suggest that what constitutes an "explanation," or even an adequate description, of a pattern formation phenomenon is more than a description of its geometry and something less than a complete molecular dissection. That is, an adequate description must, in some way, distinguish any given pattern from others that occur for fundamentally different reasons. But there is no need to have total information about a system to know the mechanisms for the pattern formation; spelling out the mechanisms involves explicitly stating which facts about the system will be taken as given. For example, in analyzing tree rings, we do not simultaneously try to explain why the seasons occur. In complicated biological situations, this may not be easy.

The examples I have discussed represent a range of different mechanisms. If there is to be a unifying theory applicable to many of these, it should be rich enough to articulate the differences as well as the similarities.

REFERENCES

Belousov, B. *Sbornik referat po radiats, meditsine 1958.* Moscow: Medzig, 1959.

Bonner, J. T. *The cellular slime molds.* Princeton: Princeton University Press, 1967.

Bourret, J. A., Lincoln R. G., & Carpenter, B. H. Fungal endogenous rhythms expressed by spiral figures. *Science,* 1969, *166,* 763.

Bourret, J. A., Lincoln, R. G., & Carpenter, B. H. Modification of the period of a noncircadian rhythm in *Nectria cinnabarina. Journal of Plant Physiology,* 1971, *47,* 682.

Busse, H. G. A spatially periodic homogeneous chemical reaction. *Journal of Physical Chemistry,* 1969, *73,* 750.

Cohen, M. H., & Robertson, A. Wave propagation in the early stages of aggregation of cellular slime molds. *Journal of Theoretical Biology,* 1971, *31,* 101. (a)

Cohen, M. H., & Robertson, A. Chemotaxis and the early stages of aggregation in cellular slime molds. *Journal of Theoretical Biology,* 1971, *31,* 119. (b)

Chevaugon, J., & Van Huong, N. Internal determinism of hyphal growth rhythms. *Transaction of the British Mycological Society,* 1969, *53.*

Dana, J. D. *Dana's system of minerology* (Vol. 3, 7th ed.). New York: Wiley, 1944–1962.

Gerisch, G. Cell aggregation and differentiation in *Dictyostelium.* In *Current topics in developmental biology* (Vol. 3). New York: Academic Press, 1968.

Gerisch, G., Malchow, D., & Hess, B. Cell communication and cyclic AMP regulation during aggregation of the slime mold, *Dictyostelium discoideum*. In L. Jaenicke (Ed.), *Biochemistry of sensory functions*. Berlin: Springer-Verlag, 1974.

Hedges, E. *Liesegang rings and other periodic structures*. London: Chapman and Hall, 1932.

Howard, L. N., & N. Kopell. Slowly-varying waves and shock structures in reaction-diffusion equations. *Studies in Applied Mathematics, 1977, 56,* 95.

Keller, E. F., & Segel, L. A. Initiation of slime mold aggregation viewed as an instability. *Journal of Theoretical Biology,* 1970. *26,* 399.

Kopell, N., & Howard, L. N. Horizontal bands in the Belousov reaction. *Science, 1973, 180,* 1171. (a)

Kopell, N., & Howard, L. N. Plane wave solutions to reaction-diffusion equations. *Studies in Applied Mathematics, 1973, 52,* 291. (b)

Liesegang, R. E. *Die Achate*. Dresden and Leipzig, 1915.

Mathur, P. B., & Ghosh, S. Liesegang rings, Part I: revert system of Liesegang rings. *Kolloid-Zeitrift, 1958, 159,* 143.

Meinhardt, H., & Gierer, A. Application of a theory of biological pattern formation based on lateral inhibition. *Journal of Cell Science, 1974, 15,* 321.

Noyes, R. M., Field, R. J., & Koros, E. Oscillations in chemical systems II: Thorough analysis of temporal oscillations in the Bromate-Cerium-Malonic Acid System. *Journal of the American Chemical Society, 1972, 94,* 8649.

Ostwald, W. *Lehrbuch der algemeinen chemie*. Leipzig: Engelman, 1897.

Pittendrigh, C. S., Bruce, V. G., Rosensweig, N. S., & Rubin, M. L. Growth patterns in *Neurospora*. *Nature, 1959, 184,* 169.

Prager, S. Periodic precipitation. *Journal of Chemical Physics, 1956, 25,* 297.

Stern, K. H. The Liesegang phenomenon. *Chemical Reviews, 1954, 54,* 79.

Stern, K. H. *A bibliography of Liesegana rings*. Washington, D.C.: U.S. Government Printing Office, 1967.

Thompson, D. W. *On growth and form*. Cambridge: Cambridge University Press, 1942.

Turing, A. M. The chemical basis of morphogenesis. *Philosophical Transactions of the Royal Society, 1952,* B *237,* 37.

Turner, J. S. Double-diffusive phenomenona. *Annual Review of Fluid Mechanics, 1974, 6,* 37–56.

Ursprung, H. The formation of patterns in development. In M. Locke (Ed.), *Major problems of development*. London: Academic Press, 1966.

Winfree, A. T. Spiral waves of chemical activity. *Science, 1972, 175,* 634.

Winfree, A. T. Polymorphic pattern formation in the fungus *Nectria*. *Journal of Theoretical Biology, 1973, 38,* 363.

Zaiken, A. N., & Zhabotinskii, A. M. Concentration wave propagation in two-dimension liquid-phase self-oscillating system. *Nature, 1970, 225,* 535.

Zimmerman, M. H., & Brown, C. L. *Trees, structure and function*. New York: Spinger-Verlag, 1971.

chapter 4

Three Levels of Mentation and the Hierarchic Organization of the Human Brain

JOSEPH ALTMAN

THREE LEVELS OF MENTATION

Several ideas are current about the problem of mind–brain relationship. Descartes's dualistic interactionism, which holds that mind has a separate existence but can affect or be affected by the brain, is still defended by many in modified forms (Beloff, 1952; Eccles, 1970; Rosenblueth, 1970; Ornstein, 1972). A more modern view is that mental states do not exist and that mental terms and concepts refer to behavioral processes or dispositions (Ryle, 1949; Shaffer, 1968). Still another modern view is that mental processes have no separate existence but are identical with certain brain processes (Place, 1956; Smart, 1959).

In this chapter I will defend a biological, two-component theory according to which specific types of mentation are integral elements of specific classes of neural activities. That is, where there is an association between mental and brain events there is also an indivisible reciprocal interdependence such that neither component of the neuropsychic process (the neural

87

PSYCHOLOGY AND BIOLOGY OF LANGUAGE AND THOUGHT
Essays in Honor of Eric Lenneberg

or the psychic) can function without the other. This general hypothesis is based on the empirically defensible view that mentation has an evolutionary history, which implies that mentation and improvements in mentation contribute to organic survival. The specific hypothesis of a reciprocal interdependence of certain classes of neural processes and certain kinds of mental activities is based on experimental evidence about the organization of neural and behavioral functions in vertebrates. The idea will be developed that routine (nonchoice) activities, whether inborn or acquired, are mediated by neural processes that do not involve mentation (apsychic functions). But when the individual has to make a choice between alternative responses, or when a singular or novel action offers existential advantages, neuropsychic mechanisms are activated, and privately experienced mental processes become involved in the determination of action.

I propose that in the evolution of vertebrates, from early beginnings to man, three hierarchically organized neuropsychic systems have emerged. The three levels will be referred to as the *pathic, iconic,* and *noetic.* Each of these systems is involved in the processing of sensory information, in satisfying the organism's needs and wants, and in generating action. I will attempt to describe in broad outlines the characteristics of mentation at each level, their relation to specific neural systems, and their functional utility in the control of behavior.

Aspects of Pathic Mentation

Pathic mentation refers to psychic functions that are best characterized as sensuous experiences or feelings and include a wide range of ego-oriented, subjective processes such as affects, moods, emotions, and passions. Pathic mentation appears in the sensory domain as protopathic sensation (Head, 1920), such as pain, itch, warmth, smells, and tastes. In all of these, information about external objects or events is linked inextricably with the feelings of pleasure or displeasure. Pathic experiences are never neutral: In their weakest form they are titillating and, when intense, they appear as an excruciating pain, a passionate desire, or a maddening rage. The evaluations produced on the pathic level are binary in nature, as exemplified by such polar mental states as like and dislike, fear and anger, love and hate; and they lead to similarly polarized opposing action patterns, such as acceptance and rejection, flight and fight, affiliation and dissociation. The organic function of pathic mentation is existential intensification and amplification: to arouse, mobilize, and sustain actions (Tomkins, 1962) and to prevent the neglect of vital goals because of distraction, discouragement, or fatigue.

I postulate that pathic mentation plays a functional role in instinctive behavior not only in man (McDougall, 1928) but even in the lowest of vertebrates. It may be an essential functional link in such action patterns as the furious attack of predatory sharks, the persistent upstream migration of homing salmon, or the untiring food gathering of a mother bird. In man, the crying of the infant demanding gratification of its hunger or relief from its discomfort exemplifies the ontogeny of pathic processes. Pathic mentation surfaces in its primordial form in adults when a person's life is threatened (choking, drowning, burning, extreme danger) or his or her wants are thwarted (extreme states of deprivation, frustration). In milder and compounded form pathic mentation is the foundation of sentiments: of our attachments to and identification with certain things and our rejection of others. The absence of affectively mediated ego-involvement leads to apathy, alienation, and mental stupor, that is, to the collapse of all higher-level mental activities.

Aspects of Iconic Mentation

Pathic mentation provides awareness either of the state of the subject or of his ego-centered assessment of objects or events. In contrast, the awareness that appears on the iconic level is object-oriented and is concerned with things or happenings. The term "iconic," which refers to visual images, is extended here to denote patterned or structured mental representations in several modalities (visual, auditory, and tactile), irrespective of whether they are directly available to the senses, as in perceptual images, or are recalled from the past, as in memory images (Richardson, 1969; Sheehan, 1972). Higher organisms have relatively little use for "stimuli" or "sensations"; what they need and what they actively seek is reliable information about the properties of objects around them and about the course of certain events. Iconic mentation plays a major role in the construction of congruent perceptual models or representations of "reality" (Craik, 1943) from the sense data available; the iconic process is the basis of our awareness or apprehension of an external world.

The impressions produced at the pathic level are diffuse or structureless, as exemplified by a piercing or dull pain, or an unanalyzable smell or taste. The impressions produced at the iconic level, in contrast, have a spatial or temporal structure, as exemplified by the texture of an object, the visual image of a flower or a fruit or, in the auditory realm, by a specific song or call. The production of structured percepts requires a series of operational accomplishments. Neural processes decay quickly (in matters of milliseconds), whereas the tactile or visual scanning of a textured three-dimensional object or the temporal integration of a sequence of sound patterns may require a relatively long time (several seconds). The task is seemingly accomplished by projection of the extracted and combined sense data on an internal "screen." This aspect of iconic processing necessitates short-term storage. But this is not enough. Percepts usually contain information that is retrieved from long-term storage of relevant past experiences. The matching of presently available sense data with memory data is necessary because the impressions that are available may be too fleeting to allow thorough scanning or they may be in flux, due to changing relations between the object and the perceiver (Gibson, 1966; Neisser, 1972). The matching process, moreover, provides not only perceptual details but also associations that are essential to assess the relevance or significance of the percept. This matching of presently available details with details retrieved from memory stores is what the imaging process is. It is a process that provides maximally enriched information about the outside world. It can be a very fast economical process because some details are rapidly filled in by memory processes.

Once the iconic production of percepts evolved, additional uses and advantages accrued. In the motivational domain, information about goal objects can be stored and retrieved, and the memory image can serve as a source of incentives and expectations (Tolman, 1932). This provides the organism with increased autonomy, enabling it to shift from respondent to operant behavior. Recall can, in turn, promote memory consolidation by allowing rehearsal of short-lived experiences. Memory images may also provide vicarious gratification, as in dreaming and the reliving of past experiences. Finally, in the action domain, memory processes of action patterns or schemata allow the acquisition and display of complex skills by chaining certain movements and actions into ever more complex ones on the basis of trial-and-error and practice.

Aspects of Noetic Mentation

While the function of iconic mentation is to construct models or representations of external things or events, noetic mechanisms enable man to go beyond the concrete image, perceived or recalled. Man forms concepts or ideas of what he perceives, assigns symbols (such as names) to them, and manipulates these vicariously while thinking and reasoning (Cassirer, 1944).

Concept formation and the generation of ideas presuppose abstracting capacity. However, abstraction and generalization are necessary but not sufficient conditions of conceptualization. Abstraction is the perceptual selection or focusing of attention on some aspect or part of the multitude of signals that reach the organism at any given time and is characteristic of all types of information processing, pathic or iconic. In conceptualization there is a systematic shift from one aspect of a percept to another in terms of categories, principles, or hypotheses in an attempt to find the class membership of the object or event and to assign the culturally determined conventional symbol of that class to it. A particular tree, others that are similar to it, and still others that are in many respects dissimilar but can meet certain explicit or implicit criteria of this class of objects, all are referred to by the adopted verbal symbol *tree*. And not only objects but, more importantly, fleeting events, recognized or suspected relations among them, the properties and functions of objects and events, and so forth, can all be similarly conceptualized and symbolized. For instance, related to the object concept of tree is the function concept of burning; importantly, the latter is applicable to many other things as well, such as coal, kerosene, or methane. The concept of tree may be related, in other contexts, to the property concepts of strength or durability, as can a class of in other ways dissimilar things, such as stone, bricks, aluminum, or steel.

Concepts are products of thinking, and thinking is not possible without concepts. In thinking, concepts are brought together that may not be manifestly related to one another as, in our previous example, a tree was associated with coal, kerosene, and methane when we were concerned with heating; and with stone, bricks, and metals when we thought of construction. One of the great benefits of thinking is this freedom of vicariously arranging and rearranging objects and events in terms of their functions and relations to one another by manipulating their symbols in the presence or absence of their referents. Thinking makes possible not only the narrative reconstruction of past events, which can be done by memory imaging, but it also allows the prediction or "fore-seeing" of future events. This becomes particularly useful when, in a given situation, alternative courses are available and the choice is made by an appropriate prediction of the outcome of each. To the extent that the concepts utilized in imaginative thinking are congruent with the characteristics and behavior of their referents (that is, they are valid), and to the extent that the inferences and judgments made are congruent with empirically validated logical operations, the charting of a future course of events by thinking has a good chance of being realizable. However, the less reliance is placed on the empirical matching and testing of the concepts used and the intellectual operations performed, the more thought becomes divorced from reality and becomes a mechanism to satisfy personal desires, as in daydreaming and fantasy. Fantasy, like directed or empirical thinking, presupposes the manipulation of complex ideas, but it is carried out for exactly the opposite purpose for which practical thinking is used, namely, as a means of escape from the real world by constructing an imaginary one. Such autistic thinking tends to be directed toward satisfying personal needs and wishes, such as becoming wealthy, wielding power, gratifying sexual needs, or achieving other desires "vicariously."

The symbol is a code in some medium (vocal, gestural, tactile, or pictorial) through which an idea, which is a transient private experience, is endowed with substantive existence such that it can be stored for future use, manipulated in thought, and transmitted to others in communication. The symbol is usually a word, a shorthand of great utility provided that it does "bring to mind" the idea that it stands for. The concept evoked by a word (or other symbol) in the thinker, speaker, or listener is its meaning. The word (or other symbol) is arbitrary in origin (in a historical sense) and need not bear any resemblance to the idea that it stands for (Locke, 1690). But there is cultural coercion so that, in a given society, words are used conventionally. Words and phrases are of great importance. When we generate simple, everyday thoughts we race from one "idea" to the next by the expedient use of conventional phrases with just fragments of the matching ideas coming to mind to ensure that the intent of the thought process is not lost. But we can use ideas for which we have no words, and our vocabulary is progressively enriched by newly coined words that express new ideas.

The cognitive use of language is predominant in private thought and in interrogative and instructive communication (seeking information from or passing information to others). But the association of language and thought is a secondary one insofar as vocalization has its origin, both phylo- and ontogenetically, as a means of social communication, not as a vehicle for the expression of thoughts. Communication starts early in the life of an animal when the young begs for food or protection and the appeal is met by the parent. Communication continues as an important regulatory force in the interaction between members of a school, flock, pack, or herd. Communication is displayed by the human infant before it gives any sign of an ability to think, when it cries in distress, to be fed, or to be relieved of its discomfort, and smiles to express its satisfaction. When true language develops in the child, replacing primitive emotional utterances and expressions, it remains a powerful vehicle for social communication. Language is used by adults as a tool for expressing moods, wishes, intents, and anxieties; as a means of resolving conflicts when threats are hurled at another or appeasement is sought. Moreover, language also has its uses in the realm of action; it can be used as a substitute for action when we instruct others to do things that we would otherwise have to do ourselves. Finally, language can also be used to express feelings and higher sentiments, since all mental processes become rationalized and intellectualized in man. This circumstance, that not only experiences with external referents but also our own activities and experiences (the role played by our eyes and ears in perception and our memories and feelings in action) can be verbalized and reflected upon is the basis of another phenomenon on this level, namely, self-awareness.

Summary

As it is schematically summarized in Figure 4.1, mentation appears on the pathic level as sensuous experience, as exemplified by protopathic sensations, desires, and passions. These uniquely emotional or affective processes provide organisms with private experiences about their own condition and their existential situation. On this level there is no awareness of an external world, of structured objects and events projected into the environment. The perception of an objective world appears on the iconic level. The iconic apprehension of the "real" world is an immediate one; that is, the subject's awareness is restricted to and preempted by the direct experience of external happenings (Sartre, 1957). This mental state can be illustrated by the nature of our subjective experience when we are so preoccupied with the pursuit of a task that we cannot reflect on what we are doing. Reflection becomes possible when the subject with noetic (conceptual and linguistic) capacities not only perceives but is also aware that he is perceiving and can

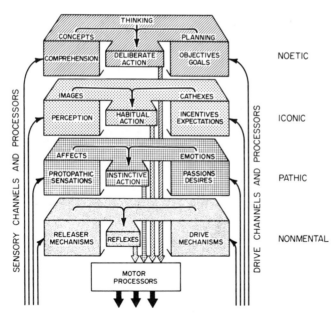

Figure 4.1.   The hierarchic integrator system of the human brain is hypothesized to have four levels, three of which are dependent on mentation. The intimate interconnections among the levels are not shown.

examine the role played by his eyes, ears, and fingers in having perceptions. This reflection soon leads to a separation of the experiencing self from the world, which is the foundation of self-awareness.

NEURAL SYSTEMS INVOLVED IN MENTATION

According to the hypothesis elaborated here, the three hierarchic levels of mentation are inextricably linked with neural systems that are, likewise, hierarchically organized (Figure 4.1). The place of this complex neuro-psychic system in relation to the neurobiologically conceptualized total behavioral system is illustrated in Figure 4.2.

Nonmental Neural Systems

There are neurally mediated activities that do not involve mentation. Some of these, for instance, reflexes, are component processes of more

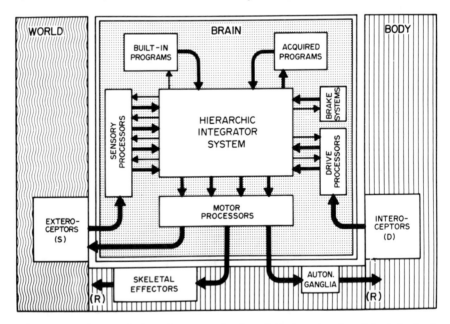

Figure 4.2. The neurobiological conceptualization of the three domains of the behavioral system: the world, the body, and the brain. Receptors are the source of stimulus (S) and drive (D) inputs to the brain; motor output, or response (R), is channeled to the scanning mechanisms of receptors, and to skeletal and visceral (or autonomic) effectors. The brain component labeled "hierarchic integrator system" is illustrated in greater detail in Figure 4.1.

complex acts and may be mediated by circuits involving relatively few neurons, that is, reflex arcs. Other nonmental or apsychic processes may be quite intricate, equaling or surpassing in complexity various behavioral acts that do involve mentation. Among such complex nonmental processes are many internal regulations (nonbehavioral processes) such as adjustments of heart rate, blood flow, water and mineral balance, and so forth, to the ongoing requirements of the body. Others are important constituents of behavioral acts. Examples are such subroutines as the mobilization and sequencing of various muscle groups during a skilled motor act, and such routines as altering a stepping cycle or shifting the body's balance during walking, running, or lifting something. Indeed, entire sequences of acts such as walking, bicycling or driving can be carried out unconsciously for varying periods, usually until some obstacle is encountered or a problem is experienced.

Among the larger central nervous structures that appear to function without mental involvement are the spinal cord, the cerebellum, and perhaps the basal ganglia. Two kinds of evidence support this. First, the functions mediated by some of these structures are not associated with mentation; for instance, spinal reflexes can be elicited in an unconscious individual or in a spinalized organism in a permanent state of stupor. Second, damage to some of these structures (for instance, the cerebellum) is not accompanied by alterations in the psychic status of the individual.

There are many brain structures whose role in mentation, if any, is unknown; others whose functioning is either suspected or known to be associated with mentation. Three kinds of interdependent evidence can be used to classify a neural structure or system as a neuropsychic one. The first evidence is that the structure in question mediates a function that involves, and cannot proceed, without mentation. The second is that artificial (for instance, electrical) stimulation of that structure produces mentation or an alteration in the individual's mental state. The third applicable evidence is that destruction or damage to the structure in question produces a permanent loss in a specific mental capacity. Ideally, all these criteria should be met before a structure is classified as a putative neuropsychic mechanism. And satisfying all these criteria still does not assure us that the structure itself belongs to this class, for it may merely be linked to another system the activation of which produces mentation. Among the structures that are strongly suspected to be components of neuropsychic systems are the cerebral cortex, septum, and amygdala in the forebrain; perhaps portions of the thalamus and hypothalamus in the diencephalon; and the central gray and reticular formation in the mesencephalon. All these structures belong to the suprasegmental central nervous system, that is, are composed of second and higher-order neurons.

We intimated before that central nervous structures that operate without mentation mediate behavioral subroutines or routine acts. Many subroutines and routines that belong to the class of inborn activities (which are based on built-in, genetic programs) are mediated by the spinal cord and its rostral medullary extension. More complex routine acts, those that are acquired through experience and training, may be dependent on such structures as the cerebellum and the basal ganglia—but much remains to be learned on this issue. However, when desires and plans cannot be reached by routine operations, when alternatives are present that call for a decision, when a solution has to be found to a new problem, then neural systems become active that depend on mentation.

The Neural Substrates of Pathic Mentation:
The Paleocephalon

There is a large body of experimental and clinical literature dealing with the identification of brain structures that are associated with one or another aspect of pathic mentation. Historically, the observation by Goltz (1892) of typical rage responses in a decorticated dog was the first evidence that emotional expression is possible in the absence of cerebral hemispheres. Subsequently, Bard (1939) showed that a rage response can be elicited from a decorticated animal even after extensive diencephalic lesions, provided that the posterior hypothalamus remains intact. Earlier stimulation studies (Karplus & Kreidl, 1910) implicated the hypothalamus; and the various hypothalamic areas involved in aggressive and defensive display were delineated by the implanted electrode experiments of Hess (1954) and others (e.g., Hunsperger, 1956). Pleasurable emotional expressions have not been reported in such stimulation studies, and it has not been satisfactorily resolved whether the hypothalamus is responsible, as a motor center, only for the expression of certain emotions or whether it is also concerned with emotional experience. The involvement of the mesencephalic reticular formation in waking and arousal, on the one hand, and somnolence and stupor, on the other, was stressed by Magoun (1963) and his associates (Moruzzi & Magoun, 1949; Lindsley, 1951). Experimental studies have shown that aggressive display can also be elicited from the mesencephalon (Romaniuk, 1965; Sheard & Flynn, 1967) and clinical work (Spiegel & Wycis, 1961; Nashold, Wilson, & Slaughter, 1974) has implicated the central gray and the region between the tectum and dorsal tegmentum in pain and related affects. Lesions in these regions may produce analgesia and relief from intractable pain. Similar effects were reported after destruction of the midline and intralaminar thalamic nuclei, and there is some electrophysiological evidence that nociceptive impulses reach this region

(Casey, Keene, & Morrow, 1974). These mesencephalic and diencephalic structures are believed to receive "nonspecific" afferents. But they may have a large innervation through the phylogenetically old, "specific" afferent system that provides somatosensory, auditory, and visual input to the tectum of the midbrain (Bishop, 1959; Altman, 1966).

In addition to these structures, several telencephalic regions have been implicated in émotional behavior. Klüver and Bucy's (1939) studies led to the identification of the amygdala as an important component of the "emotional circuit" (Papez, 1937). Stimulation of the amygdala is reported to produce aggressive behavior (Egger & Flynn, 1963; Fernandez de Molina & Hunsperger, 1962); taming effects, reduced emotionality; and changes in social behavior were reported after bilateral amygdaloid lesions (Schreiner & Kling, 1953; Rosvold, Mirsky, & Pribram, 1954; Kling, 1972). Contrariwise, septal lesions produce heightened (though transient) rage susceptibility (Brady & Nauta, 1953). The demonstration by Olds and Milner (1954) that rats with electrodes implanted in the septum will engage in protracted self-stimulation indicates that activation of this brain region is rewarding, presumably because it is pleasurable. Indeed, Heath (1964, 1972) reported that stimulation of the septum in human patients produces euphoria. Olds and Olds (1963) mapped the rewarding and aversive sites of the brain of rats; these sites essentially outline the various components of the limbic system that are involved not only in the expressive but apparently also in the experiential aspects of pathic mentation.

In summary, there is accumulating evidence that a series of suprasegmental structures including (a) the central gray and reticular formation (and possibly the tectum) in the mesencephalon; (b) the medial thalamus and hypothalamus in the diencephalon; and (c) an inner telencephalic belt (composed of the amygdala and septum, and probably portions of the rhinencephalon, cingulate gyrus and the hippocampus) constitute a system whose functioning is intimately associated with pathic mentation. Since most components of this system, the *paleocephalon* (Edinger, 1911; Altman, 1966), are present in lower vertebrates, whereas components of the newer system (the *neencephalon*) are ill-developed or absent, the neurological evidence is reconcilable with our previous hypothesis that mentation in lower vertebrates is predominantly (if not exclusively) pathic in nature. The operation of the paleocephalon produces and is dependent on sensuous experience, a private or inner intensifying mechanism that assures that situations *felt* to be harmful (those that produce pain, fear, displeasure) are avoided or fought off; while those that are *felt* to be beneficial (those that produce comfort, pleasure, desire) are preserved or pursued. Pathic experience is felt intensely as one's own. It is referred diffusely to some part of the body (as to the heart or stomach in the case of love or hate) or is projected with varying degrees of precision to some organ or tissue (as in the case of pain).

The Neural Substrates of Iconic Mentation:
The Neencephalon

In lower vertebrates like fishes, the bulk of the afferent input from the distal receptors terminates in the tectum of the mesencephalon. Input to the thalamus is rudimentary and so is the transmission of somatosensory, auditory, and visual information to the telencephalon. Beginning with the most primitive mammals, such as marsupials, there was a progressive trend to channel afferents from the tectum to the various thalamic relay nuclei, whence they are relayed to the neocortex. In higher mammals, this neocortical pathway became the dominant input channel of the nervous system. Coupled with this change was the progressive growth of the neocortex, the enlargement of its "silent" or "association" areas and of its efferent outflow, the pyramidal tract. A question often posed is why, for instance, optic input to the optic tectum (superior colliculus) has become, as it were, obsolete and why evolutionary pressures prevailed to reroute these fibers to the lateral geniculate nucleus and the striate cortex? I propose that this rerouting reflects an evolutionary switch from an exclusive reliance on pathic processing of exteroceptive information to iconic processing. If this is correct, the questions that one would like to have answers to are, first, what is the subjective consequence of this change from pathic to iconic processing? and, second, what demonstrable differences and behavioral advantages accrued from the evolution and increased reliance on this new neuropsychic processing system? We do not have satisfactory answers to these questions, but a few indirect lines of evidence might be worth considering here.

There is at least one sensory system in mammals (including man) that has no thalamocortical representation, namely, the olfactory system; there are several others that either have no representation or only a minor one, namely, the gustatory system, the vestibular system, and perhaps the pain mechanisms. If one examines the subjective nature of olfaction, for instance, it becomes evident (as we discussed before) that smell is a protopathic sensation, not a percept; that is, it lacks articulable structured details and it does not produce an awareness of the object quality of the source stimulus. We have no difficulty in distinguishing the fragrance of a lemon from the fragrance of a rose, but only in terms of a unitary Gestaltless impression—not the way we distinguish visually a lemon tree from a rose bush. Smells do not provide us with structural information about objects; only data about their presence, their intensity, and our subjective–affective reactions to them.

It could be argued that smells provide structureless sensuous impressions because of the ephemeral nature of the olfactory medium. Indeed this may be the reason why neencephalic mechanisms, which are concerned with the perceptual reconstruction of an object world, never evolved for olfaction. Contrariwise, the optical medium is naturally fitted for patterned representation. And because our visual experiences are fundamentally structured in character, it is difficult for us to imagine what the subjective nature of a Gestaltless visual experience might be, unless it were the kind that can be artificially produced in a *Ganzfeld*. This dichotomy between structureless sensuous impression and structured object perception may have been the thrust of Lashley's (1931, 1935) attempt to demonstrate that the superior colliculus mediates brightness discrimination while the striate cortex mediates pattern discrimination. However, the conclusion that after removal of the striate cortex only light flux discrimination is possible (Klüver, 1942) has been repeatedly challenged (Smith, 1938; Spear & Braun, 1969; Levey, Harris, & Jane, 1973). Certainly lower vertebrates like fish (Herter, 1953) can learn to make pattern discriminations, even though their vision is predominantly tectally mediated. Thus the conclusion is inescapable that tectal representation in lower vertebrates, and perhaps in many mammals (Ferrier and Cooper, 1976), does allow behavioral response to some structural aspects and the topographic properties of a visual stimulus. But is it possible that subjectively tectal mechanisms provide only sensuous impressions—not iconic perception? Perhaps visual experience on this level is analogous to pain, which provides clues about the locus and spatial extent of tissue damage but little if anything about the object. An indirect line of evidence that iconic processes, indeed, may be absent in lower vertebrates comes from retinal inversion studies (Stratton, 1897; Snyder & Pronko, 1952; Kohler, 1964). We argued earlier that one of the functions of iconic mentation is the modification and enrichment of a given momentary impression of an object by memory traces derived from previous encounters, by information gained from other sense organs, and by experience obtained from previous handling and manipulation of that object. The subjective percept is a composite of these and probably other contributions to the momentary impression. And it must be these modifications and enrichment that make it possible for a human subject wearing distorting or inverting goggles not only to adapt to them after a while but, after prolonged experience, to perceive the visual world subjectively as undistorted and right-side up. Apparently the iconic percept can be divorced from the specifics of orientation of the retinal image by experience provided by the other senses. In contrast, Sperry's (1951) studies showed that lower vertebrates, such as newts and frogs and perhaps also chicks (Kohler, 1964), are unable to make these adaptations because they rely on tectal mechanisms.

Accordingly, we shall tentatively suggest that with the evolution of the neencephalic processing system it has become possible to form iconic percepts through an amalgamation of scanned images with memory images and other information. The integrated product is, as it were, a "phantom" produced on an internal phosphorescent screen but one which, importantly, is not perceived internally (as in the head) but is projected out into the external world.

The Neural Substrates of Noetic Mentation:
The Anthropocephalon

Communication is prevalent among social animals; it may indeed be a prerequisite of social existence. The absence of symbolic language in the animal world must, therefore, be due to factors other than an inability to vocalize, gesture, or otherwise communicate. It is presumably due to an inability to generate ideas and attach symbols to them. It seems as if the neuropsychic mechanisms that mediate linguistic processes are absent in subhuman vertebrates, with the exception of some higher primates in which rudiments of symbolic capacity have been demonstrated (Gardner & Gardner, 1969, 1975; Premack, 1971, 1976; Fouts, 1973).

The idea that special brain mechanisms mediate language skills goes back to clinical observations in the early nineteenth century when it was noted that brain injuries that result in right hemiplegia are associated with language disorders. This view was promoted by Broca (1865) who believed he had identified a region in the left frontal cortex which when extensively damaged produces motor aphasia. Subsequently Wernicke (1874) claimed that pathologies in a region of the left temporal cortex produce sensory aphasia. Broca's and Wernicke's views have been challenged with regard to both strict cortical localization and dissociability of the aphasias. However, the available clinical evidence justifies two conclusions: First, unlike so many other functions, linguistic processes are unilaterally represented in the left hemisphere of right-handed patients; second, the probability of language disorder is high when brain trauma encroaches on the areas now named after Broca and Wernicke and low when other cortical regions are affected (Conrad, 1954; Russell & Espir, 1961; Lenneberg, 1967).

The unilateral representation of language is supported by clinical evidence, by experiments performed during surgical operations in man, by the psychological examination of patients after sectioning of the corpus callosum, and by psychological studies in normal human subjects.

Penfield (1966; Penfield & Roberts, 1959) reported that stimulation of the language areas in the left hemisphere of unanesthetized patients produced either vocalization or interference with speech production. Such effects were not obtained in corresponding regions in the right cerebral cortex; there stimulation led, rather, to flashbacks of past experiences. The unilateral representation of linguistic skills is not surprising if one considers that unlike most other motor systems, which are composed of paired lateral organs, the mouth and tongue and the rest of the vocal apparatus form a single or unpaired organ system. Indeed, nonlinguistic vocalization in birds is unilaterally represented in the brain (Nottebohm, 1971).

The predominantly unilateral representation of linguistic functions in the human cerebral cortex and the diverging functional specialization of the left and right hemispheres were dramatically demonstrated by Sperry and his associates. Sperry (1961) and Myers (1961) found in studies in monkeys that cutting the corpus callosum prevents the interhemispheric transfer of memory and learning. Soon after this demonstration of specific "split brain" effects, a "disconnection syndrome" was suggested by observations in a patient with callosal infarction (Geschwind & Kaplan, 1962) and in another with surgical transection of the forebrain commissures (Gazzaniga, Bogen, & Sperry, 1962). These observations tended to contradict previous conclusions (Akelaitis, 1944) that commissurotomy in man leads to no obvious neurological or psychological dysfunctions. Subsequent systematic studies (Gazzaniga, Bogen, & Sperry, 1965; Sperry, Gazzaniga, & Bogen, 1969; Sperry, 1974) brought strong evidence in favor of the hypothesis of hemispheric specialization in man. When visual stimuli were presented tachistoscopically (to prevent scanning) to the left-half visual field, that is, to the disconnected right or minor hemisphere, these stimuli could not be identified verbally and were seemingly not perceived. However, when the patient was allowed to communicate by nonverbal means he could respond adequately with his left hand. When the visual stimuli were presented to the disconnected left or major hemisphere, there were no difficulties with verbal identification. Similar observations were made when objects were palpated with the left or right hand. The conclusions that were drawn from these initial studies were, first, that after callosal sectioning the two hemispheres process information separately; and second, that the mode of information processing is different in the two hemispheres. Apparently the minor hemisphere is superior to the major hemisphere in many perceptual tasks. Examples are copying or drawing test figures and building block designs (Bogen & Gazzaniga, 1965); identifying unfolded three dimensional objects visually after they are palpated tactually (Levy-Agresti & Sperry, 1968); or completing fragmented visual shapes by finding the missing parts by palpation (Nebes, 1972). The patients tended to be accurate with their left hand (controlled by the minor hemisphere) and often performed on a chance level with their right hand.

The differing and sometimes conflicting operation of the two hemispheres was most strikingly demonstrated by using chimeric stimuli (Levy, Trevarthan, & Sperry, 1972). When visual figures are split in the middle and presented to the right or left hemisphere, the missing half of the image tends to be filled in by each hemisphere according to a general principle of perceptual completion. When conflicting half images are presented to the two hemispheres, each perceives different things in the same position at the same time. When the task is the visual matching of an image, such as a face or a nondescript pattern, to a similar item, the minor hemisphere is usually dominant. But when interpretation, understanding and verbalization are essential, the patient's response tends to be dominated by the disconnected major hemisphere.

Other investigators have been successful in showing differences in the way the two hemispheres process perceptual information in normal human subjects. There are the early findings, which at the time were not interpreted in terms of cerebral dominance, that when stimuli are presented tachistoscopically to either the left or the right visual field verbal material is recognized more accurately from the right visual field (Heron, 1957; Mishkin & Forgays, 1952). Subsequent studies that confirmed the superiority of the left hemisphere for verbal functions (Kimura, 1961) showed that visual tasks related to spatial perception—such as line orientation, depth perception, visual point localization—are more efficiently processed by the right than the left hemisphere (Kimura, 1966; Kimura and Durnford, 1974). In another approach, the involvement of one or the other hemisphere is inferred from the speed of the normal subject's reaction time. The idea is that tachistoscopically presented tasks will be processed faster if directly presented to the hemisphere involved in their processing and will be processed more slowly if presented to the opposite hemisphere, because that requires added crosshemispheric transfer. Several studies (Geffen, Bradshaw, & Wallace, 1971; Rizzolatti, Umiltà,& Berlucchi, 1971) have shown that the left hemisphere processes information faster when the task is verbal, whereas nonverbal, like pictorial, material is processed faster by the right hemisphere.

From his extensive studies Sperry (1974) concluded that the major hemisphere mediates symbolic functions, such as speech, writing, and calculation. This is the hemisphere that has primary control over the manipulative and executive motor system (the right hand) in normal subjects and to which the patient turns after commissurotomy. The minor hemisphere mediates such functions in an elementary manner, as shown by the comprehension of only simple words or counting only up to 20. However, the minor hemisphere is also a conscious system and is superior in tasks, which, to quote Sperry (1974), "involve the apprehension and processing of spatial patterns, relations and transformations. They seem to be holistic and unitary rather than analytic and fragmentary . . . and to involve concrete perceptual insight rather than abstract, symbolic, sequential reasoning." Sperry adds: "However, it yet remains for someone to translate in a meaningful way the essential right-left characteristics in terms of the brain process . . . [p. 11]."

The results of these and related observations seem to suggest that in man the minor hemisphere specializes in the iconic processing of sensory information, what Hughlings Jackson called "visual ideation" (quoted from Milner, 1974), whereas the major hemisphere specializes in noetic processing. This would explain the superiority of the minor hemisphere in spatial and nonverbal perceptual tasks and the dominance of the major hemisphere in linguistically mediated tasks. This formulation appears to be compatible with the ideas of Bruner (1966) regarding the ontogeny of thinking and the conceptualization of hemispheric specialization by Bower (1970) and Seamon (1974).

Psychobiologists have long puzzled over the fact that, in spite of great evolutionary transformations in the mental capacities of man, all that neuroanatomists have been able to demonstrate is a quantitative increase in the mass of the cerebral cortex. There are few, if any, new cytoarchitectonic areas and certainly no new morphologically distinct brain structures, to account for the emergence of qualitatively new mental capacities in man. Apparently, instead of evolving altogether new brain regions, what happened was that as the mass of the cerebral cortex substantially increased (it more than trebled in weight from *Australopithecus* to *Homo sapiens*; Tobias, 1971), one entire hemisphere was assigned to a new function. In terms of our previous hypothesis, iconic mentation is mediated by both cerebral hemispheres in subhuman mammals but in man iconic processing is largely restricted to the "minor" hemisphere and noetic processing is carried out by the "major" or "dominant" hemisphere, the *anthropocephalon*.

Lateral hemispheric specialization in man became possible as the result of several trends in primate evolution. As the eyes gradually moved from a lateral to a medial position, the entire visual field became redundantly represented in both hemispheres. Moreover, one hemisphere, usually the left, also receives most of the necessary tactile information since there is a predominant reliance on one hand, usually the right, in palpating and manipulating objects. The unilateralization of manipulatory activities led to one hemisphere taking charge of those functions on which man's superiority in the animal world rests, namely, the making and using of tools. It is from this hemisphere that noetic functions are controlled and also the non-lateralized (midline) vocal apparatus. The opposite hemisphere takes charge of constructing a concrete perceptual world, such as images of objects, spatial maps, and the like.

That an entire hemisphere can adopt a new function without evident reorganization of its structure suggests that it is extremely plastic or, to use Penfield's term (1966), "uncommitted." But it cannot be entirely plastic, since there is evidence for a powerful biological disposition for the development of language (Lenneberg, 1967). Perhaps the major hemisphere contains two components, specialized regions that mediate basic linguistic and conceptual skills, and plastic regions that allow the assimilation of the language, the thought patterns, and other transmitted practices of one culture or another.

SUMMARY

Empirical evidence has been presented in support of the hypothesis that the three classes of mental functions, the pathic, iconic, and noetic, are associated with three hierarchically organized neural systems, the paleocephalon, neencephalon, and anthropocephalon. The organization of these three neural systems, together with a subordinated system that mediates routine functions without mentation, is schematically illustrated in Figure 4.3 as an evolutionary sequence in vertebrates. Nonmental, routine functions are coordinated by the gray matter of the spinal cord, and increasing importance is assumed during evolution, perhaps as an interfacing mechanism, by the cerebellum and basal ganglia. Pathic functions are mediated by the paleocephalon, which consists of various brainstem structures, and, perhaps again as an interfacing mechanism, an evolving limbic system. The lemniscal and pyramidal pathways and the thalamus and the cerebral hemispheres are the organs of iconic processing in subhuman

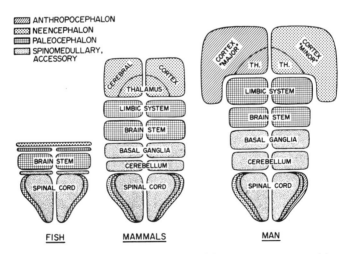

Figure 4.3. Schematic illustration of the evolution of the major components of the quadrupartite nervous system. The evolving input and output channels between the segmental, spinomedullary system ("spinal cord") and the paleo-, neen-, and anthropocephalon are represented by strips bordering the spinal cord. The cerebellum and basal ganglia are conceptualized as accessory mechanisms that mediate routine functions.

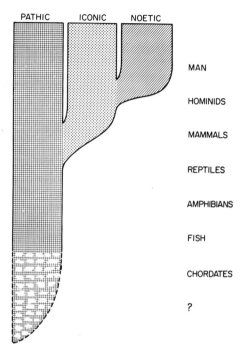

Figure 4.4. A hypothesis of the evolution of mentation. It is based on the identification of the emergence of the pathic, iconic, and noetic levels of mentation with the successive effervescence of the paleocephalon, neencephalon, and anthropocephalon, respectively, in vertebrate phylogeny.

mammals. In man, iconic functions are mediated by the minor hemisphere and its accessory systems, while noetic processing is the function of the major hemisphere. If the sequence presented is a realistic representation of the evolution of the brain in vertebrates, and if the neuropsychic correlations described are valid, then the evolution of mentation illustrated in Figure 4.4 may be justified. That the phylogenetic trend described may have its ontogenetic parallels in man deserves careful examination.

REFERENCES

Akelaitis, A. J. A study of gnosis, praxis and language following section of the corpus callosum and anterior commissure. *Journal of Neurosurgery,* 1944, *1,* 94–101.

Altman, J. *Organic foundations of animal behavior.* New York: Holt, 1966.

Bard, P. Central nervous mechanisms for emotional behavior patterns in animals. *Research Publications, Association for Research in Nervous and Mental Disease,* 1939, *19,* 190–218.

Beloff, J. *The existence of mind.* London: McGibson, 1962.

106   JOSEPH ALTMAN

Bishop, G. H. The relation between nerve fiber size and sensory modality: phylogenetic implications of the afferent innervation of cortex. *Journal of Nervous and Mental Diseases*, 1959, *128*, 89–114.
Bogen, J. E., & M. S. Gazzaniga. Cerebral commissurotomy in man: minor hemisphere dominance for certain visuospatial functions. *Journal of Neurosurgery*, 1965, *23*, 394–399.
Bower, G. H. Analysis of a mnemonic device. *American Scientist*, 1970, *58*, 496–510.
Brady, J. V., & Nauta, W. J. H. Subcortical mechanisms in emotional behavior: Affective changes following septal forebrain lesions in the albino rat. *Journal of Comparative Physiology and Physiological Psychology*, 1953, *48*, 412–420.
Broca, P. Du siège de la faculté du langage articulé. *Bulletin of Social Anthropology*, 1865, *6*, 377–393.
Bruner, J. On cognitive growth. In J. S. Bruner, R. R. Olver, & P. M. Greenfield (Eds.), *Studies on cognitive growth*. New York: Wiley, 1966.
Casey, K. L., Keene, J. J., & Morrow, T. Bulboreticular and medial thalamic unit activity in relation to aversive behavior and pain. In J. J. Bonica (Ed.), *International symposium on pain*. New York: Raven Press, 1974.
Cassirer, E. *An essay on man*. New Haven: Yale University Press, 1944.
Conrad, K. New problems of aphasia. *Brain*, 1954, *77*, 491–509.
Craik, K. J. W. *The nature of explanation*. London: Cambridge University Press, 1943.
Eccles, J. C. *Facing reality*. New York: Springer, 1970.
Edinger, L. *Vorlesungen über den bau der nervösen zentralorgane der menschen und der tiere* (Vol. 1, 8th ed.). Leipzig: Barth, 1911.
Egger, M. D., & Flynn, J. P. Effect of electrical stimulation of the amygdala on hypothalamically elicited attack behavior in cats. *Journal of Neurophysiology*, 1963, *26*, 705–720.
Fernandez de Molina, A., & Hunsperger, R. W. Organisation of the subcortical system governing defensive and flight reactions in the cat. *Journal of Physiology (London)*, 1962, *160*, 200–213.
Ferrier, R. J., & Cooper, R. M. Striate cortex ablation and spatial vision. *Brain Research*, 1976, *106*, 71–85.
Fouts, R. S. Acquisition and testing of gestural signs in four young chimpanzees. *Science*, 1973, *180*, 978–980.
Gardner, R. A., & B. T. Gardner. Teaching sign language to a chimpanzee. *Science*, 1969, *165*, 664–672.
Gardner, R. A., & Gardner, B. T. Early signs of language in child and chimpanzee. *Science*, 1975, *187*, 752–753.
Gazzaniga, M. S., Bogen, J. E., & Sperry, R. W. Some functional effects of sectioning the cerebral commissures in man. *Proceedings of the National Academy of Sciences*, 1962, *48*, 1765–1769.
Gazzaniga, M. S., Bogen, J. E., & Sperry, R. W. Observations on visual perception after disconnection of the cerebral hemispheres in man. *Brain*, 1965, *88*, 221–236.
Geffen, G., Bradshaw, J. L., & Wallace, G. Interhemispheric effects on reaction time to verbal and nonverbal stimuli. *Journal of Experimental Psychology*, 1971, *87*, 415–422.
Geschwind, N., & Kaplan, E. A human cerebral deconnection syndrome. *Neurology*, 1962, *12*, 675–685.
Gibson, J. J. *The senses considered as perceptual systems*. Boston: Houghton Mifflin, 1966.
Goltz, F. Der Hund ohne Grosshirn. *Archives für die gesamte Physiologie*, 1892, *51*, 570–614.
Head, H. *Studies in neurology*. London: Hodder and Stoughton, 1920.
Heath, R. G. Pleasure response of human subjects to direct stimulation of the brain: physiologic and psychodynamic considerations. In R. G. Heath (Ed.), *The role of pleasure in behavior*. New York: Hoeber, 1964.

Heath, R. G. Pleasure and brain activity in man. *Journal of Nervous and Mental Diseases*, 1972, *154*, 3–18.

Heron, W. Perception as a function of retinal locus and attention. *American Journal of Psychology*, 1957, *70*, 38–48.

Herter, K. *Die Fischdressuren und ihre sinnesphysiologischen grundlagen.* Berlin: Akademie Verlag, 1953.

Hess, W. R. *Diencephalon: Autonomic and Extrapyramidal Functions.* New York: Grune and Stratton, 1954.

Hunsperger, R. W. Affektreaktionen auf elektrische Reizung in Hirnstamm der Katze. *Helvetica Physiologica et Pharmacologica Acta*, 1956, *14*, 70–92.

Karplus, J. P., & A. Kreidl. Gehirn and Sympathicus. II. Ein sympathicuszentrum im Zwischenhirn. *Pflügers Archiv für die gesamte Physiologie*, 1910, *135*, 401–416.

Kimura, D. Cerebral dominance and the perception of verbal stimuli. *Canadian Journal of Psychology*, 1961, *15*, 166–171.

Kimura, D. Dual functional assymetry of the brain in visual perception. *Neuropsychologia*, 1966, *4*, 275–285.

Kimura, D., & Durnford, M. Normal studies on the function of the right hemisphere in vision. In S. J. Dimond & J. G. Beaumont (Eds.), *Hemisphere function in the human brain.* New York: Wiley, 1974.

Kling, A. Effects of amygdalectomy on social-affective behavior in non-human primates. In B. E. Eleftheriou (Ed.), *The neurobiology of the amygdala.* New York: Plenum Press, 1972.

Klüver, H. Functional significance of the geniculo-striate system. *Biological Symposium*, 1942, *7*, 253–299.

Klüver, H., & Bucy, P. C. Preliminary analysis of functions of the temporal lobes in monkeys. *Archives of Neurology and Psychiatry*, 1939, *42*, 979–1000.

Kohler, I. *The formation and transformation of the perceptual world* (trans. by H. Fiss.). New York: International University Press, 1964.

Lashley, K. S. The mechanism of vision: IV. The cerebral areas necessary for pattern vision in the rat. *Journal of Comparative Neurology*, 1931, *53*, 419–478.

Lashley, K. S. The mechanism of vision. XII. Nervous structures concerned in the acquisition and retention of habits based on reactions to light. *Comparative Psychology Monograph*, 1935, *11*, 43–79.

Lenneberg, E. H. *Biological foundations of language.* New York: Wiley, 1967.

Levey, N. H., Harris, J., & Jane, J. A. Effects of visual cortical ablation on pattern discrimination in the ground squirrel *(Citellus tridecemlineatus). Experimental Neurology*, 1973, *39*, 270–276.

Levy, J., Trevarthen, C., & Sperry, R. W. Perception of bilateral chimeric figures following hemisphere deconnection. *Brain*, 1972, *95*, 61–78.

Levy-Agresti, J., & Sperry, R. W. Differential perceptual capacities in major and minor hemispheres. *Proceedings of the National Academy of Sciences*, 1968, *61*, 1151.

Lindsley, D. B. Emotion. In S. S. Stevens (Ed.), *Handbook of experimental psychology.* New York: Wiley, 1951.

Locke, J. *Essay concerning human understanding.* 1690. [A. C. Fraser (Ed.), London: Oxford University Press, 1894.]

Magoun, H. W. *The waking brain* (2nd ed.). Springfield, Mass.: Thomas, 1963.

McDougall, W. *An introduction to social psychology* (21st ed.). London: Methuen, 1928.

Milner, B. Introduction. In F. O. Schmitt & F. G. Worden (Eds.), *The neurosciences: third study program.* Cambridge: MIT Press, 1974.

Mishkin, M. & Forgays, D. G. Word recognition as a function of retinal locus. *Journal of Experimental Psychology*, 1952, *43*, 43–48.

Moruzzi, G. & Magoun, H. W. Brain stem reticular formation and activation of the EEG. *Electroencephalography and Clinical Neurophysiology*, 1949, *1*, 455–473.

Myers, R. E. Corpus callosum and visual gnosis. In J. F. Delafresnaye (Ed.), *Brain mechanisms and learning*. Oxford: Blackwell, 1961.

Nashold, B. S., Wilson, W. P., & Slaughter, G. The midbrain and pain. In J. J. Bonica (Ed.), *International symposium on pain* (Vol. 4). New York: Raven Press, 1974.

Nebes, R. D. Dominance of the minor hemisphere in commissurotomized men in a test of figural unification. *Brain*, 1972, *95*, 633–638.

Neisser, U. Changing conceptions of imagery. In P. W. Sheehan (Ed.), *The function and nature of imagery*. New York: Academic Press, 1972.

Nottebohm, F. Neural lateralization of vocal control in a passerine bird. I. Song. *Journal of Experimental Zoology*, 1971, *177*, 229–262.

Olds, J., & Milner, P. Positive reinforcement produced by electrical stimulation of septal area and other regions of rat brain. *Journal of Comparative Physiological and Psychology*, 1954, *47*, 419–427.

Olds, M. E., & Olds, J. Approach-avoidance analysis of rat diencephalon. *Journal of Comparative Neurology*, 1963. *120*, 259–295.

Ornstein, J. H. *The mind and the brain: a multi-aspect interpretation*. The Hague: Nijhogg, 1972.

Papez, J. W. A proposed mechanism of emotion. *Archives of Neurology and Psychiatry*, 1937, *38*, 725–743.

Penfield, W. Speech, perception and the uncommitted cortex. In J. C. Eccles (Ed.), *Brain and conscious experience*. New York: Springer, 1966.

Penfield, W., & Roberts, L. *Speech and brain mechanisms*. Princeton: Princeton University Press, 1959.

Place, U. T. Is consciousness a brain process? *British Journal of Psychology*, 1956, *47*, 44–50.

Premack, D. Language in chimpanzees? *Science*, 1971, *172*, 808–822.

Premack, D. *Intelligence in ape and man*. Hillside, N.J.: Erlbaum, 1976.

Richardson, A. *Mental imagery*. New York: Springer, 1969.

Rizzolatti, G., Umiltà, C., & Berlucchi, G. Opposite superiorities of the right and left cerebral hemispheres in discriminative reaction time to physiognomical and alphabetical material. *Brain*, 1971, *94*, 431–442.

Romaniuk, A. Representation of aggression and flight reactions in the hypothalamus of the cat. *Acta Biologia of the Polish Academy of Sciences*, 1965, *25*, 177–186.

Rosenblueth, A. *Mind and brain: a philosophy of science*. Cambridge: MIT Press, 1970.

Rosvold, H. E., Mirsky, A. F., & Pribram, K. H. Influence of amygdalectomy on social interaction in a monkey group. *Journal of Comparative Physiological and Psychology*, 1954, *47*, 173–178.

Russell, W. R. & Espir, M. L. E. *Traumatic aphasia*. London: Oxford University Press, 1961.

Ryle, G. *The concept of mind*. London: Hutchinson, 1949.

Sartre, J.-P. *The transcendence of the ego: an existentialist theory of consciousness* (trans. by F. Williams & R. Kirkpatrick). New York: Noonday Press, 1957.

Schreiner, L., & Kling, A. Behavioral changes following rhinencephalic injury in cat. *Journal of Neurophysiology*, 1953, *16*, 643–659.

Seamon, J. G. Coding and retrieval processes and the hemispheres of the brain. In S. J. Dimond & J. G. Beaumont (Eds.), *Hemisphere function in the human brain*. New York: Wiley, 1974.

Shaffer, J. A. *Philosophy of mind*. Englewood Cliffs, N.J.: Prentice-Hall, 1968.

Sheard, M., & Flynn, J. P. Facilitation of attack behavior by stimulation of the midbrain of cats. *Brain Research*, 1967, *4*, 324–333.

Sheehan, P. W. (Ed.). *The function and nature of imagery*. New York: Academic Press, 1972.

Smart, J. J. C. Sensations and brain processes. *Philosophical Review,* 1959, *48,* 141–156.

Smith, K. U. Visual discrimination in the cat: VI. The relation between pattern vision and visual acuity and the optic projection centers of the nervous system. *Journal of Genetic Psychology,* 1938, *53,* 251–272.

Snyder, F. W., & N. H. Pronko. *Vision with spatial inversion.* Wichita: Kansas University Press, 1952.

Spear, P. D., & Braun, J. J. Pattern discrimination following removal of visual neocortex in the cat. *Experimental Neurology,* 1969, *25,* 331–348.

Sperry, R. W. Mechanisms of neural maturation. In S. S. Stevens (Ed.), *Handbook of experimental psychology.* New York: Wiley, 1951.

Sperry, R. W. Cerebral organization and behavior. *Science,* 1961, *133,* 1749–1757.

Sperry, R. W. Lateral specialization in the surgically separated hemispheres. In F. O. Schmitt & F. G. Worden (Eds.), *The neurosciences: third study program.* Cambridge: MIT Press, 1974.

Sperry, R. W., Gazzaniga, M. S., & Bogen, J. E. Interhemispheric relationships: The neocortical commissures; syndromes of hemisphere disconnection. In P. J. Vinken & G. W. Bruyn (Eds.), *Handbook of clinical neurology* (Vol. 4). Amsterdam: North Holland, 1969.

Spiegel, A. E., & Wycis, H. T. Stimulation of the brain stem and basal ganglia in man. In D. E. Sheer (Ed.), *Electrical stimulation of the brain.* Austin: University of Texas Press, 1961.

Stratton, G. Vision without inversion of the retinal image. *Psychological Review,* 1897, *4,* 341–360.

Tobias, P. V. *The brain in hominid evolution.* New York: Columbia University Press, 1971.

Tolman, E. C. *Purposive behavior in animals and men.* New York: Appleton-Century, 1932.

Tomkins, S. *Affect, imagery, consciousness.* New York: Springer, 1962.

Wernicke, C. *Der aphasische Symptomencomplex.* Breslau: Cohn and Weigert, 1874.

chapter 5

Motor Programming and Language Behavior

SIMEON LOCKE

Central among Eric Lenneberg's many important contributions to the study of language was his firm commitment to a biological base. At a time when major interest was directed toward the relation between language and mind (Chomsky, 1968) he, in contrast, was keenly aware of the behavioral heritage of language, and of language as behavior. In 1967 he wrote "I believe there is evidence that behavior has the same history and the same origin as form and physiological processes; in fact, the division between physiological function and behavioral function is an artifact of our mode of looking at animals, and these functions shade into each other and are, thus, objectively indistinguishable [Lenneberg, 1967]." This suggests a continuity between physiological processes and behavior. And, in turn, behavior (such as language) may be considered continuous with mind. With Sherrington (1952), Lenneberg might have said "Mind is always an inference from behavior."

Lenneberg's was an interesting and a rather fresh view in a period when studies were largely concerned with the structure of language or with its abnormalities following cerebral lesions. For if carried to its logical extreme,

111

PSYCHOLOGY AND BIOLOGY OF LANGUAGE AND THOUGHT
Essays in Honor of Eric Lenneberg

it suggests that a great deal can be learned about language by examining the principles of organization of the nervous system—its physiology and its behavior. These should reflect in some way the kinds of processes and organization which underlie language and its production. This oblique approach to the study of the relation between language and the nervous system can be justified not only because direct assessment has been so disappointing, but more importantly, because language is viewed as but one expression of a set of organizational principles which underlie all neurological function and its overt expression, behavior.

Behavior, whatever else it means, implies movement. It is movement which is organized, goal directed, and creates an action system. Customarily, movement is thought to be "represented" at certain places in the nervous system and modulated or "rerepresented" at others. The representation is certainly not isomorphic with the movement; nor are the places of representation to be conceived in a literal sense. Rather they are allegorical levels of neurological function or, if a spatial model must be used, the anatomical substrate of the system under consideration (Weiss, 1969). With accession of neurological structure, with refinement of neurological function, and with rerepresentation of the modules of behavior, systems grow and change. Low-level systems, controlled and dominated from above, become incorporated in the generation of new functions determined by the new systems, which they influence in turn. In the context of the larger interaction the smaller system loses its autonomy to regain it again following neurological lesions and "reflex release." A specific movement is represented throughout the system that underwrites it, and not at any particular "level." A lesion at *any* level of the system disrupts the movement represented in that system; what the level of lesion does determine is the residual capability inherent in the integrated system that has been released.

Something is known about this organization in the case of movement. Various levels of function determine the posture of the organism—a static state—and associated muscle tone, which is a bias, a set, or a readiness to change. Movement constitutes a transition between postures and requires sequencing. It is the sequencing that determines the goal-directed aspects of the action system and converts random movement to meaningful behavior. Sequencing is inherent at each level of neurological function and should not be construed as a high-level activity (represented, for example, in cortex) imposed on low-level function. Sequenced behavior occurs at each level of neurological performance, and is a constituent of the central program at each level of organization. With acquisition of capability, the latitude, modifiability, and facultative aspects of the sequencing increase imposing delicacy and increased meaning on behavior.

Some of the anatomy which underlies the organization of movement is known. Flexion is the prepotent posture released by spinal section. Extension, which can also be obtained from isolated spinal cord is enhanced by input from neck and labyrinthine receptors (Denny-Brown, 1966). Brainstem contributions in the monkey course in a lateral and ventromedial pathway to terminate on the internuncial spinal grey. The ventromedial system is concerned with maintenance of erect posture, integrated body and limb movements, and the course of progression. The lateral brainstem pathway is responsible for independent distal limb movements and flexion of the extended limb. Fibers of cortical origin overlap those of brainstem projections and terminate, as well, directly on spinal motor neurons, further fractionating and amplifying distal control (Brinkman & Kuypers, 1973). The specifics of the connections are not important for our purposes; what matters is to appreciate the cascading input of fiber systems, each widening the available receptive fields and accounting for the potential of behavior nesting within behavior at each level of representation.

In cortex, the efferent zones which control movement at a given joint are close together, organized in columns, have sharp boundaries, and receive afferent input from skin, joints, and muscles involved in the movements produced by microstimulation (Asanuma & Rosen, 1972; Goldring & Ratcheson, 1972). This input, often a reafference secondary to output, signals the movement the organism has made and helps distinguish it from movement generated from without (Bruner, 1969). Feedback of this sort is not essential for the realization of the fundamental motor program. The spinal scratch reflex, for example, occurs despite complete deafferentation of the scratching limb, indicating that the response is inherent in a central pattern of reflex activation and not in a feedback mechanism (Denny-Brown, 1966).

If the motor program is independent of feedback, the question arises as to what function the reafferent input serves. Current thinking suggests that it functions as a regulating system that compares the results achieved with an antecedent plan and allows for the generation of an error signal and compensation in the case of mismatch (Luria, 1966a). Apparently, the process is something of this sort. Exposure of the organism to the objective environment results, by way of tuned receptors (Luria, 1966b), in a widespread cortical response. Information is referred from cortex to cerebellum and basal ganglia (DeLong, 1974; Kornhuber, 1974) which project by way of nucleus ventralis lateralis of thalamus to motor cortex. Motor cortex triggers an appropriate motor program, long in advance of overt movement (Evarts, 1975), to meet the requirements of the objective situation. The more diverse the environmental stimuli, the richer the afferent input; the more complex the structure of movement required, the more conscious its character (Luria, 1966a). A corollary discharge (Teuber, 1960) links "motor cortex" to appropriate cortical "sensory" areas, and constitues an analogy of the predicted results of action, serving as a comparator against which the reafferent signal may be matched.

This plan, or prediction, constitutes the intent of the organism. And the serial order of behavior is determined by the intent. "The intention to act or the ideas to be expressed determine the sequence" wrote Lashley (1951). Intent is signaled by pyramidal tract neurons which determine "selectivity of motor behavior depending upon decisions made by the subject (Yingling, 1975)." The cells are not always activated by the same sensory stimuli, are not active during all movements of a given muscle group, discharge only conditionally, and are considered responsible for holistic commands for action (Mountcastle, Georgopoulos, Sakata, & Acuna, 1975). The commands are not detailed instructions for behavior; they are programs for sequencing subprograms which are contained in units, commanded from above, and which appear in strategic order guided by feedback and feedforward mechanisms related to environmental input. Such command potentials occur in human voluntary activity. A "readiness potential" appears well in advance of voluntary movement; it is bilateral and widespread over parietal and precentral regions. This is followed by "premotor positivity," also bilaterally and widespread, which precedes movement at a shorter interval. Only then does a third potential, limited to the contralateral motor area, appear (Kornhuber, 1974). Similar command potentials may appear before speech; they vary in morphology according to the phoneme uttered (although this may be an artifact generated by tongue muscles) (Ertle & Schafer, 1967, 1969). This should not be surprising, for

> Fluent narrative speech in man is a complex psychological process. To enable man to progress from the naming of individual objects to produce fluent narrative speech, it is not enough for him to understand and master various logico-grammatical structures. He must first prepare a provisional scheme or program of what he has to say, including the order of the successive stages of his narration. All the concrete elements of his discourse must be given their proper place in this program and each link of this narrative must be replaced at the proper time by the next [Luria, 1966a].

Now, the ability to formulate a plan and intentionally generate goal-directed behavior in response to environmental stimuli presupposes a central representation of perception considerably more abstract than the physical agents which generated it (Koestler, 1969). This abstraction occurs increasingly at successive stages of input and results, in part, from feedback operation on the input devices. Information selection and decision making occur at each stage of input, from the tuned receptor to the most central representation, and must be done with reference to some criterion. Stated somewhat differently, the information chosen, the decisions made, and the abstractions which result must have meaning to the organism, and this

meaning presumably occurs in relation to some aspect of biological significance. In turn, it generates abstract commands that eventuate in concrete
performance that also has meaning determined by biological significance.
The complex movements of goal-directed behavior are grounded in a motor
plan which is responsive to the afferent array provided by the stimulus field.
"A train of motor acts results therefore from a train of successive external
situations. The movements are not meaningless; they carry each of them an
obvious meaning [Sherrington, 1947]." The meaning of behavior, as determined by the meaning of the input, represents a propositional relationship
between organism and environment. Each operates on the other to determine
the ultimate result of the interaction. The organism appreciates the
proposition—that is, what the relationship "proposes" in terms of biological
significance—and behaves accordingly. In this sense, the environmental
input can be conceived as having a semantic aspect. Now, it is true that
semantics deals "primarily with linguistic knowledge and knowledge about
the world that is described by sentences," but ". . . there is a sense of the
term 'semantics' that refers to conceptual structures in a general way
[Greeno, 1972]." This general sense of semantics must antedate the acquisition of language, both pylogenetically and ontogenetically, and may well
serve as the biological foundation on which language is erected. Less
metaphorically put, it is semantics in the second sense of the term that
determines the operations of the organism on the environment; language, as
it evolves, is put to the service of this kind of semantics as yet one more
conceptual structure to represent the world; and simultaneously it becomes
a motor mechanism, goal directed, to operate on the environment. In its
evolution, one would guess, phonology and syntax become incorporated as
accession of neurological function allows greater abstraction of input, with
reduction of immediacy and inflexibility of response. The biological implications are less urgent at higher levels of functions, for the immediate needs of
the organism can be handled by movement subprograms at lower levels.

Evidence for the interaction between the "command" or "predictive"
cortical programs and associated subroutines in language function is inferen-
tial but can be found in both acquisition and dissolution of language function. "Infants learn their mother tongue by first determining, independent of
language, the meaning which a speaker intends to convey to them, and then
working out the relationship between the meaning and the expression they
heard. In other words, the infant uses meaning as a clue to language, rather
than language as a clue to meaning [McNamara, 1971]." In dissolution of
language function, with which I am more familiar, the evidence exists in
several familiar clinical situations and has, curiously, escaped the attention
of those neurologists who continue to look exclusively for dissolution of
language structure as a consequence of cortical lesions. The evidence is

fragmentary, and often hard to quantify, but can be construed as indicating that in a number of disorders which are accompanied by language dissolution, major programs or subprograms, not all of which are necessarily primarily linguistic, may be affected in isolation, thereby exposing aspects of the hierarchy not otherwise seen. Conversations with patients in the early stages of a diffuse dementing disorder such as Alzheimer's disease, for example, have a peculiar unsettling quality. It is as if the two parts of the dialogue are operating in parallel and are only rarely intersecting. Linguistically, the patient's output is acceptable enough; sentences are well formed, words are perhaps limited but properly used. There is, however, a "two dimensional" aspect about the output suggesting a dissociation between the meanings of words and the meanings of what they represent. And this can be seen from the other side as well, when the patient verbalizes quite properly a response to a hypothetical situation, but then lacks the ability to so perform. This is not apraxia in the usual sense, nor is it a deficit in sequencing. The disorder consists, it appears, of difficulty in formulating the detailed aspects of a plan even though the verbal aspects are unimpaired.

A second view of the same sort of phenomenon can be seen in some aphasic patients in whom a focal lesion is alleged to produce an isolated disorder of language. And yet, these patients often have an unequivocal disorder of eye movements in response to nonverbal visual stimuli (Tyler, 1969), suggesting that the disorder is considerably more widespread than one of language alone; it may be that the language impairment is representative of a prelinguistic abnormality or, contrariwise, that the nonlinguistic behavioral impairment is a consequence of an interruption of the internal language system. With further dissolution, palilalic repetition may occur. In the severe dement this may be ceaseless monosyllabic reiteration; in the aphasic it occurs as variations on a neologism (Caplan, Kellar, & Locke, 1972), and in the schizophrenic the longer more variable utterances are known as "clang associations." But in all, the presumption is that the self-generated auditory stimulus, usually ineffective as a releaser of verbal behavior, is serving at some comparatively low level to bypass the normal actuating mechanism, and to trigger a subprogram. Simultaneously, vision, which customarily serves as a releaser, is now no longer required, so the dement babbles as much in the dark as in the light (Locke, 1975; Locke, Caplan, & Kellar, 1973).

Just as reafferent signals determine the accuracy of a limb movement by correlating it with a motor plan, so in the case of speech, reafferentation occurs and presumably utilizes auditory as well as proprioceptive feedback. It is, we suspect, the improper utilization of this reafferent signal that accounts for palilalic reiteration. What makes the situation particularly intriguing in the case of speech is suggested by the Russian studies on its regulatory function. What happens normally, they suggest, is that the reafferent function acquires more and more of the symbolic aspect of speech, and diffuses to govern more and more generalized behavior. "The regulatory function is steadily transferred from the impulse side of speech to the analytic system of elective significative connections which are produced by speech [Luria, 1961]." What starts out as a motor function, obeying the principles that govern all motor activity—of extracting meaning from environmental input and generating a meaningful response—now goes on to produce meaning comparatively independent of initial environmental input. This meaning, first as an acoustic percept and later as internalized speech, is projected back on the environment, whether external or internal, to serve as new input to initiate a new plan or to modify an old one. It thus governs behavior by "planning" it in a very physiological way, substituting speech for the more fundamental modality input. It is recycling of this sort that allows for the generative aspects of speech and of behavior, recombining a finite number of motor components into an infinite number of sequences.

It would seem that speech and language respond to the same neurological principles that govern all motor behavior. Motor responses, hierarchically programmed, are released as a consequence of the biological meaning of stimulus input. Analysis of meaning, in this sense, occurs well in advance of the phylogenetic or ontogenetic acquistion of language. In this sense all behavior has a semantic aspect. Elaboration of this semantic component of neurological function occurs in parallel with neurological development and results ultimately in the release of behavior from immediate correspondence with environmental stimuli. It serves as the foundation on which language is built. The phonological aspect develops at a lower neurological level to be pressed into the service of the language system in the same way that spinal and brainstem programs of movements are incorporated into higher-level goal-directed behavior. Although the evidence to substantiate much of this point of view has been obtained only during the last 10 years, Eric Lenneberg was far sighted in his certainty the evidence would be forthcoming, for it was his confident aim "to discover biological principles that explain why a single specie displays behavior that is unique in the animal kingdom [Lenneberg, 1967]."

REFERENCES

Asanuma, H. & Rosen, I. Topographical organization of cortical afferent zones projecting to distal forelimb muscles in monkey. *Experimental Brain Research*, 1972, *14*, 243–256.
Brinkman, J. & Kuypers, H. G. J. M. Cerebral control of contralateral and ipsilateral arm, hand and finger movements in the split brain rhesus monkey. *Brain*, 1973, *96*, 653–674.

Bruner, J. S. On voluntary action and its hierarchical structure. In A. Koestler & J. R. Smythies (Eds.), *Beyond reductionism*. New York: Macmillan, 1969.

Caplan, D. Kellar, L., & Locke, S. Inflection of neologisms in aphasia. *Brain,* 1972, *95*, 169–172.

Chomsky, N. *Language and mind*. New York: Harcourt, 1968.

De Long, M. R. Motor functions of the basal ganglia: single unit activity during movement. In F. O. Schmitt & F. G. Worden (Eds.), *The neurosciences: third study program*. Cambridge: MIT Press, 1974.

Denny-Brown, D. *The cerebral control of movement*. Liverpool: Liverpool University Press, 1966.

Ertl, J., & Schafer, E. W. Cortical activity preceding speech. *Life Science,* 1967, *6*, 473–479.

Ertl, J., & Schafer, E. W. Cortical activity preceding speech. *Life Science,* 1969, *8*, 559.

Evarts, E. V. Activity of cerebral neurons in relation to movement. In D. Tower (Ed.), *The nervous system* (Vol. I). New York: Raven Press, 1975.

Goldring, S., & Ratcheson, R. Human motor cortex: Sensory input data from single neuron recording. *Science,* 1972, *175*, 1493–1495.

Greeno, J. G. On the acquisition of a simple cognitive structure. In E. Tulving (Ed.), *Organization of memory*, New York: Academic Press, 1972.

Koestler, A. Beyond atomism and holism—the concept of the holon. In A. Koestler & J. R. Smythies (Eds.), *Beyond reductionism*. New York: Macmillan, 1969.

Kornhuber, H. H. Cerebral cortex, cerebellum and basal ganglia. An introduction to their motor functions. In F. O. Schmitt & F. G. Worden (Eds.), *The neurosciences: third study program,* Cambridge: MIT Press, 1974.

Lashley, K. S. The problem of serial order in behavior. In L. A. Jeffress (Ed.), *Cerebral mechanisms of behavior*. New York: Wiley, 1951.

Lenneberg, E. H. *Biological foundations of language*. New York: Wiley, 1967.

Locke, S. Speech behavior—a foundation of language. *Language and Speech,* 1975, *18*, 270–271.

Locke, S., Caplan, D., & Kellar, L. *A study In neurolinguistics*. Springfield, Ill.: Thomas, 1973.

Luria, A. R. *The role of speech in regulation of normal and abnormal behavior*. New York: Liveright, 1961.

Luria, A. R. *Human brain and psychological processes*. New York: Harper & Row, 1966. (a)

Luria, A. R. *Higher cortical functions in man*. New York: Basic Books, 1966. (b)

McNamara, J. The cognitive strategies of language learning. In T. Andersson (Ed.), *Conference on child language*. Quebec: Les Presses de l'Universite, 1971.

Mountcastle, V. B., Lynch, J. C., Georgopoulos, A., Sakata, H., & Acuna, C. Posterior parietal association cortex of the monkey: Command functions for operations within extrapersonal space. *Journal of Neurophysiology,* 1975, *38*, 871–909.

Sherrington, C. S. *The integrative action of the nervous system*. Cambridge: Cambridge University Press, 1947.

Sherrington, C. S. Introductory. In P. Laslett (Ed.), *The physical basis of mind*. Oxford: Basil Blackwell, 1952.

Teuber, H. L. Perception. In J. Field & H. W. Magoun (Eds.), *Handbook of physiology* (Section I). Washington, D.C.: American Physiological Society, 1960.

Tyler, H. R. Effective stimulus exploration in aphasic patients. *Neurology,* 1969, *19*, 105–112.

Weiss, P. The living system: Determinism stratified. In A. Koestler & J. R. Smythies (Eds.), *Beyond reductionism*. New York: Macmillan, 1969.

Yingling, C. Motor programs and feedback in control of movement. *BIS Conference Report,* 1975, *35*, 65–73.

chapter 6

Aphasia and the Concept of
Brain Centers

O. L. ZANGWILL

In his remarkable book on the *Biological Foundations of Language*
(1967), the late Eric Lenneberg devoted an important chapter to the neurology of speech. Lenneberg pointed out that it would be intellectually satisfying if we could deduce the nature of the brain mechanisms of language from
a careful survey of neurological disorders but is reluctantly forced to conclude that this is not possible. There is, he argued, too much discrepancy
between the conceptual systems of neurologists and behavioral scientists to
enable one to specify in any satisfactory way the neurological correlates of
behavioral events. Further, cerebral lesions are so variable in their effects
that firm localization of specific syndromes becomes exceedingly difficult.
"Clinically," he pointed out, "we encounter an almost kaleidoscopic combination of idiosyncratic failure or sparing of particular skills which renders
precise correlation between pathological anatomy and pathological verbal
behavior very difficult [p. 222]."

While it is hard to quarrel with these views, it would be wrong to
suppose that Eric Lenneberg had lost hope that the nature of language would
ever be clarified by consideration of its disorders. For one thing, as Len-

119

PSYCHOLOGY AND BIOLOGY OF LANGUAGE AND THOUGHT
Essays in Honor of Eric Lenneberg

neberg pointed out, the apparent lack of congruence between behavioral and neurological sciences is not a true discordance: It is merely a consequence of the fact that the theoretical framework of each science has evolved without proper knowledge of the other. Indeed, Lenneberg seemed to be in no doubt that the brain is the instrument of behavior, including linguistic behavior, and that when neurological and behavioral concepts are more adequately aligned we shall achieve that "coalescence of neurology and psychology" to which Lashley looked forward. In this connection, Lenneberg (1967) had no doubt that a measure of cerebral localization of psychological function truly exists. "Too much has been learned about specific brain functions during the past few years to consider seriously the idea that any component of the brain lacks specific physiological function [p. 209]." The real question, he asked, is what these functions may be and whether they can be discovered through observation of whole, complex behavior patterns. I call this question "Lenneberg's question," and my object in this chapter is to outline some possible ways in which one might begin to answer it.

BRAIN CENTERS AND CONNECTIONS

As I see it, the concept of cortical localization of psychological function, in its modern form at least, has been with us ever since neurologists, following the lead of Marc Dax and Paul Broca, came to see aphasia as linked with damage to one cerebral hemisphere only, usually the left but occasionally the right and, moreover, with certain less or more circumscribed portions of that hemisphere. In spite of Hughlings Jackson's well-known dictum that localizing a defect is something very different from localizing a function, these facts were very generally taken to mean that the various aspects of language are discretely localized in the cortex and might be selectively affected by focal brain lesions. Although the concept of specific "brain centers" governing the various aspects of language is out of fashion today, it provided the first comprehensive neurological model of language and if only for this reason merits our consideration.

What is a "brain center"? In common with most people, I long thought that the whole idea was no more than an aftereffect of phrenology, a hangover from Gall's speculative attempt to parcel out the cortex into discrete areas, each of which could be viewed as the seat of a mental faculty. Although Gall's ideas undoubtedly had influence, I think it is true to say that the concept of a brain center owes much less to phrenology than to the theory of reflex action, as it evolved in the course of the nineteenth century. David Ferrier, for example, writing in 1876, referred to the brain and spinal cord as the "cerebrospinal centers" and pointed out that both the spinal cord as a whole and its component segments are capable of a degree of independent action entirely comparable to that of a primitive invertebrate nervous system. It is the central components of these spinal reflexes that he designated as "centers" for the acts elicited by peripheral excitation.

In much the same way, Ferrier ascribed the control of essential vital activities, such as swallowing, respiration, and regulation of the heart rate, to similar (if more complex) centers located in the medulla and hind-brain. Indeed for Ferrier and others of his time, it is probably true to say that a "center" was envisaged as the seat of integration of a less or more complex adaptive reflex mechanism—if you like, the "C" in CNS. Integration, which was later given more specific meaning by Sherrington (1906), was, of course, viewed as something purely physiological and any reference to vital forces or psychical powers was rigidly excluded.

Nonetheless, this purely physiological concept of a brain center soon became modified as experimental techniques began to be applied to the analysis of cortical function. It became, as it were, contaminated by psychology. For example, Ferrier himself believed that the cortical sensory areas, as defined by early ablation experiments, were truly organs of perception, their stimulation resulting in physical modifications that "coincide with subjective phenomena." He likewise viewed the motor cortex, as demarcated by his own experiments and by those of Fritsch and Hitzig, as being truly part of the mechanism producing voluntary movement and, to this extent, conjoined with psychical activity. Although brain centers remained physiological, the possibility of their possessing psychological correlates was thus explicitly admitted.

Not unnaturally, the doctrine of brain centers was eagerly embraced by early students of aphasia. These men, picturesquely described by Henry Head (1926) as the "diagram makers," evidently believed that all disorders of language could be classified in terms of affections of independent centers or of the pathways between them. Clearly, such an approach lends itself well to the construction of diagrams, and between 1870 and 1910 diagrams of alleged brain centers and their interconnections steadily increased in number and complexity—and, some might say, implausibility. But in the course of this evolution, the very concept of a center underwent further psychological contamination. What had begun as a focus of reflex integration turned into a system of nerve cells and fibers designed to classify sensory information, to store memories, and to generate and coordinate motor output. Certain of these functions, moreover, could be defined only in psychological terms, and this implied a clear departure from the reflex arc concept. It was this more than anything else that led to the ultimate downfall of the whole doctrine.

Let us look in a little more detail at the schemes of explanation produced by the diagram makers. W. H. Broadbent, a British neurologist, provides a good example of the thinking of his time. Writing in 1879, he begins by insisting that speech, like all sensorimotor acquisitions, depends upon a cell-and-fiber system, the activities of which are governed by the principles of reflex action. The motor coordinations that issue in articulated speech are, he suggests, controlled by the corpus striatum (or possibly Broca's area) and are formed under the influence of auditory impressions relayed from the thalamus to an auditory perceptive center, thought to be located in the first temporal convolution (Wernicke's area). The latter is where, in Bastian's (1869) classic phrase, "words are revived as sound impressions." Broadbent further postulated at least two supraordinate centers, one concerned with the categorization of sensory input from all modalities (this he called an "idea" center), the other with "propositionizing," that is, the formulation and expression of propositional speech. Thus an attempt was made to marry the thinking of Hughlings Jackson, who was not, of course, himself a diagram maker, with the prevailing doctrine of brain centers. But we are left with the notion that some higher centers, at least, have wholly psychical functions, and the original concept of a purely reflex integrative mechanism has, in consequence, been virtually abandoned.

The justification of the diagram makers' explanation of aphasia lay of course in the relative specificity of the dysphasic syndromes that were distinguished by the neurologists of the period and their apparent relation to injury or disease of relatively circumscribed areas of the brain. Among these were classical motor aphasia, in which comprehension is relatively well preserved; classical sensory aphasia, marked especially by speech errors and paraphasias that the patient is powerless to correct; and conduction aphasia, marked by intact comprehension but failure in repetition of spoken speech. So-called "pure" word-deafness and word-blindness were later adduced as powerful evidence for the existence of discrete perceptive centers linked to the mechanisms of speech. Nonetheless, the ideas of the diagram makers have largely lost their appeal, mainly on account of the strong attack made upon them by Henry Head (1926) and his powerful advocacy of Jacksonian thinking, with its very much more cautious views on the nature of language and the cerebral localization of speech. The later, and very influential, thinking of K. Goldstein (1948) likewise tended in the same direction.

When I first began to work in the sphere of aphasia, I must admit that I was considerably under the spell of Hughlings Jackson and Henry Head.

However, like Eric Lenneberg, I was much struck by the way in which relatively circumscribed types of speech disorder might occur in consequence of focal injuries of the brain. Head's writings did not always prove to be a reliable guide to the symptomatology of aphasia and, like Norman Geschwind more recently, I was led for a time to take much more seriously the ideas of the diagram makers and to envisage the possibility, if not of speech centers, at any rate of aspects of linguistic function with discrete cortical representation. Indeed I have been very much impressed by Geschwind's analysis of disconnection syndromes, in particular those that may be associated with lesions of the corpus callosum (Geschwind & Kaplan, 1962). Nonetheless, I still find myself highly critical of the doctrine of brain centers, at all events in the form in which it was advocated by the diagram makers. Yet if we reject this notion, we cannot, except in purely structural terms, answer the question of what is disconnected from what.

THE LOCALIZATION OF SPEECH

It seems to me that a further, and perhaps very important, implication of the doctrine of centers was the belief that a center is *punctate,* that is, it constitutes a highly circumscribed integrative focus. The respiratory center in the medulla, for instance, was for long envisaged as a *noeud vital,* a very small area of brain tissue governing action whose maintenance was essential to life. In the same way, the eliciting of specific muscular movements by stimulation of points on the motor cortex seemed to suggest to many a highly punctate representation of muscular action. Yet as has often been pointed out, there is no necessary reason for envisaging motor control in this way. Hughlings Jackson, indeed, most certainly did not do so, even though his own observations on Jacksonian epilepsy largely stimulated Ferrier to undertake his original stimulation experiments. Nonetheless, this conception of a brain center as highly circumscribed, possibly inherited from Gall's phrenology, undoubtedly influenced early students of aphasia in their search for the centers governing speech.

Not all diagram makers, however, took this view. Although Broca insisted that articulate speech was governed by a small part of the third left frontal convolution, Bastian (1898) pointed out that a center is not necessarily punctate and that it may be envisaged as a functionally unified nervous network of variable extension. This is, I think, a valuable idea. It suggests that, instead of searching for highly specific behavioral deficits, each of which is correlated with a cerebral lesion of determinate location, we should do better to try to define the total extent of brain cortex within which lesions may occasion disorder of language. Only then, when the character of the disorder has been properly specified, does it become proper to seek more specific localization of the component functions involved in language.

Inspired by these rather vague reflections, I turned first to the question of the prefrontal cortex. I had been worried for a long time by the claims made by several distinguished neurosurgeons, in particular Jefferson (1949) that excisions of the left frontal lobe produce effects on psychological function no different from, or at any rate no more severe than, those of the right frontal lobe. It seemed to me that even if the left frontal lobe has no inherent superiority over its fellow, the very fact that it forms part of the dominant hemisphere should not be totally without influence in the event of its excision. Might not, therefore, left frontal lobectomy be expected to have certain psychological sequelae not found following comparable operations on the right hemisphere?

Review of the Literature

The first step was to review the literature to see whether there was any evidence of a differential effect of unilateral prefrontal lesions. Not entirely to my surprise, I soon came upon such evidence, precisely in the sphere in which one might most reasonably expect to find it, namely, that of language and speech. This evidence came from two sources: first, the earlier clinical studies of the effects of penetrating unilateral brain wounds, more especially those undertaken in Germany during and after World War I (Feuchtwanger, 1923; Kleist, 1928); and second, later psychometric studies of patients who have undergone excisions of frontal cortex in the surgical treatment of focal epilepsy (Milner, 1964).

I have considered this material elsewhere (Zangwill, 1966) and will review it here only very briefly. The earlier German work, although largely qualitative, seems to show that a degree of impairment in expressive speech, if seldom sufficiently marked as to justify a diagnosis of aphasia, is far more common after left-sided than after right-sided prefrontal injury. It involves appreciable loss of spontaneity in speech (though not necessarily in overall motor activity) and a difficulty in verbal expression, especially noteworthy if the content is complex or abstract, often associated with an apparent impoverishment in verbal thinking. Articulation is not impaired, though there is sometimes a trace of agrammatism. In more recent studies, Luria (1966) has emphasized that in patients with left prefrontal damage, conversational speech loses its fluency and may become curiously fragmented, as if the retrieval of each separate word requires a special volitional impulse. As he picturesquely puts it, "the patient speaks like a hobbled horse runs [p. 206]."

Luria further refers to the absence of a scheme of expression, well seen if the patient is asked to retell a story or make a short speech on a specified topic. He considers the disturbance to lie essentially in the dynamic structure of speech.

Luria's acute observations find support from the results of the simple verbal fluency tests reported by Milner (1964) and Benton (1968). Although I have done no systematic work using these tests, their evidence of a marked depression in verbal fluency (retrieval of names of objects within a prescribed category) following left, though not right, prefrontal lesions is entirely in accord with my own experience.

From these somewhat scattered observations, I think one may safely conclude that minimal expressive language disorder may result from left frontal lobe lesions anterior to Broca's area. At the least, this suggests that the left prefrontal cortex in some way participates in the generation of fluent, well-organized expressive speech. Although conventionally excluded from the "speech area," I think this area of cortex deserves inclusion in the total cell-and-fiber system of the left hemisphere involved in the generation of propositional language.

The next step in my search for the gross neural correlates of linguistic disorder came about purely by serendipity. It involves the question of Broca's area itself and its role in the production of speech. For many years, I had unreflectingly accepted the traditional view that this region of the brain and its subjacent connections provide the essential neurological basis of articulate speech. Recently, however, I have had the opportunity of studying two cases in which Broca's area was either excised or completely undercut in the course of operation for tumor involving the left frontal lobe. A preliminary report of these two cases has been published (Zangwill, 1975). It may be said that both the patients were fully right-handed and in neither was there a familial history of sinistrality. One patient was slightly dysphasic before operation and both were totally aphasic for a day or two after it. This aphasia, however, was purely transient. Four weeks postoperatively, neither patient showed any disorder of speech or writing on ordinary neurological examination, and the only noteworthy feature on psychological testing was a loss in fluency of the type described by Milner (1964). Indeed the picture was strikingly reminiscent of that shown by cases of left prefrontal excision anterior to Broca's area. I may add that two further and very similar cases have since been seen in which, despite operative excision of Broca's area, neither patient showed appreciable dysphasia either before or after operation.

These findings have occasioned much surprise and some disbelief. Certainly the evidence is far from conclusive, and in neither case has the pathology been verified at necropsy. Furthermore, it was not thought appropriate in either case to give a preoperative Wada test, and corticography was not undertaken at operation. Yet such findings as I have described should occasion little surprise. As early as 1914, von Monakow concluded that "the available facts exclude the theory that lesions strictly confined to Broca's area give rise to complete and chronic aphasia [p. 734]." More recently, Hécaen and Consoli (1973) have reviewed 12 cases of verified lesions involving Broca's area and have concluded that severe and persistent aphasia was present only in the cases in which the lesion was extensive and involved subcortical white matter. In 5 cases similar to ours, in which the lesion was purely cortical, only mild and transitory aphasia was in evidence.

THOUGHT AND LANGUAGE

It would be impossible to dispute the fact, first clearly appreciated by Wernicke (1874), that striking disorder in the understanding and expression of speech in the absence of defect in articulation, modulation, and fluency is produced by lesions of the posterior region of the left temporal lobe. Wernicke's syndrome, which comprises defect of comprehension, paraphasia, alexia, and agraphia, was for a long time referred to as sensory or receptive aphasia, it being implicitly assumed that paraphasic and related speech errors owe their origin to defect of comprehension; that is, the patient through failure to recognize his speech errors becomes incapable of monitoring his own speech output. But we now appreciate that the position is a good deal less simple than this. The incidence of speech errors is poorly correlated with the severity of receptive loss; some Wernicke aphasics, indeed, produce relatively little paraphasia in spite of severe disorder of comprehension. Others understand fairly well though their speech is so full of jargon as to be virtually incomprehensible. Further, while it is quite evident that relatively circumscribed disorders of speech may be produced by posterior temporal lobe lesions, of writing by posterior parietal lobe lesions, and of reading by occipital or occipito-parietal lesions of the dominant hemisphere, it would be a bold man who ventured to localize such complex linguistic skills exclusively in these limited areas of the brain cortex.

The search for precise localization of these relatively specific defects has, I believe, its roots in the older theories of punctate language centers and serves to retard rather than advance our understanding of the neural activities actually involved in language. Damage to the left temporal lobe, especially when it is relatively mild, may produce striking alterations in the understanding and use of language that may tell us far more about its neurological organization than the occasional case of "pure" word-deafness, word-blindness, or florid jargon aphasia. For example, I described some years ago striking defects in the understanding and explanation of idioms, proverbs, and figures of speech in patients with mild or recovering temporal lobe aphasia (Zangwill, 1964). In these patients, there may be little, if any, handicap in ordinary spontaneous speech, yet surprising difficulty is encountered on these very simple intellectual tasks. For example, the patient may repeat an idiom or proverb over and over again, evidently recognizing it yet being quite unable to find other words in which to express its meaning. Often the patient will say that he knows perfectly well what the phrase means yet completely fails to explain it. Occasionally, however, he will say that, although he has heard it hundreds of times, he is not absolutely sure if he knows what it means; that is, the defect is not necessarily one of verbal formulation and expression but may involve an element of failure in understanding. Although I suspect that such a patient is by no means incapable of using appropriately an idiom or proverb whose meaning he is unable to explain, there is no doubt that he has suffered a genuine loss in the flexibility of his language and in his capacity to recode information and communicate it in appropriate form to others. This is an example of what I like to call a defect in the intellectual use or application of language, rather than a defect in language itself.

Luria (1966) has described somewhat similar intellectual deficiencies in many left temporal patients, which he attributes to a combination of high-grade deficits in phonemic speech structure and short-term verbal memory. Although abstract intellectual capacity may be largely preserved, the patient fails on many tasks that entail discursive intellectual activity wholly dependent on language. (For examples, see Luria, 1966, pp. 118–122.) He considers these difficulties to be due to "the constant alienation of word meanings, the instability of word-values and the impossibility of retaining traces of word associations and sequence [Luria, 1966, p. 121]." Although I believe that a certain element of intellectual loss is implied in such a deficit, I agree with Luria that basic conceptual processes in cases of left temporal lobe lesion are, in general, intact.

This relative dissociation of intellectual and linguistic disability is well brought out in cases of temporal lobe aphasia with grossly paraphasic speech. Kinsbourne and Warrington (1963) have described patients with florid jargon aphasia who were nontheless able to perform at an average level on a diagrammatic intelligence test (Raven's Progressive Matrices, 1938). The contrast between correct solution of the problem and the patient's totally incomprehensible account of how he arrived at it was indeed

striking. More recently, I have had occasion to observe a laboratory techni-
cian with chronic jargon aphasia who was, nevertheless, capable of dis-
charging his duties to the complete satisfaction of his employers (Hatfield &
Zangwill, 1975). Here again, the contrast between the patient's excellent
performance of his duties and his totally incomprehensible description of
them was indeed dramatic.

It is when we turn to posterior parietal lesions, however, that we see
disorders that approximate more closely to circumscribed patterns of intellectual loss. Here again, the study of more or less specific, localized deficit-
syndromes, such as constructional apraxia or the Gerstmann syndrome, has
tended to divert attention from the disorders of language and thought that are
so commonly associated with parietal lesions. For example, the form of
aphasia designated by Head (1926) as *semantic* is by no means uncommon
and justifies far closer attention than it has so far received. This is not a
disorder of comprehension in the narrow sense as seen in temporal lobe
dysfunction. Such patients with semantic difficulties fully understand individual words and sentences, though they do not always grasp the overall
significance of what is heard or read. They find it hard to appreciate the
development of a line of thought or to follow an argument. Not uncom-
monly, similar difficulties may be encountered in the understanding of maps
and ground plans or, indeed, in some aspects of spatial orientation (Paterson
& Zangwill, 1944). As Luria (1966) has demonstrated so ably, such patients
can no longer fully grasp logico-grammatical relationships, more especially
in the spatial sphere. For this reason, they no longer fully understand
instructions based upon compass directions or discrimination of right from
left. They may likewise fail to distinguish between grammatical constructions with an attributive genitive case, for example, between "father's
brother" and "brother's father." As one of Luria's patients put it: "Of course
I know what a brother and a father mean, but I cannot imagine what the two
are together [Luria, 1966, p. 157]."

I do not think our understanding of these deficits, which lie somewhere
on that hazy borderline between the intellectual and the linguistic, will be
assisted by undue concentration upon the localization of the lesions which
bring them about. As has been said so well, localization of a lesion does not
imply localization of a function, let alone explain its nature. It merely tells us
where to look. I would certainly regard the posterior zones of the classical
speech area as being especially concerned not merely with the understanding of speech but with understanding in a broader and more fundamental
sense. But such understanding itself cannot be understood in terms of
centers, as, for example, Bastian's centers for ideas and for the formulation of
propositions. I think it can be understood only in terms of the nature and

functions of the entire left cerebral hemisphere, which in the course of human evolution appears to have acquired special responsibilities for the initiation and execution of linguistic skills.

THE RIGHT HEMISPHERE
AND LANGUAGE

What of the right cerebral hemisphere and its role in language? As is well known, the right hemisphere can subserve the acquisition of speech in young children who have sustained early damage to the left. Indeed this was specifically predicted by Broca (1861), who regarded the two hemispheres as being essentially equipotential at birth. Moreover, we now know from the work of Roger Sperry and his associates (Gazzaniga & Sperry, 1967; Gazzaniga & Hillyard, 1971; Sperry, Gazzaniga, & Bogen, 1969; Zaidel, 1976, 1977) that the right hemisphere possesses appreciable powers of comprehension, though its capacity for expressive speech seems to be very much more limited, indeed to be often virtually negligible. Whether this incapacity is due to true lack of competence or to a suppression exercised by the dominant hemisphere is uncertain, but in view of the somewhat more adequate powers of speech exhibited by patients who have undergone excision of the left hemisphere as compared with the linguistic capacity of the isolated right hemisphere in cases with section of the cerebral commissures, an explanation in terms of suppression might seem the more plausible. At the same time, the fact that right hemispherectomy in adults does not appear to affect speech might suggest that, in the right-handed adult at least, the right hemisphere plays no essential part in governing language.

This conclusion may, however, be too simple. In the first place, the right hemisphere possesses some measure of speech comprehension, and it might, therefore, be suggested that it is involved to some extent in the linguistic activity of the individual whose brain is intact. That it may do so is suggested by the fact that cerebral dominance appears to operate essentially with regard to expressive as opposed to receptive speech functions. It has been evolved, one may surmise, essentially to ensure "singleness of purpose" in motor behavior, and appears to relate primarily to lateral preference, manipulative skill, and the expression of speech. Comprehension, on the other hand, is more "automatic," in the Jacksonian sense of the term, and no pressing biological advantage would seem to dictate that it be lateralized to one or the other hemisphere. Further, severe "word-deafness," though it has been reported to occur with purely left-sided lesions, is most commonly seen with bitemporal lesions or with left temporal lesions involving the corpus callosum. At all events, it cannot necessarily be concluded that speech comprehension in the healthy individual does not involve the activity of both temporal lobes. Nor can it be concluded that so-called inferior speech, that is, expletives, stereotyped utterances, and other non-propositional forms of linguistic expression, which are so commonly spared in aphasia, is not generated by either cerebral hemisphere or conceivably by both together.

SUMMARY

1.   Following Lenneberg, the question is asked whether specific brain functions can be identified through observation of gross behavioral change. An attempt is made to answer this question in terms of the cerebral localization of various types of deficit in linguistic capacity following injury or disease of the brain.

2.   It is pointed out that failure to distinguish between localization of a deficit and localization of a function has resulted in the assumption of specific brain centers, to which psychological in addition to purely physiological functions came to be ascribed. Disorders of speech consequently came to be regarded in terms of affections of independent centers or of the connections between them. Although long out of fashion, this line of thinking has reemerged in connection with recent work on disconnection syndromes in animals and man.

3.   It is argued that too great an emphasis upon the localization of highly circumscribed aspects of language may impede rather than promote our understanding of its neurology. If the minor or more subtle disorders of language are included, it would seem that an area of the dominant hemisphere considerably larger than the classical "speech area" is involved in linguistic activity. This area certainly includes the prefrontal cortex anterior to Broca's area.

4.   Evidence is adduced that lesions of Broca's area result in permanent aphasia only if the subjacent white matter is involved. Circumscribed cortical excisions involving this area produce at most a transient motor aphasia.

5.   Some characteristic deficits in the understanding and use of language in mild cases of aphasia involving the prefrontal, posterior temporal, and posterior parietal cortex, respectively, are outlined. These may best be described not as intellectual deficits per se, nor yet as linguistic deficits per se, but as limitations in the intellectual uses and applications of language.

6. The role of the right cerebral hemisphere in language is briefly discussed. It is argued that its participation in the understanding of speech and in some relatively primitive aspects of linguistic expression in the healthy individual cannot be ruled out.

REFERENCES

Bastian, H. C. On the various forms of loss of speech in cerebral disease. *British and Foreign Medico-Chirurgical Review*, 1869, *403*, 209–236, 470–492.

Bastian, H. C. *Aphasia and other speech defects*. London: H. K. Lewis, 1898.

Benton, A. L. Differential behavioural effects in frontal lobe disease. *Neuropsychologia*, 1968, *6*, 53–60.

Broadbent, W. H. A case of peculiar affection of speech, with commentary. *Brain*, 1879, *1*, 484–503.

Broca, P. Perte de la parole. Ramollissement chronique et destruction partielle du lobe anterieur gauche du cerveau. *Bulletin de la Société d'Anthropologie*, 1861, *2*, 235–238.

Ferrier, D. *The functions of the brain*. London: Smith, Elder, 1876.

Feuchtwanger, E. Die funktionen des stirnhirns. In O. Förster & K. Willmanns (Eds.), *Monographen aus der gesamtgebiete der neurologie und psychiatrie*. Berlin: Springer, 1923.

Gazzaniga, M. S., & Hillyard, S. A. Language and speech capacity of the right hemisphere. *Neuropsychologia*, 1971, *9*, 273–280.

Gazzaniga, M. S., & Sperry, R. W. Language after section of the cerebral commissures. *Brain*, 1967, *90*, 131–148.

Geschwind, N., & Kaplan, E. A human cerebral disconnection syndrome. *Neurology*, 1962, *12*, 675–685.

Goldstein, K. *Language and language disturbances*. New York: Grune & Stratton, 1948.

Hatfield, F. M., & Zangwill, O. L. Occupational resettlement in aphasia. *Scandinavian Journal of Rehabilitation Medicine*, 1975, *7*, 56–60.

Head, H. *Aphasia and kindred disorders of speech*. London: Cambridge University Press, 1926.

Hécaen, H., & Consoli, S. Analyse des troubles du langage an cours des lesions de l'aire de Broca. *Neuropsychologia*, 1973, *11*, 371–388.

Jefferson, G. Localization of function in the cerebral cortex. *British Medical Bulletin*, 1949, *6*, 333–340.

Kinsbourne, M., & Warrington, E. K. Jargon aphasia. *Neuropsychologia*, 1963, *1*, 27–37.

Kleist, K. *Gehirnpathologie*. Leipzig: Barth, 1928.

Lenneberg, E. *The biological foundations of language*. New York: Wiley, 1967.

Luria, A. R. *Higher cortical functions in man*. London: Tavistock, 1966.

Milner, B. Some effects of frontal lobectomy in man. In J. M. Warren & K. Akert (Eds.), *The frontal granular cortex and behavior*. New York: McGraw-Hill, 1964.

Monakow, C. von. *Die lokalisation im grosshirn*. Wiesbaden: Bergmann, 1914.

Paterson, A., & Zangwill, O. L. Disorders of visual perception associated with lesions of the right cerebral hemisphere. *Brain*, 1944, *67*, 331–358.

Raven, J. C. *Progressive matrices*. London: H. K. Lewis, 1938.

Sherrington, C. S. *The integrative action of the nervous system*. Cambridge: University Press, 1906. (Reprinted 1947.)

Sperry, R. W., Gazzaniga, M. S., & Bogen, J. E. Interhemispheric relationships: the neo-cortical commissures: syndromes of hemisphere disconnection. In P. J. Vinken & G. W. Bruyn

(Eds.), *Handbook of clinical neurology* (Vol. 4). Amsterdam: North Holland, 1969.

Wernicke, C. *Der aphasische symptomenkomplex.* Breslau: Cohn and Weigert, 1874.

Zaidel, E. Auditory vocabulary of the right hemisphere following brain bisection or hemidecortication. *Cortex,* 1976, *12,* 191–211.

Zaidel, E. Unilateral auditory comprehension on the token test following cerebral commissurotomy or hemispherectomy. *Neuropsychologia,* 1977, *15,* 1–18.

Zangwill, O. L. Intelligence in aphasia. In A. V. S. de Reuck & Maeve O'Connor (Eds.), *Disorders of language.* London: Churchill, 1964.

Zangwill, O. L. Psychological deficits associated with frontal lobe lesions. *International Journal of Neurology,* 1966, *5,* 395–402.

Zangwill, O. L. Excision of Broca's area without persistent aphasia. In K. J. Zülch, O. Creutzfeld, & G. C. Galbraith (Eds.), *Cerebral localization.* Heidelberg and New York: Springer-Verlag, 1975.

chapter 7

Lenneberg, Locke, Zangwill, and the Neuropsychology of Language and Language Disorders

AARON SMITH

In introducing his extraordinary work entitled *Biological Foundations of Language* (1967), Eric Lenneberg wrote:

> This book must be understood as a discussion rather than a presentation of the biological foundations of language. The exact foundations are still largely unknown. On the other hand, I considered this book to be the right place to evaluate critically some of the most common claims . . . the topic seemed to me to be important enough to warrant a detailed discussion [p. viii].

Like Zangwill, Lenneberg rejected the "classical" theory of the localization of speech ("There is no clear cut evidence that Broca's area is more specifically related to speech than other areas adjacent to it [p. 61]."), as well as today's versions of the nineteenth-century cerebral cartography of language functions. At the time he wrote his book, however, Lenneberg did believe that, in the normally matured brain, the biological structures mediating language functions are developed exclusively in the left hemisphere. Citing studies by Ajuriaguerra (1957), Hécaen and Ajuriaguerra (1963), and Teuber (1962), Lenneberg (1967) wrote: "In the absence of pathology, a

133

PSYCHOLOGY AND BIOLOGY OF LANGUAGE AND THOUGHT
Essays in Honor of Eric Lenneberg

polarization of function between the right and left takes place during childhood, displacing language entirely to the left and certain other functions
predominantly to the right [p. 153]." Thus, he concluded that although
aphasia acquired after the age of 18 may be recovered from within 3 to 5
months after onset, such recovery is due to physiological restoration rather
than to a learning process: "Symptoms that have not cleared up by this time
are, as a rule, irreversible [p. 143]."

For students training to become speech therapists, this was a depressing
conclusion. They were further dismayed by a report by Sarno, Silverman,
and Sands (1970) describing effects of speech therapy on 31 stroke patients
with severe aphasia. Citing Lenneberg, they reported that speech therapy
was of no benefit.

My studies of the initial and later effects of right and left hemispherectomy for lesions incurred in infancy or in adulthood, and studies of
patterns of language deficits as well as effects of therapy on adults with
chronic aphasia, had shown very different results. On learning of my findings, Lenneberg requested reprints and expressed great interest. He wrote
that he had no data to support the view that language therapy was of no
value to the adult with chronic aphasia, and invited me to visit his laboratory
to discuss details of our studies, our techniques of testing, and the like.

Eric Lenneberg's deeper interest in discovering what was true than in
defending his published views impressed me greatly. Not only did it reflect
his intellectual honesty; it was evidence that his extraordinary range of
knowledge resulted, in part at least, from his recognition of the critical
importance of keeping an open mind. Thus the invitation to discuss the
presentations by Locke and Zangwill in this volume meant far more to me
than a simple appeal to my vanity. It symbolized some of the particular
attributes that stamped Eric Lenneberg as a rare and gifted human being.

THE BIOLOGICAL FOUNDATIONS
OF LANGUAGE

Locke's construction of an allegorical model of sequential motor programming underlying the organization of brain functions in general and
language in particular (Chapter 5 of this volume) and Zangwill's "Aphasia
and the Concept of Brain Centers" (Chapter 6 of this volume) illustrate two
different but related approaches to the problems of elucidating the biological
foundations of language—or, in Zangwill's apt term, to "Lenneberg's question."

Locke's bold and elaborate model describes the hierarchical development and organization of anatomical structures into discrete autonomous mechanisms of specific functions. The lower level (sensory and motor) subfunctions are the first to develop; as they become organized, these subfunctions are integrated, forming the more complex mechanisms underlying the higher (cognitive) functions. The stupendously complex neural processes of normal expressive and receptive language functions thus emerge when the various autonomous mechanisms are organized and integrated. Although he emphasizes the motor aspects ("movement which is organized, goal directed, and creates an action system"), Locke views his model not only as applying to the development of language, but also as reflecting an organizational principle that underlies all neurological function and its overt expression, behavior. Since a specific movement is represented throughout the system that "underwrites" it, a lesion at any level disrupts the movement represented in that system. What the level of the lesion determines is "the residual capability inherent in the integrated system that has been released." However, like Zangwill, Locke cautions against a simplistic geographical or "where" approach, or any suggestion of circumscribed cortical or subcortical areas in which the different language functions have been variously localized since the nineteenth century.

Instead, in keeping with Jackson's dynamic concepts of brain functions, Locke describes the various movements as being "represented" (presumably to varying degrees) in different neuroanatomically organized configurations (or mechanisms). ("The representation is certainly not isomorphic with the movement; nor are the places of representation to be conceived in a literal sense.") His view that "the general sense of semantics must antedate the acquisition of language and may well serve as the biological foundation on which language is erected" is consistent with Chomsky's observation that "a grammar is no more learned than, say, ability to walk is learned [Chomsky, 1967, p. 81]."

Many of us were taught that the highly complex grammatical processes involved in the development of normal speech and comprehension are acquired as a result of the development of early mental, cognitive, or intellectual capacities; that the complex grammar of speech is learned much as, say, reading and writing, as opposed to walking, are "learned". But Lenneberg (1964) called attention to the development of functional speech and comprehension in mentally retarded children whose IQ was 50 at age 12 and about 30 at age 20; similarly, my studies of patients with left or right hemispherectomy for infantile epileptogenic lesions revealed development of correct grammatical speech and comprehension in cases in which verbal and nonverbal reasoning capacities were below the lowest limits of standardized intelligence tests (Smith, 1972).

Locke's model represents an integration of a variety of theoretical constructs from the relatively recent literature in an effort to define specific principles that determine the development and organization of the human brain structure–function relationships underlying language processes. Although Locke's focus does not include consideration of the evidence in clinico-anatomic correlation studies of aphasics, Zangwill, in a similar effort, reviews the findings and interpretations of such studies from Dax and Broca to the present.

Zangwill's motif in his review of selected studies from the vast literature is the question posed by Lenneberg's observation that too much has been learned about specific brain functions to doubt that any component of the brain lacks specific physiological function. Thus, Zangwill's object is to outline some of the possible ways in which one might begin to answer "Lenneberg's question."

This question has, of course, loomed before all students of human brain functions. How does the brain work? In 1543, Vesalius, founder of modern neuroanatomy, wrote:

> But how the brain performs its functions in imagination, in reasoning, in thinking, and in memory . . . I can form no opinion whatever. Neither do I think that anything more will be found out by anatomy or the methods of those theologians who deny to brute animals all powers of reasoning and indeed all facilities belonging to what we call the chief soul [p. 255].

Over three centuries later, Goltz (1888) added, "The research into the functions of the various parts of the brain is a very old question. Many have tried and many have erred [p. 130]."

In the continuing elucidation of the anatomy, pathology, and physiology of the central nervous system since then, Zangwill's integration of psychology and neurology in his studies of the effects of focal brain lesions has contributed greatly to the emergence of clinical neuropsychology as an independent discipline. His views in this volume reflect the cumulative results of his more than 30 years of outstanding studies of aphasia, as well as his early recognition of the role of the long-ignored right hemisphere. With Paterson (Paterson & Zangwill, 1944, 1945), Zangwill provided the first compelling psychological evidence to confirm Hughlings Jackson's conclusions (based on clinical observations) that the right hemisphere "leads" in nonlanguage visual ideational functions. Zangwill's redemption of status of the lowly right hemisphere (variously described as nondominant, minor, subordinate, silent, and as the weaker, less clever, dependent brother) has continued since then. In Chapter 6, he discusses his evolving views on the role of the right hemisphere in language functions in children and adults, as well as on the varieties of language disorders resulting from variously situated lesions in the left hemisphere and on the relationships between thought and language, views based on his studies of aphasic and nonaphasic adults with such lesions.

As in his earlier review, aptly titled "Diagram Makers Old and New" (1971), Zangwill remains impressed with Geschwind's analyses of disconnection syndromes, and recalls that, for many years, he unreflectingly accepted the traditional view that Broca's area and its subjacent connections provide the essential neurological basis of articulate speech. However, he cites his studies (Zangwill, 1975) of two right-handed adults with excision or complete undercutting of Broca's area who showed no disorder of speech or writing on ordinary neurological examination 4 weeks postoperatively. (Such anatomically verified "negative" cases are increasingly numerous; Zangwill has reported two more since his 1975 paper.) Such findings, he notes, should occasion little surprise—as early as 1914, von Monakow concluded: "The available facts exclude the theory that lesions strictly confined in Broca's area give rise to complete and chronic aphasia." Thus Zangwill finds himself "highly critical of the notion of brain centers, at least in the form advocated by the Diagram Makers." But, he notes, the difficulty is that "If we reject this notion, we cannot, except in purely structural terms, answer the question of what is disconnected from what."

Von Monakow (1911) went much further than simply rejecting the localization of speech in Broca's area. Based on extensive and careful clinico-anatomical studies, he concluded

> The general conception that in the visual sphere we have centers for the optic perception and images, in the auditory sphere that for the perception of tones, and in Broca's and Wernicke's centers the memory images of word sounds, the center for intelligence in the frontal lobe, and that the corresponding functions perhaps are satisfied in these circumscribed centers—is to be declined with certainty; in the future, it will probably generally be called naive, and it was called so by a few intelligent researchers since the very beginning of investigations of localization [p. 232].

In his prediction, von Monakow anticipated the trenchant criticisms of the classical localization theory by Walshe: "The original experimentalists were more concerned with the 'where' than the 'how'. . . . The fixed mosaic survived to become the object of a cult of dogmatic finality with those who continued to believe in it [Walshe, 1965, pp. 8–9]."

Walshe called attention to three distinct modes of localization described by von Monakow: (a) anatomical localization of cell stations and tracts; (b) localization of symptoms by clinico-pathologic investigations; and (c) the most difficult of the three, true localization of function. "Nothing," von Monakow observed, "has so obscured the problems of cerebral localization or led it so far astray, as the confusion between these three different modes, and the loose use of the term 'localization' without due definition of what precisely is being located [Walshe, 1965, p. 15]."

In his brief references to the work of Sherrington and of Bastian, Zangwill suggests possible ways we may begin to approach the problems of the "how" and "where," as well as the "what," in efforts to elucidate the principles underlying the "disorganization" of cerebral functions resulting from focal brain lesions. In rejecting the notion of the brain as a fixed mosaic, he quotes Bastian's (1898) view that a center "may be envisaged as a functionally unified nervous network of variable extension."

Like Bastian, Gowers used the term *center*, but explicitly cautioned that he used it in a physiological, not a geometric, sense. He defined a center as a combination of cells subserving a given function. However, he also noted that *such cells may serve a mutiplicity of functions*, and, further, that *the same cells may variously participate to different degrees in different centers.* He also emphasized that a single functional center (or, in current terms, an organized cerebral mechanism mediating a given complex of functions) "may consist of elements that are anatomically distant—even situated in different hemispheres [Gowers, 1885, pp. 4–5]."

This, as Zangwill observed, is a valuable idea indeed. It represents an advance in efforts to define the principles underlying the organization of the specific higher-level and lower-level cerebral functions into discrete brain mechanisms mediating the diverse language and nonlanguage functions; the principles underlying the disorganization (and determining the nature of aberrations) of such functions; and the capacities for reorganization of the various language and nonlanguage functions following insults to the brain in various stages of its maturation.

Most students of brain functions have paid scant attention to the role of the right hemisphere in language functions. In elaborating his earlier concepts of the development of hemispheric specialization in specific language functions, Zangwill (see Chapter 6 of this volume) observes: "Cerebral dominance appears to operate essentially with regard to expressive as opposed to receptive speech functions. . . . Comprehension . . . is more 'automatic' in the Jacksonian sense of the term, and no pressing biological advantage would seem to dictate that it be lateralized to one or the other hemisphere." He notes that right hemispherectomy in right-handed adults does not appreciably affect speech, suggesting that "the right hemisphere plays no essential part in governing language." But he draws attention to a tacit assumption in early animal experiments that has persisted in subsequent studies of initial and later effects of brain lesions in children and adults: If the destruction of a specific area of the brain does not result in abolition or chronic impairment of a specific function, then the destroyed area apparently plays no essential or discernible role in that function. In addition to being too simple, he notes, this conclusion may often be unwarranted.

In a little noted but remarkable essay entitled "The Factor of Safety in the Nervous System," Campbell (1960) cited Meltzer's (1906–1907) observations of the large safety factor in the duplication of the kidneys and other paired human organs. In extending this principle to the nervous system, he cited studies of the auditory system by Mettler, Finch, Girden, and Culler (1934) showing that destruction of 50% of the hearing apparatus reduced measured auditory acuity by only 2 or 3%; and summarized the results of hemispherectomy in cats in a study with Bogen (Campbell, 1960):

> Perhaps the most exciting prospect which I can report of our inquiry into hemispherectomy is the possibility of a sizeable advance in the physiology of cortical function. . . . With the *possible* exception of speech, function is mediated by both cerebral hemispheres, each of which is sufficient for the whole function. The obvious factor of safety furnished by this complete duplication is multiplied many times by the particular way that the two organs are joined [pp. 114–115].

Studies of hemispherectomy for pre- , peri- , or early postnatal lesions have demonstrated that at birth the presence of two intact human cerebral hemispheres constitutes a safety factor—at least for the higher cognitive cerebral functions—similar to that for renal function provided by the two kidneys, but with one important difference. Because of the progressive specialization by the left hemisphere in speech, reading, writing, and, apparently to a much lesser degree, in comprehension, and by the right hemisphere in visual ideational and other nonlanguage cognitive functions, the safety factor is gradually diminished. In considering the processes involved in this "polarization of function between right and left [Lenneberg, 1967, p. 153]," Zangwill notes that although the adult right hemisphere possesses appreciable powers of comprehension, "its capacity for expressive speech seems very much more limited, indeed often virtually negligible." He adds, however, "Whether this incapacity is due to true lack of competence or to a suppression exercised by the dominant hemisphere is uncertain." In view of the more adequate powers of speech of adults after left hemispherectomy "as compared with linguistic capacity of the isolated right hemisphere in cases with section of the cerebral commissures, an explanation in terms of suppression might seem the more plausible."

The first reported case of left hemispherectomy for tumor (Zollinger, 1935) revealed that comprehension *and speech* were present immediately after surgery in a 43-year-old woman. Although the patient died 17 days later, improvement of expressive and receptive language functions continued throughout the short survival period. Thus, over four decades ago,

Lereboullet (1936) pointed out, "From a physiologic point of view, this case proves that the dogma of localization of word centers is not absolute, and that the right hemisphere contributes to this function [p. 360]." In almost all of the few subsequent cases of left dominant hemispherectomy including two adults who survived 18 and 24 months postoperatively, relative preservation of comprehension and continuing improvement in language functions until recurrence of the tumor have been reported. Since there are as yet no reported cases of long survival after excision of a normally developed left "dominant" hemisphere, the extent of the capacities of the right hemisphere and other intact residual structures to compensate for the loss of language functions is unknown (Burklund & Smith, 1977).

I have been engaged in systematic studies of initial and later effects of left and right hemispherectomy in 58 children and adults since 1965, and in (a) neuropsychological studies of language and associated nonlanguage defects in 282 patients with chronic aphasia; and (b) the effects of intensive language therapy on such deficits in 160 patients since 1967. Not surprisingly, in his analyses of the complex interacting factors that continue to confound efforts to define the nature of language and of its biological foundations by consideration of its disorders, Zangwill discusses areas in which my research deeply interested Lenneberg.

PLASTICITY OF HEMISPHERIC FUNCTIONS OF THE INFANT BRAIN

The conclusion reached by Lenneberg (1967) and others that there is, at birth, perfect equipotentiality of the two cerebral hemispheres with respect to ultimate competence in language functions has been challenged in a few studies of comparisons of later effects of perinatal lateralized lesions and of right versus left hemispherectomy for such lesions (cited by Smith & Sugar, 1975; and by Smith, 1977). Reciprocal patterns of symptoms, with attenuated development of language skills after focal perinatal lesions or excision of the left hemisphere versus attenuated development of nonlanguage functions after focal perinatal lesions or excision of the right hemisphere, are cited as evidence that the plasticity of the infant brain has been overrated and that the adult pattern of reciprocal specialization of the hemispheres exists even before birth.

Comparisons of neuropsychological test performances of 27 patients with left and 17 patients with right hemispherectomy for perinatal lateralized epileptogenic lesions (Smith, 1977), however, support Lenneberg's concept of perfect equipotentiality of the infant cerebral hemispheres. In fact, the more rapid development of language functions than nonlanguage functions in 21 of the 27 patients with left hemispherectomy and in 15 of the 17 with right hemispherectomy indicates a hierarchy in which the development of language functions takes precedence over that of nonlanguage functions. The results of these studies have demonstrated that only one intact hemisphere—either the right or the left—and other residual neural structures after hemispherectomy for perinatal lesions will suffice (i.e., can provide the neuroanatomic substrata necessary) for the development of normal adult language and nonlanguage skills.

PLASTICITY OF HEMISPHERIC FUNCTIONS OF THE ADULT BRAIN

According to Lenneberg, the equipotentiality of the hemispheres systematically diminishes from perfect equipotentiality (from birth to 20 months); to marked signs of reduction of equipotentiality (ages 11 to 14 years); to none for language functions (mid-teens to senium) (Lenneberg, 1967, p. 181). This view is similar to Zangwill's earlier observation (1964) that "It is at least plain that the right hemisphere in the dextral adult retains little or no capacity to subserve spoken language. Were it otherwise, reeducation in aphasia would be a great deal more effective than it is [p. 109]." In his report on two cases with excision or undercutting of Broca's area, Zangwill (1975) observed:

> The relatively short course of the illness and the rapid restitution of speech in both patients render it highly improbable, to say the least, that the nondominant hemisphere can have played any significant role in the recovery process. We thus seem obliged to conclude that speech restitution was due to the participation of those parts of the left hemisphere which had survived injury [pp. 261–262].

In contrast to the sudden destruction of brain tissues wrought by penetrating missiles or precipitate cerebrovascular infarctions, however, the underlying lesions in both of Zangwill's patients were slowly developing neoplasms. As early as 1836, Dax noted that although sudden destruction of left hemisphere structures resulted in marked aphasia, slowly developing lesions in the same regions often failed to produce aphasia. Thus he anticipated Jackson's discovery that the "momentum" of a lesion, "not only the quantity of nervous elements destroyed, but the rapidity of their destruction [Jackson, 1880]" is an important determinant of the nature and severity of its sequelae. The "rapid" recovery of speech and other language functions in Zangwill's two cases may indeed be due to suddenly augmented roles of residual intact parts of the motor, speech, and other mechanisms in the left hemisphere mediating speech and other language functions. However, the slowly evolving nature of the underlying lesions also suggests the possibility of a similar role played by right hemisphere mechanisms, which may have started in the early stages of the developing neoplasms.

The capacities of the right hemisphere for recovery of speech have been periodically emphasized from the time of Gowers ("Loss of speech due to permanent destruction of the speech region in the left hemisphere has been recovered from, and that recovery was due to supplemental action of the corresponding right hemisphere is proved by the fact that in some of these cases, speech has been again lost when a fresh lesion occurred in this part of the right hemisphere [Gowers, 1885, pp. 131–132]"), to recent studies of traumatic aphasics ("When the right side of the brain remains undamaged, remarkable recoveries may occur in these young men, but when both parietal lobes are injured . . . the possibilites for recovery are greatly reduced [Russell & Espir, 1961, p. 141]"), to my own continuing studies of stroke patients with chronic aphasia ("The right hemisphere plays an important role in auditory comprehension and in recovery of language functions in children and adults with aphasia. Failure to recover may therefore reflect inhibition or disruption of the capacities of the right hemisphere to compensate for diminished language functions immediately following damage to left hemisphere mechanisms [Smith, 1971, pp. 203–204]."

Only two dextral adults have survived more than 1 year after excision of a normally developed left "dominant" hemisphere (for malignant tumor). The varying degrees of their recovery of singing and of the different language functions (until recurrence of the tumor in the lower residual right-sided structures and the rapid deterioration of all recovered language functions) have been described by Smith (1966), Smith and Burklund (1966), and Burklund and Smith (1977). It is obvious that in these two cases, the restitution of speech and other language functions to varying degrees cannot be attributed to the motor speech system and other mechanisms of the left hemisphere. The significant if not major role of the right hemisphere in recovery of speech in most cases of aphasia has also been indicated in recent studies of the effects of intracarotid barbiturate injections by Mempel, Srebrezynska, Subszynska, and Zarski (1963), Kinsbourne (1971), and Czopf (1972). In the largest series, Czopf reported that in 22 dextral aphasics with left hemisphere lesions, right carotid artery injections abolished speech in 10, moderately worsened speech in 9, and had no effect in 3.

DIASCHISIS, CHRONIC APHASIA, AND CONSTRUCTIONAL DYSPRAXIA

In rejecting the nineteenth-century "classical" concepts of localization of cerebral functions in circumscribed cortical areas, von Monakow (1911) also wrote, "However the problem will develop in the future, I am convinced that it will not be able to do without the dissociation of function by diaschisis. . . . Diaschisis is the basic dynamic principle, it forms a bridge between those phenomena which can be localized distinctly and those which cannot [p. 250]."

In simple terms, *diaschisis* is the radiation of the disruptive effects of acute or chronic focal lesions in the brain—and, according to Sherrington (1906), in the spinal cord—resulting in the reduction or suspension of functions of anatomically intact structures that are geographically remote from the lesion. Von Monakow (1914) later documented the frequency and importance of diaschisis in efforts to localize cerebral lesions as well as cerebral functions. Subsequently, numerous studies have documented the radiation of the effects of focal lateralized lesions that disrupt the functions of anatomically intact mechanisms in the opposite as well as the same hemisphere. More recently, the validity of von Monakow's observations was confirmed in studies of hemispheric blood flow and cerebral metabolism in adults with diverse types of lateralized lesions (Smith, 1972, 1975).

Chronic attenuation of the functions of an anatomically intact hemisphere due to the radiation of pathological influences from the diseased opposite hemisphere have been demonstrated in numerous studies of hemispherectomy, providing compelling evidence of the validity of von Monakow's definition of diaschisis. As reported by Smith and Sugar (1975) and Smith (1977), comparisons of preoperative and postoperative EEG, neurological and psychological studies of hemispherectomy patients have repeatedly confirmed the sudden and striking improvement in the chronically depressed functions of the residual hemisphere following excision of the diseased hemisphere. Smith and Sugar (1975) also noted that these same conditions apply in unoperated cases of children and adults with lateralized cerebral lesions.

Our studies of adults with chronic aphasia also emphasize the importance of diaschisis. For example, of 122 dextral adults with chronic aphasia (mean duration 18 months) after vascular lesions reportedly restricted to the left hemisphere, Purdue Pegboard and Double Simultaneous Stimulation tests revealed that 70 (57%) had obvious signs of *left-sided sensory and motor deficits,* indicating persisting involvement of the mechanisms in the right hemisphere mediating these functions. Not surprisingly, comparisons of language *and* nonlanguage functions showed significantly greater impairment than in the 52 with normal left-sided sensory and motor functions.

The effects of diaschisis were also indicated by the presence of constructional dyspraxia in 34 aphasics with presumably unilateral left-sided lesions. This nonlanguage defect in adults is usually associated with postrolandic lesions in the right hemisphere. Its occasional appearance in patients with left-sided lesions and associated language deficits has been interpreted as evidence of an atypical pattern of hemispheric specialization in which the development of the mechanisms underlying visual constructional as well as language functions had somehow all been crowded into the left hemisphere. (However if this assumption is true, what functions does the right hemisphere perform in such cases?) The 122 aphasics consisted of 54 without and 68 with right hemiplegia. Yet of the 34 aphasics with constructional dyspraxia, 29 had right hemiplegia (indicating generally larger lesions in the left hemisphere than in nonhemiplegic aphasics); and 29 had *left-sided* sensory and/or motor defects. Although the mean age of the 122 aphasics was 50 years, the mean age of the 34 aphasics with constructional dyspraxia was 56 versus 46 for the remaining 88 aphasics. Not surprisingly, comparison of these two groups showed significantly greater impairment in speech, comprehension, reading, and writing by the 34 constructional dyspraxics. Von Monakow reported that the severity and duration of diaschisis increase with age and with the magnitude as well as the irritative nature of the lesions. In view of (a) the high proportion of left-sided sensory and/or motor deficits (29/34 or 85.3%), indicating *right* hemisphere involvement; (b) the similarly high proportion of right hemiplegics (also 29/34 or 85.3% with aphasia and associated severe right-sided motor deficits), indicating generally *larger* lesions in the left hemisphere than in nonhemiplegics; and (c) the increasing incidence of constructional dyspraxia with advancing age, constructional dyspraxia is apparently caused by attenuation of right hemisphere functions as a result of unsuspected involvement of the *right as well as the left hemisphere*. This may be due to diaschisis (as suggested by the striking compatibility of the findings with those reported by von Monakow) and/or to unsuspected lesions in the right hemisphere. Computerized axial tomographic studies of 14 stroke patients with persisting aphasia (Yarnell, Monroe, & Sobel, 1976) have revealed unsuspected right as well as multiple left hemisphere lesions in three patients; recovery of language functions in these three patients was poorer than in those with lesions restricted to the left hemisphere.

The confounding effects of diaschisis in efforts to localize either cerebral disease or functions were described in clinicopathologic correlation studies of 48 patients with lateralized and bilateral cerebrovascular lesions by Davison, Goodheart, and Needles (1934). Noting that effects of diaschisis are more marked in the acute stages of such lesions, they cited the differences between Henschen and von Mayerdorf in their localization of function. After clinicopathologic correlations of some 1200 cases of motor aphasia, Henschen and von Mayerdorf concluded by localizing speech motor functions in two totally different regions!

DEVELOPMENT OF STANDARDIZED LANGUAGE AND NEUROPSYCHOLOGICAL TESTS

In contrast to the highly subjective and variable assessments of language disorders by means of clinical interviews by Broca, Wernicke, Lichtheim, and the early map makers, the development of standardized language tests by Eisenson (1954), Schuell (1955), Wepman and Jones (1961), and Porch (1967) provided objective measures of the nature and degree of impairment in speech, verbal comprehension, reading, and writing in aphasics. Although the term "center" is not now used, it is implied in current descriptions of presumably discrete aphasic syndromes in which, depending on the site of the lesion in the left hemisphere, some language functions are impaired while others are intact. For example, Broca's motor and Wernicke's conduction and anomic aphasias are frequently so described, and Geschwind has reported, "The localization of these forms of aphasia has been confirmed repeatedly [Geschwind, 1970, p. 941]." It is therefore interesting to note that studies of thousands of aphasics with the standardized language tests cited have failed to confirm the existence of such discrete syndromes. Our own standardized and comprehensive neuropsychologic, audiologic, and language examinations of 126 stroke patients with chronic aphasia (mean duration 18 months) from 1967 to 1972 revealed impairment in all four language components in 125. Moreover, with a few although notable exceptions, they revealed generally comparable degrees of impairment in speech, comprehension, and reading, with greater impairment in writing.

In contrast to the eclectic approach of Eisenson, Schuell, Wepman, and Porch, the more recent language test by Goodglass and Kaplan (1972) was designed according to the preconception of discrete, classical, anatomically differentiated syndromes. Goodglass and Kaplan also observed, "The bulk of clinical material for quantitative studies comes from cases in which *large lesions* are the rule, implicating simultaneously, functionally diverse areas. *Small lesions* producing *isolated disorders* have a smaller effect in any study which groups all cases together [Goodglass & Kaplan, 1972, pp. 2–3, emphasis added]."

The differences between my findings and those of Goodglass and Kaplan are not the result of differences in populations with respect to age, chronicity, or education; these were successively ruled out. However, in examining more than 400 aphasics with various language tests, I have yet to find a single pattern of language deficits that corresponds to Wernicke's initial definition of conduction aphasia or to subsequent modifications by Goodglass and Kaplan and others (neither did Wernicke himself, who first hypothesized this syndrome on theoretical grounds; nor have numerous subsequent investigators). In reply to my inquiry in 1974, Goodglass wrote that except for 11% with global aphasia, his latest statistics continued to show discrete syndromes in 89%, including 11% with conduction aphasia. Our studies, however, continue to reveal generally comparable degrees of impairment in speech, comprehension, and reading, usually associated with more severe impairment in writing.

ANATOMICAL BASES OF VARIATION
IN APHASIC DISTURBANCES

The unresolved historical controversies on the anatomical bases of the quantitative and qualitative variations in aphasic disturbances may seem academic. In addition to their practical implications for diagnostic studies, however, the prevailing views are especially important for considerations of treatment of the loss of our capacities to communicate with others, that results in such severe isolation and human disability. If the different language functions are indeed localized in brain centers in the left hemisphere exclusively, then efforts to improve language functions in adults with chronic aphasia due to destruction of such centers encourage false hopes and are wasteful.

I initially shared the widespread skepticism about the value of language therapy for aphasics, as described in the report of the results of our program of intensive residential language therapy after the first 5 years (Smith, Champoux, Leri, London, & Muraski, 1972). However, in contrast to emotional or personality disorders, language disorders are amenable to objective measurements. Eighty chronic aphasics were given therapy; the Schuell and other language and nonlanguage tests were administered before and after treatment, and performance was compared. Fifteen untreated patients were also tested, and retested after a comparable interval of time. Not only was there marked and statistically significant improvement in language functions by the treated aphasics, but the specificity of the effects of language therapy was evident from the negligible gains on the nonlanguage tests. Although language functions were still noticeably impaired in all 80 patients after therapy, the significant improvement in their ability to communicate resulted in striking psychological and social changes in their personal lives. Initial follow-up studies of 36 surviving stroke patients also revealed resumption of gainful full-time employment by 9, and part-time employment by 4 for the first time since the onset of aphasia. Not surprisingly, the 15 untreated aphasics showed negligible changes or slight losses on language tests, and none was employed. In the overwhelming majority of our cases, the degrees of impairment in speech, verbal comprehension, and reading, as noted, are remarkably comparable (writing is generally more severely impaired). Thus, Zangwill's description of the "relative specificity" of aphasic syndromes is most apt. Although he describes differences in effects of variously restricted lesions within and beyond the "language zone" in the left hemisphere, the thrust of his evolving concepts as presented in Chapter 6 is consistent with the summation of Lenneberg's experiences and observations (1967): "It is hard to escape the conclusion that the nervous activity that mediates specific behavior patterns and experiences is never confined to any one cerebral locus. Behavior must be the product of interaction and integration of function of many components of the brain [p. 214]."

In coining the term "Lenneberg's question" and in his suggestions of possible ways we may begin to answer it, Zangwill emphasizes the importance of integrating the clinical and experimental approaches of neurology and psychology to resolve historical problems of brain structure–function relationships that border on both disciplines. In the preface to *Biological Foundations of Language* (1967), Lenneberg wrote

> This book attempts to reinstate the concept of the biological basis of language capacities and to make the specific assumptions so explicit that they may be subjected to empirical tests. In many instances I have not been able to do more than formulate questions and to show that they are not spurious. There is no research as yet that provides answers to them. But I hope I have been able to show what types of investigations might lead to new insights and thus, perhaps, give new directions to old inquiries. A particularly promising approach seems to be the systematic evaluation of patients with various deficits, especially the deaf and mentally retarded.

In seeking out evidence that did not agree with his assumptions, Lenneberg provides a salutary model for the many students of brain functions who become invested in their own findings. And in his recommendation of systematic neuropsychological evaluations of patients with specific deficits, he adds one of the most important suggestions for future approaches to answering "Lenneberg's question."

REFERENCES

Ajuriaguerra, J. de. Language et dominance cérébral. J. Francais d'Oto-Rhino-Láryngologie, 1957, 6, 489–499.

Bastian, H. C. A treatise on aphasia and other speech defects. New York: Appleton, 1898.

Burklund, C. W., & Smith, A. Language and the cerebral hemispheres: Observations of verbal and nonverbal responses during 18 months following left ("dominant") hemispherectomy. Neurology, 27, 1977, 627–633.

Campbell, B. The factor of safety in the nervous system. Bulletin of Los Angeles Neurological Society, 25, 1960, 109–117.

Chomsky, N. The general properties of language. In C. H. Millikan & F. L. Darley (Eds.), Brain mechanisms underlying speech and language. New York: Grune and Stratton, 1967.

Czopf, J. Role of the non-dominant hemisphere in the restitution of speech in aphasia. Archiv für Psychiatrie und Nervenkrankheiten, 1972, 216, 126–171. .

Davison, C., Goodheart, P., & Needles, W. Cerebral localization in cerebrovascular disease. Association for Research in Nervous and Mental Disease, 1934, 13, 436–465.

Dax, M. Lesions de la moite gauche de l'encephale coincidait avec l'oublie des signes de la pensee. Lu au Congres Meridional tenu a Montepellier en 1836. Gazette Hebdomadaire de Medecine et de Chirugie, 1865, 33, 259–262.

Eisenson, J. Examining for aphasia. New York: Psychological Corporation, 1954.

Geschwind, N. The organization of language and the brain. Science, 1970, 170, 940–944.

Goltz, F. On the functions of the hemispheres. Pflügers Archiv für die gesamte Physiologie, 1888, 42, 419–467. (Trans. by G. von Bonin in Some papers on the cerebral cortex, Springfield, Ill.: Thomas, 1960.)

Goodglass, H., & Kaplan, E. The assessment of aphasia and related disorders. Philadelphia: Lea and Febiger, 1972.

Gowers, W. R. Diagnosis of disease of the brain and of the spinal cord. New York: William Wood, 1885.

Hécaen, H., & de Ajuriaguerra, J. Les gauchers: prévalence manuelle et dominance cérébrale. Paris: Presses Universitaires de France, 1963.

Jackson, J. H. On affections of speech from disease of the brain. Brain, 1915, 38, 147–174.

Kinsbourne, M. The minor cerebral hemisphere as a source of aphasic speech. Archives of Neurology, 1971, 25, 302–306.

Lenneberg, E. H. A biological perspective of language. In E. H. Lenneberg (Ed.), New directions in the study of language. Cambridge: MIT Press, 1964.

Lenneberg, E. H. Biological foundations of language. New York: Wiley, 1967.

Lereboullet, J. Removal of left cerebral hemisphere. Paris Medical, 1936, 1, 358–360.

Meltzer, S. J. The factors of safety in animal structure and animal economy. Harvey Lectures, 1906–1907, 139–169.

Mempel, E., Srebrezynska, J., Subszynska, J., & Zarski, S. Compensation of speech disorders by the non-dominant cerebral hemisphere in adults. Journal of Neurology, Neurosurgery and Psychiatry, 1963, 26, 96.

Mettler, F. A., Finch, G., Girden, E., & Culler, F. A. Acoustic value of the several components of the auditory pathway. Brain, 1934, 57, 475–483.

Monakow, C. von. Localization of brain functions. Journal fur Psychologie und Neurologie 1911, 17, 185–200. (Trans. by G. von Bonin in Some papers on the cerebral cortex, Springfield, Ill.: Thomas, 1960.)

Monakow, C. von. Die lokalization im grosshirn und der abbau der funktion durch kortikale herde. Wiesbaden: J. F. Bergmann, 1914.

Paterson, A., & Zangwill, O. L. Disorders of visual space perception associated with lesions of the right hemisphere. Brain, 1944, 67, 331–358.

Paterson, A., & Zangwill, O. L. A case of topographical disorientation associated with unilateral cerebral lesion. *Brain*, 1945, *68*, 188–212.

Porch, B. *Porch index of communicative ability.* California: Consulting Psychologists Press, 1967.

Russell, W. R., & Espir, M. L. E. *Traumatic aphasia.* Oxford: Oxford University Press, 1961.

Sarno, M. T., Silverman, M., & Sands, E. Speech therapy and language recovery in severe aphasia. *Journal of Speech and Hearing Research*, 1970, *13*, 607–623.

Schuell, H. *Minnesota test for differential diagnosis of aphasia, researched.* Minneapolis: University of Minnesota, 1955.

Sherrington, C. *The integrative action of the nervous system* (1st ed.). New Haven: Yale University Press, 1906.

Smith, A. Speech and other functions after left (dominant) hemispherectomy. *Journal of Neurology, Neurosurgery and Psychiatry*, 1966, *29*, 467–471.

Smith, A. Objective indices of severity of chronic aphasia in stroke patients. *Journal of Speech and Hearing Disorders*, 1971, *36*, 167–207.

Smith, A. Dominant and nondominant hemispherectomy. In W. L. Smith (Ed.), *Drugs, development and cerebral function.* Springfield, Ill.: Thomas, 1972.

Smith, A. Neuropsychological testing in neurological disorders. In W. J. Friedlander (Ed.), *Advances in neurology* (Vol. 7). New York: Raven Press, 1975.

Smith, A. Symbol-digit substitution processes in chronic aphasia. *Neuroscience Abstracts*, 1976, *2*, 436.

Smith, A. *Language and nonlanguage functions after right or left hemispherectomy for cerebral lesions in infancy.* Paper presented at the Fifth Annual Conference of the International Neuropsychological Society, Santa Fe, February 1977.

Smith, A., & Burklund, C. W. Dominant hemispherectomy. *Science*, 1966, *153*, 1280–1282.

Smith, A., Champoux, R., Leri, J., London, R., & Muraski, A. *Diagnosis, intelligence and rehabilitation of chronic aphasics* (Final Report, Research Grant SRS 14-P-55198/5-01). University of Michigan, 1972.

Smith, A., & Sugar, O. Development of above normal language and intelligence 21 years after left hemispherectomy. *Neurology*, 1975, *25*, 813–818.

Teuber, H.-L. Effects of brain wounds implicating right or left hemisphere in man: hemisphere differences and hemisphere interaction in vision, audition, and somesthesis. In V. B. Mountcastle (Ed.), *Interhemispheric relations and cerebral dominance.* Baltimore: Johns Hopkins Press, 1962.

Vesalius, A. *De humani corporis fabrica*, 1543. [Trans. by M. Foster, *Lectures on the history of physiology.* Cambridge: Cambridge University Press, 1901.]

Walshe, F. M. R. Current ideas in neurobiology and 'neuropsychology': A study in contrasts. In F. M. R. Walshe (Ed.), *Further critical studies in neurology.* Baltimore: Williams and Wilkins, 1965.

Wepman, J. M., & Jones, L. V. *Studies in aphasia: an approach to testing.* Chicago: Education-Industry Service, 1961.

Yarnell, P., Monroe, P., & Sobel, L. Aphasia outcome in stroke: A clinical neurological correlation. *Stroke*, 1976, *7*, 516–522.

Zangwill, O. L. The current status of cerebral dominance. *Association for Research in Nervous and Mental Disease*, 1964, *42*, 103–113.

Zangwill, O. L. Diagram makers old and new. *Totus Homo*, 1971, *3*, 53–58.

Zangwill, O. L. Excision of Broca's area without persistent aphasia. In K. J. Zulch, O. Creutzfeldt, & G. C. Galbraith (Eds.), *Cerebral localization.* New York: Springer-Verlag, 1975.

Zollinger, R. Removal of left cerebral hemisphere. *Archives of Neurology and Psychiatry*, 1935, *34*, 1055–1064.

chapter 8

A New Paradigm of Reference[1]

ROGER BROWN

EARLY RESEARCH IN THE PROCESS OF NAMING

Eric Lenneberg and I started our research careers together. "A Study in Language and Cognition," the paper we coauthored, stands near the beginning of Eric's list of publications as it does of mine. As matters turned out, we never worked together as coauthors again, but for nearly a decade our experiments, though independently planned, seemed always to be closely related. Both of us were studying linguistic reference, the process of naming. Not many other psychologists were interested in reference in the late 1950s, so it did not seem unreasonable to me for a possible publisher of my manuscript, *Words and Things*, to ask me: "Just what readership do you have in mind for this book?" I had never thought of such a question and when I had to, my answer was: "Well, . . . there's Eric Lenneberg."

[1] The research for this chapter was supported by Grant GSOC-7309150, "Later Preschool Stages in the Development of a First Language," from the National Science Foundation.

151

PSYCHOLOGY AND BIOLOGY OF LANGUAGE AND THOUGHT
Essays in Honor of Eric Lenneberg

"A Study in Language and Cognition" has had many interesting consequences, especially in the 1970s, and it was the story of these consequences
I chose to tell for the journal *Cognition*, when its editors asked me to write a
memorial tribute to Eric Lenneberg in the form of a substantive article
(1976). As I worked back to the few early studies of reference in the 1950s
and then forward to the more numerous studies in the 1960s and especially
in the 1970s, it seemed to me that there was a larger story to tell. The old
model of reference has, I think, lost its ascendancy. There is now a new
paradigm, more accurate, consequential, and interesting than the old one.
For myself, it has been like a last act of friendship from Eric to have
recovered my interest in linguistic reference as a consequence of reviewing
his work.

A NEW PARADIGM

The principal creators of the new paradigm are, perhaps, Eleanor
Heider (now Eleanor Rosch), Carolyn Mervis, Brent Berlin, Jeremy Anglin,
and Michael Posner. In this chapter, there is no space for the empirical
matrix that gives the paradigm most of its appeal, but only space enough to
describe the paradigm itself, together with what I believe will prove to be
two developmental laws employing the concepts of the paradigm.

Figure 8.1 is a minimally complex view of reference. It is not historically
earlier than any other view and probably has never been championed by
anyone who thought long enough about the subject to write a book about it.
The "words and things" view is more like a serviceable encapsulation for all
the sensible people who get along nicely with very little epistemology and
less semantics. To them, it is clear that the world is made up of a number of

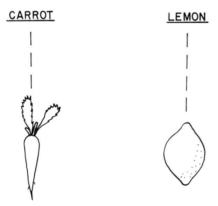

CARROT   LEMON

Figure 8.1. Words and things.

things, each of which has a name in the local language, and the child's job is to get the pairs together in his mind.

It is a minimal complication to notice that each referent thing has more than one name, as in Figure 8.2. The same thing that may be called a *carrot* may also appropriately be called a *vegetable* or, using a constructional process to build a more specific name, *the carrot in Figure 8.2.*

If we happen to notice that names like *carrot, lemon, vegetable,* and *fruit* apply to more than one referent and, in fact, are used for sets or classes of referents and that these classes are on different taxonomic levels, such that carrots are a subset of vegetables and lemons of fruit, then we have Figure 8.3, which depicts the essentials of the old paradigm. Sets or classes are enclosed in unbroken lines to represent the fact that membership in the extension is conceived to be determinate. Any given entity either is or is not a member of the class of lemons or the class of fruits. Membership depends on satisfaction of the intension, the definition of the class. The intensions in the figure are culled from dictionaries and are not really entirely satisfactory. However, they serve to illustrate a familiar relation between a set and any of its subsets: The extension or referent members of the subset must be smaller than the extension of its containing set (there are fewer carrots in the world than there are vegetables), whereas the intension of the subset will list more attributes than the intension of the set (carrots have more in common than do all vegetables). This, I think, is the gist of the old paradigm for studies of concept formation and linguistic reference.

I will introduce the properties of the new paradigm one at a time, because it is the case, at present, that they are not bound together by

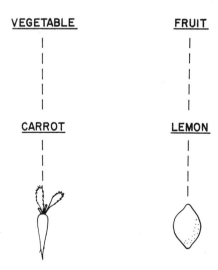

Figure 8.2. Things have more than one name.

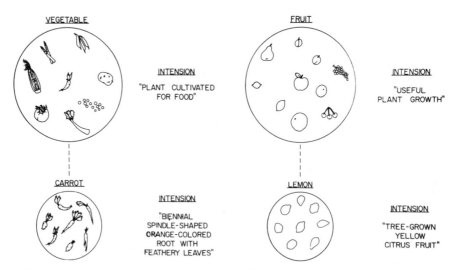

Figure 8.3. Names apply to classes; the old paradigm.

complete mutual entailment. Before doing so, however, I should like to dwell for a moment on Eric Lenneberg's doctoral research as it was reported in 1957 in the journal *Behavioral Science*. Not because Eric would want me to claim priorities on his behalf—priorities never interested him much. It is historically interesting, however, to find that the new paradigm has been with us right along. But, for whatever reasons, it was formerly in the shadows.

Eric's thesis concerned the naming of color chips in English by adult speakers and also the learning of new names and new categories. Figure 8.4, taken from the published report of Eric's thesis (Lenneberg, 1957), shows how 27 adult speakers of English named a set of color chips varying in hue alone. The immediately relevant point it makes is that each color term turns out to be applicable to some range of hues and that, among these hues, some are always *better* (more nearly prototypical) examples of the term than are others. One does not usually think of any one member of a proper set, like the set of triangles, as being any better than any other.

Reflecting on these results, Eric thought how little they seemed to have in common with the experimental study of concept formation. In the usual experiment, new, initially nonsensical terms, would be introduced; for instance, *piffles* and *puffles*. Subjects would be told that some of the referent objects or pictures before them were *piffles* and some *puffles*. The problem was to learn to name each referent correctly, and this could be done by discovering the implicit rule governing the use of the words. Ordinarily, the concept was already known; the only problem was to retrieve it from

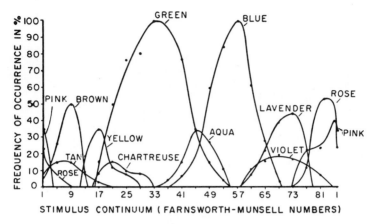

Figure 8.4. Frequency distribution of color names elicited from 27 subjects. [Reprinted from *Behavioral Science*, Volume 2, No. 1, 1957, by permission of James G. Miller, M.D., Ph.D., Editor.]

memory or, at most, to make a necessary conjunction of several already known concepts. There was never any indeterminacy, any "fuzziness" of boundary as it were, and never any variation in degree of membership. But what if all or many or most *natural* referential terms, by which I mean terms allowed freely to evolve, were like color terms in having fuzzy boundaries and degrees of prototypicality? Why, then, it would be almost as if concept formation had never been studied! And at this point, roughly, Eric's attention was captured by other problems. Others, in the 1970s, have taken up just where he stopped, and I will return now to introducing the new paradigm, one property at a time.

In Figure 8.5, the class of vegetables alone is used to illustrate a fuzzy concept. The enclosing line is broken and bent to suggest the fact that while there are some things like carrots and peas that are surely vegetables, there are others, like pickles and garlic and dandelions, whose membership is not certain in our minds. When I sketched this figure, I had no actual prototypicality ratings to rely upon and so consulted my own intuition. Now I do have ratings from Rosch (1975) for 56 presumptive vegetables. When these are rank ordered, it turns out that peas are the most prototypical vegetable, with carrots next. Pickles, garlic, and dandelions all rate very low, and just where the line should be drawn is unclear.

In Figure 8.6, depicting only carrot and vegetable, I have drawn the enclosing circles as solid lines, making the membership determinate rather than fuzzy; and the carrot class is represented as a proper subset of vegetable rather than as a subset in the terms of fuzzy-set theory as set forth by L. A. Zadeh (1965, 1971). I have done this because it is perfectly possible to

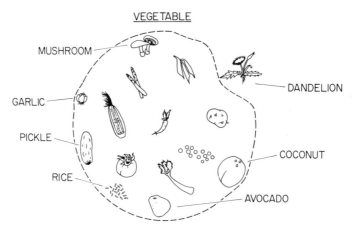

Figure 8.5. Membership in a referent class may be fuzzy rather than determinate.

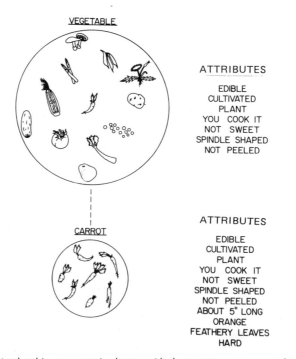

Figure 8.6. Membership may vary in degree with the prototype represented as unity.

combine the determinate membership and subset definitions of proper set theory with the notion that members vary in prototypicality. In fact, many interesting problems are to be found just here.

The set, "United States senators," is a proper set with a determinate membership, and it functions as such when votes are counted in the Senate. However, these facts have not prevented us from thinking of some senators as being more truly senatorial than others. Probably the prototypical senator is from a Southern state and has been in the Senate for a good many years, since that is the way the South votes. Certainly, too, the prototypical senator is a male and perhaps somewhere around 60 years old, with white hair worn rather long—Senator Sam Ervin, at the time of the hearings on Watergate, was just right. There need not, however, be a living perfect prototype; we can imagine him from the instances that do exist. The comedian, Fred Allen, created, some years ago, a "Senator Claghorn" who was somewhere between prototype and caricature.

Proper sets and fuzzy sets defined over the same extension also interact interestingly whenever an academic tries to define his discipline in the first chapter of a textbook. He feels that it ought to have a clear definition, but as it is not a theoretical term, but rather a term that has been allowed to evolve naturally, probably there is no attribute or conjunction of attributes that will characterize all the work called psychological or sociological or physiological. Even medical diagnoses, though doctors strive to make determinate classes of them, are also words and may become fuzzy. It has been shown that the word *schizophrenic* is applied to overlapping but far from identical sets of persons in London and in New York City (Cooper, Kendell, Gurland, Sharpe, Copeland, & Simon, 1972). And there is no doubt that some schizophrenics are more schizophrenic than others. There is something a little amusing about fuzzy boundaries and a range of prototypicality, but I have never heard anyone say that he does not understand these ideas or that there is nothing in his thinking that corresponds to them.

Apparently none of Rosch's (1975) subjects found it unnatural to rate 56 presumptive vegetables for prototypicality. Since I had not seen the actual ratings when preparing my illustrations, my placement of particular vegetables within the vegetable class is not quite accurate. Peas, as the most prototypical, should be dead center, with carrots located off to the side. Green beans, asparagus, corn, and celery are all somewhat less prototypical—in that order—and pickle ranks 49th, garlic is 53rd, dandelion is 54th, and rice is 56th. It is worth noting that the instances of the subclass "individual carrots" could also be rated for prototypicality, though I have no such ratings, but only my intuition.

Books for very young children and also illustrations in the dictionary are good sources to consult for examples of prototypes. Let me interpolate at this point a picture, Figure 8.7, that accompanies the entry *bird* in the fifth edition (1943) of *Webster's Collegiate Dictionary*. Was there ever a more quintessential bird? Yet, in this 1943 dictionary, it is not identified as belonging to any real bird species at all. Certainly it does not do justice to chickens and penguins and is very hard on the ostrich and emu. However, even dictionary-making progresses, and the parallel entry in the seventh edition (1967) of the same dictionary reads: "bird (waxwing)." In fact, then, the illustration is a picture of a real species and not of the essence of birdsville.

But what species has been selected to illustrate the entry "bird"? The waxwing, though little known by name, closely resembles Rosch's most prototypical cases: the robin, sparrow, and bluejay. How odd it would be if the entry read: "bird (flamingo)" with an illustration to match. Yet why not, if dictionary makers had no sense of prototypicality, since, in proper set theory, a flamingo is just as representative of a bird species as is the waxwing. While one may presume to doubt that the compilers of the seventh edition dictionary knew exactly why they had to make certain modifications in earlier editions, the few changes I have sampled all point to a shift from the inadequate, idealized old paradigm of reference to the psychologically more realistic new paradigm.

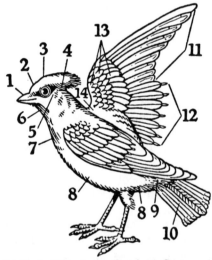

Bird. 1 Bill; **2** Forehead; **3** Crown; **4** Occipital Region; **5** Auricular Region; **6** Throat; **7** Breast; **8, 8** Abdomen; **9** Under Tail Coverts; **10** Tail; **11** Primaries; **12** Secondaries; **13** Upper Wing Coverts; **14** Scapulars.

Figure 8.7. Drawing used to illustrate the entry *bird*. [By permission. From *Webster's Collegiate Dictionary*, Fifth Edition©1936 by G. & C. Merriam Co., Publishers of the Merriam-Webster Dictionaries.]

When members of a set vary in degree, we cannot very well have an intension, or a defining rule that applies to all alike. What we have instead is a set of attributes, none of which is true of all instances, but each of which relates some instances to others. These are like Wittgenstein's family resemblances. The attributes, or family resemblances, will serve independently to order instances for prototypicality. Rosch and Mervis (1975) have shown that the more attributes an item has in common with other members of the category, the more it will be considered a good and representative member, or prototype, of the category. Their method essentially was to correlate prototypicality ratings of an item with a weighted measure of family resemblance, weighted for the degree to which the item shared attributes with other members of the category; the various correlations were all close to .90. This is the essence of the method, but for a full understanding, the original article should be consulted.

In the vegetable category of Figures 8.3, 8.5, and 8.7, the centrality of carrots cannot be due to the attribute of edibility, which they share with all other vegetables, but is due presumably to such features as their spindle shape, which they share with celery, string beans, asparagus, and cucumbers; their cooked and raw edible allomorphs; the fact that they are roots rather than leaves and that they come in a certain range of sizes. Each of these features relates them to some subset of other members, never to all at once, but, in the end, to most of the fairly central members of the family. However, the color of carrots—orange—is very much against them, whereas the green of the pea is just right for most vegetables, and that must be one reason why peas just edged out carrots for rank 1. In combination—as the familiar restaurant vegetable, peas-and-carrots—they have a prototypicality that makes the mind reel. The composite photograph that is the carrot is a pretty typical vegetable. We can glimpse here a kind of concept formation that might proceed in a manner quite distinct from that imagined for proper sets. Candidates for concept membership probably are not tested against some rule of admission but are rather, perhaps, compared with a few good prototypes or conceivably given a composite family resemblance score.

THE BASIC OBJECT LEVEL

In Figure 8.8, only two levels are represented, and one of these is the level of the basic object. It is necessary to keep your eye on the central prototypical lemon in the subclass and to know that the lemon in the class of fruits, which appears off center and on the left, is to be regarded as that very same individual lemon. We have then a single referent, which may be

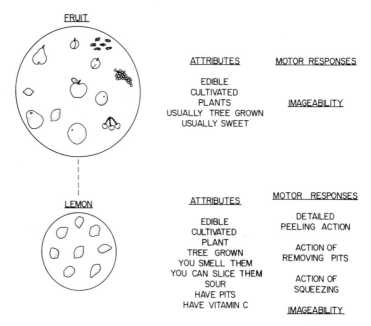

FRUIT

ATTRIBUTES   MOTOR RESPONSES

EDIBLE
CULTIVATED
PLANTS   IMAGEABILITY
USUALLY TREE GROWN
USUALLY SWEET

LEMON

ATTRIBUTES   MOTOR RESPONSES

EDIBLE   DETAILED
CULTIVATED   PEELING ACTION
PLANT
TREE GROWN   ACTION OF
YOU SMELL THEM   REMOVING PITS
YOU CAN SLICE THEM
SOUR   ACTION OF
HAVE PITS   SQUEEZING
HAVE VITAMIN C
                          IMAGEABILITY

Figure 8.8. One of the names appropriate to a referent categorizes it at the basic object level.

named in either of two ways: as a kind of "fruit" and as a "lemon." Only one of these names is on the basic object level, and that is "lemon." The concept of the basic object level is an elaboration and deepening of the notion, developed in my early paper (1958) "How Shall a Thing Be Called?" that one name, from the names appropriate to a referent, is felt to be its real name, its truest name. (To forestall an easy misunderstanding, the basic object level is not conceived to fall consistently at any particular taxonomic level.)

As developed by Eleanor Rosch and her associates (1976), the basic object level, at least for some large number of referents, is not arbitrary, but rather is determined by the nature of physical reality. Objects in the physical world are precisely *not* like a set of Vigotsky blocks, materials that were invented for the experimental study of concept formation. Vigotsky blocks vary in shape, color, and size, and the full set consists of combinations of attribute values such that no one categorization is more salient than another and the experimenter is free to impose the groupings he chooses. Rosch's view is that sets of concrete objects not intended for experimental purposes, whether manufactured or biological, do not usually make one categorization as likely as another. There are correlations among attributes such as to favor some categorizations over others.

In particular, sets of objects not manufactured for experimental pur-poses do not usually realize all possible combinations of attribute values. As I understand Rosch et al. (1976), they think of natural objects as rather like a handful of change. Our coins vary in size, hue, and inscription, but not in such a way as to realize all possible combinations. There is no brown-colored quarter, no small, thin half-dollar, no silver penny. On the contrary, the attribute values are correlated so that only brown coins of a certain size are inscribed "one cent," and so on. As a result, if a handful of change is thrown on the table, it breaks up perceptually into natural categories that are, in fact, the functioning categories of economic exchange.

Whether the basic object level is or is not, in some degree, constrained by the nature of the physical world, Rosch and her associates have not yet, to my knowledge, found a way to test this idea directly. I think they may make the claim as energetically as they do for the purpose of counteracting Benjamin Whorf's picture of a totally unformed passive reality ("a patient etherized upon a table?") which languages are free to dissect as they like. I doubt that they think there is no cultural relativism in cognition, but I am sure they do think there is a good deal of universalism.

How, in fact, have Rosch and her associates defined the basic object level? The full story is a complex, utterly fascinating research program described in the journal Cognitive Psychology (Rosch et al., 1976). Nine taxonomic hierarchies were used. There were in each hierarchy one superordinate term (e.g., furniture), three middle-level terms thought to be at the basic object level, such as table, lamp, and chair, and for each of these middle-level terms two subordinates, such as kitchen table and dining room table, floor lamp and desk lamp, kitchen chair and living room chair, which makes a total of 10 terms for each taxonomy. Rosch's prediction was that the basic object-level terms would be distinguished from their superordinates by three behavioral characteristics. Subjects would be able to name more attributes, including both perceptible characteristics and uses (in about 1.5 min) for the referents of an object-level term like table than for the referents of its superordinate furniture. Subjects would be able to describe or act out more motor responses made in connection with a basic-level term like bicycle than for its superordinate vehicle. Finally, a composite of four photographs of referent instances for an object-level term like apple, the photographs being normalized for size and all in a canonical position, would be more easily recognized than four such photographs of different instances for the superordinate fruit. This last procedure was an attempt at operationalizing what Rosch thinks of as the superior "imageability" of referents at the object level. As you will have been able to judge from the examples, all of this worked out perfectly.

The behavioral distinction between object-level terms and their subordinates, for example, *apple* and *McIntosh apple* is less pronounced in the results. Rosch's general thought (Rosch *et al.*, 1976) is that while the subordinates might often have as many, or even more, attributes and characteristic motor responses and be more nearly imageable, the gain would be slight and not generally worth the trouble of making the finer discrimination. This is one of several points where I find room for serious argument. Clearly, "specialists" of all kinds, from wine tasters to stamp collectors, do find it possible and worth the trouble to make discriminations much finer than those pitched at the object level of people in general. In fact, Rosch and her associates found that for their particular terms, the subordinates were not always as rich in attributes, responses, and imageability as the basic object terms, and when they were more so in any of these respects, they were not significantly more so.

There are several difficulties and problems with all this, but this is not the place to discuss them. I, myself, am satisfied that in general the basic object level can be determined for taxonomies in these behavioral ways, and that the terms thus identified are the terms people in general intuitively feel to be the real names for the referents in question.

In Figure 8.8, there is just one referent and two terms. As you can see, there are more attributes and motor responses at the level *lemon* than at the level *fruit*. The illustrator, who works mostly with biologists and so was already outraged by what I had asked him to do, dug in his heels when I suggested that he sketch a composite photograph of four fruits, say a lemon, a banana, a pineapple, and a bunch of grapes.

In Figure 8.9 I have cut back to the original carrot and lemon. For both of these things, the terms *carrot* and *lemon* are the basic object-level terms, whereas *vegetable* and *fruit* are not. However, on the basic object level, the particular carrot is not prototypical of the class of carrots, and for that reason has consistently been drawn off center. The particular lemon, on the other hand, is prototypical of lemons, and so has consistently been positioned dead center in its semantic space. The main point made by this figure is that the particular carrot that is not prototypical in the class of carrots is prototypical in the class of vegetables and has so been represented. On the other hand, the particular lemon that is prototypical among lemons is not the prototypical fruit; that honor belongs to the apple.

These are the basic concepts of the new paradigm: fuzzy boundaries, varying prototypicality, and the notion of basic object level. It is aesthetically pleasing to note that if the concept of basic object level is correct, if there is one truest, real name for things and the level of this truest name is determined as such by physical reality, then we return to our beginnings and find that the simplest reference model, the one I have called "words and things," is quite a good encapsulation of the apparently most adequate model.

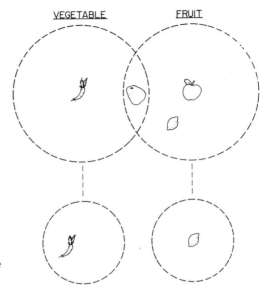

Figure 8.9. Interrelations in the new paradigm.

USES OF THE NEW PARADIGM

A new paradigm ought to fill an old paradigmer's head with new ideas. The paradigm of reference does that for me. I will limit speculation to two semantic progressions of childhood. Holding the referent constant, one can ask in what order its various possible names will be offered by adults and learned by children. I think the answer is that the object-level name will always come first, with names more concrete and also names more abstract following after, in no obviously lawful order. The second progression involves holding the name constant and asking in what order referent instances will be selected and learned. I think the answer is that instances will be selected in an order from high prototypicality to low. There is some evidence for the first proposal; not much as yet for the second.

The Progression of Names for a Fixed Referent

Rosch and her associates (1976) have collected extensive naming data from adults utilizing the nine taxonomies already described for which basic object-level terms had been independently determined. Each maximally subordinate referent in a taxonomy, such as *claw hammer* in a taxonomy that rises to *hammer* at the basic object level and *tool* at the most superordinate level, can be named with perfect appropriateness at three possible levels: A *claw hammer* is a *hammer* and is also a *tool*. A *McIntosh apple* is an *apple* as well as a *fruit*. It follows, since there are six maximally subordinate referents in each taxonomy, that 54 pictures constitute the full set from which the nine taxonomies were constructed.

Adult subjects were allowed to shuffle through the deck of pictures and were then asked just to give the name of each object. Notice that the preliminary look through the deck might well have suggested that each picture ought to be named distinctively, though this was not said. The question was whether the basic object name would have an intuitive "rightness" sufficient to override the implicit suggestion to discriminate more finely—and it did so. A total of 530 basic object-level names were given and only 10 names of any other sort. There is additional evidence from Rosch *et al.* (1976) and even more direct evidence from Jeremy Anglin (1977) since he had mothers name pictures for their own 2-year-old children. The picture is constant: Adults name at the basic object level unless expressly diverted from doing so, for reasons Anglin discusses.

Are basic level names the ones that children first learn? There is abundant evidence that they are. Rosch and her group borrowed from us the full set of 31 half-hour transcriptions for the child Sarah belonging to the period I (1973) have called Stage I. They extracted from the transcriptions all occurrences of terms included at any level of the nine taxonomies for which they had independently defined the basic object level. Almost every word in Sarah's noun lexicon that appeared in the nine taxonomies was at the basic object level. In addition, Mervis (in Rosch *et al.*, 1976) determined that 3-year-olds asked to name pictures from the nine taxonomies did as the adults had done: They used only basic object names.

Finally, is there anything to suggest that the basic object level for referents is, quite apart from names, the first level of categorization for reasons of physical similarity? Rosch and Mervis (1975) did a simple sorting task of a kind never done before. Because they wanted to work with children as young as 3 years, they used a simplified version of sorting, the "oddity task," which simply requires that two objects of the same kind be put together and the odd item set aside. The completely novel feature of the task was that the two objects to be put together were not, as has usually been the case, linked only at a superordinate level. That kind of problem would lay out a dog and a cat and a car; the correct pairing would, of course, be dog and cat, as both are animals (the common superordinate). However, Rosch and Mervis used another sort of triad: two referents belonging together at the basic object level, such as two cats—quite different, but still cats—and one dog.

This kind of pairing at the basic object level was done correctly by 90% of 3-year-olds and 100% of older children. It is of particular significance that very many children could make object-level pairings when they could not supply the correct name for the objects. It looks very much as if there may be a great many referent classes that are founded in physical reality and constructed in the child's mind before he learns to name them.

The Progression of Referent Instances for a Given Name

For this progression my hypothesis is that instances will be selected in an order from the more prototypical in the direction of the less prototypical. Relevant research is in progress but not yet complete. Nevertheless, I dare guess that it will prove to be a law of semantic development simply because it makes such good intuitive sense.

Let us consider the 10 natural taxonomies for which Rosch (1975) has provided prototypicality ratings for 50–60 instances. The 10 categories are: furniture, fruit, vehicle, weapon, vegetable, carpenter's tool, bird, sport, toy, and clothing. Consider just the category furniture. It has 60 members, ranging from chair and sofa at the highest level of prototypicality, to hassock and buffet about in the middle, and fan and telephone at the bottom. All of these names of kinds of furniture are at the basic object level.

At first guess, one might think the prediction I have made clearly wrong. I said, after all, that the order of progression would be from higher prototypicality to lower prototypicality. A casual look at the instances of furniture suggests that it will not always or even usually be so. The prototypicality of *refrigerator,* for instance, is very low (rank 54) whereas *ottoman* is rank 25. But surely refrigerators, objects found in most households, will be named before ottomans—whatever *they* are. There are many such likely reversals. The order of naming seems mainly to depend on what furniture is in the child's home.

The facts are right; it is just the prediction that has been misunderstood. I know that it can be misunderstood in this way because when I first formulated it I promptly misunderstood it in just this fashion. What has been briefly forgotten is that the prediction requires that the word be held constant. With the word constant, I think instances to which to apply the word, for children, will generally proceed in an order of decreasing prototypicality. The problem, you see, is learning the meaning of the word *furniture;* that is the word that is to be held constant. So we are not concerned with the naming of the refrigerator, as such, at its object level, but with the naming of refrigerator *as an* instance of furniture. *That* is not going to happen soon or often. It surely is true that a chair, a sofa, a couch, a table—yes, and even an ottoman—will be classified as kinds of furniture before a refrigerator or a radio or a telephone will be, ubiquitous though these latter objects be. They will all surely be named early as objects, but not as instances of *furniture*. To convey to a child a first understanding of *bird*, few parents would reach out for the nearest ostrich. And it is the same with the other categories, so I have little doubt that the principle will stand.

There is more that I could say about the uses the new paradigm has for me in the study of language development. There is mounting evidence that the finding is equally suggestive in many areas of psychology.

REFERENCES

Anglin, J. M. *Word, object, and conceptual development.* New York: Norton, 1977.

Brown, R. W. How shall a thing be called? *Psychological Review,* 1958, *65,* 14–21.

Brown, R. W. *A first language; the early stages.* Cambridge: Harvard University Press, 1973.

Brown, R. W. Reference—In memorial tribute to Eric Lenneberg. *Cognition,* 1976, *4,* 125–153.

Brown, R. W., & E. H. Lenneberg. A study in language and cognition. *Journal of Abnormal and Social Psychology,* 1954, *49,* 454–462.

Cooper, J. E., Kendell, R. E., Gurland, B. J., Sharpe, L., Copeland, J. R. M., & Simon, R. *Psychiatric diagnosis.* New York and London: Oxford University Press, 1972.

Lenneberg, E. H. A probabilistic approach to language learning. *Behavioral Science,* 1957, *2,* 1–12.

Rosch, E. Cognitive representations of semantic categories. *Journal of Experimental Psychology: General,* 1975, *104,* 192–233.

Rosch, E., & Mervis, C. B. *Children's sorting: A reinterpretation based on the nature of abstraction in natural categories.* Unpublished manuscript, 1975.

Rosch, E., & Mervis, C. B. Family resemblances: Studies in the internal structure of categories. *Cognitive Psychology,* 1975, *7,* 573–605.

Rosch, E., Mervis, C. B., Gray, W., Johnson, D., & Boyes-Braem, P. Basic objects in natural categories. *Cognitive Psychology,* 1976, *8,* 382–439.

Webster's Collegiate Dictionary (5th ed.). Springfield, Mass.: Merrian, 1943.

Webster's Collegiate Dictionary (7th ed.). Springfield, Mass.: Merriam, 1965.

Wittgenstein, L. *Philosophical investigations.* New York: Macmillan, 1953.

Zadeh, L. A. Fuzzy sets. *Information and Control,* 1965, *8,* 338–375.

Zadeh, L. A. Quantitative fuzzy semantics. *Information Science,* 1971, *3,* 159–176.

chapter **9**

Pastness[1]

GEORGE A. MILLER

PASTNESS AS A SEMANTIC PHENOMENON

"Apparently," Lenneberg (1967) commented in a discussion of language development in children, "*pastness* is first learned as a semantic phenomenon [p. 304]." This chapter is an attempt to explicate the semantic phenomenon he had in mind.

Lenneberg's comment appeared in the following context. He had observed that young children will often use so-called strong verbs in both their present and preterit forms, for example, *go* and *went,* even before they have learned to add the inflection *-ed* as an expression of pastness.[2] When the *-ed* suffix appears, it is not only used to form the preterit of regular verbs, e.g.,

[1] Preparation of this chapter was supported, in part, by Grant No. GM21796 from the Public Health Services to The Rockefeller University.

[2] The inflection *-ed* represents three allomorphs (/t/, /d/, /ɪd/) that a child must learn to use appropriately, but this side of the problem will be neglected in order to concentrate on semantic aspects of the learning process.

PSYCHOLOGY AND BIOLOGY OF LANGUAGE AND THOUGHT
Essays in Honor of Eric Lenneberg

walked, but may also be added to strong verbs, resulting in such forms as *goed* and *wented.* Lenneberg cites the work of Berko (1958) as evidence for overgeneralization of this morphological rule.

I assume that Lenneberg viewed a child at the preinflectional stage as considering *go* and *went* to be semantically related but morphologically distinct—if these distinctions from the analysis of adult language can be legitimately adapted to describe a child's state of knowledge. For example, an adult may think of verbs like *rise* and *raise* as being semantically related but morphologically independent: Semantically, *raise* is the causative of *rise,* it is *rise*-plus-a-concept-of-causeness; morphologically, however, *raise/raised/raising* and *rise/rose/risen/rising* are unrelated. The child, to parallel this account, may think of *went* as *go*-plus-a-concept-of-pastness; morphologically, however, the two words are as unrelated for the child as *raise* and *rise* are for the adult. The evidence for semantic relatedness is that children seem to use *go* and *went* appropriately. The evidence for morphological independence is the subsequent overgeneralization of -*ed* to both forms.

Lenneberg was interested in this overgeneralization primarily as evidence that language development involves learning and applying rules, not rote memorization or imitation. Since a child does not hear *goed* or *wented* in adult speech, their occurrence in child speech is strong evidence that children are not simply memorizing or imitating fragments of adult speech. In shifting the focus of his comment away from the process of learning syntactic rules and toward the semantic phenomenon of pastness, I am doing some violence to his intent. There are some semantic puzzles in his account, however, which I think he would have liked to resolve; I hope this is an appropriate occasion on which to point them out.

To quote Lenneberg in full, "Apparently, *pastness* is first learned as a semantic phenomenon, and it is most saliently labeled in the case of the linguistically ancient suppletive forms in which the word for the past is phonetically totally different from the present. Once the semantic past is linked to the -*ed* form, a rule is generated and then applied universally [p. 304]." Setting aside the question of universality, I take this to mean that children who use *went* correctly must have acquired a concept of pastness and are conceptually prepared to associate it with -*ed* when they learn some such rule as:

(1)   *The concept of pastness is added to a verb by adding* **-ed** *to it.*

There are two parts to learning a rule. The obvious part is learning what the rule is. The part that is sometimes neglected by theorists is learning when to apply the rule. In the case of Rule (1) the child's principal problem is learning which verbs to apply it to. There are some English verbs, like *cost, cut, hit, hurt, let, put, set,* that are exactly the same in the present as in the past; it is necessary to learn that the rule does not apply to those verbs. There are some English verbs, like *break, dig, give, see, take* and many others, where pastness is signaled by a vowel change; it is necessary to learn that the rule does not apply to those verbs either, but something else does. Learning all these exceptions to the -*ed* rule takes a child several years; overgeneralizations are not entirely absent from the speech of first graders.

Note, however, that another aspect of learning when to apply the rule is learning that -*ed* is added to verbs. This aspect tends to be overlooked because children have little trouble with it. Yet we would not want to assume that children have any clear idea of which words are verbs—that they say to themselves, "Since this is a verb, maybe I can add -*ed* to it." Rather, we assume that children have some implicit grammatical (structurally dependent) intuition about each member of this class of words that are later categorized as verbs; these words feel like they ought to take -*ed* endings. I recognize that this is a very unsatisfactory way to put it, but I doubt that I could improve it even with an extended interruption of my argument. But if professional linguists can have reliable intuitions about language, why not 2-year-old children?

The puzzles I want to call attention to are semantic. Let me list three. First, temporal relations are abstract, but children are notorious for the concreteness of their language, for their preoccupation with observable things and events here and now. We have little evidence that preinflectional children have learned pastness as a semantic phenomenon other than the linguistic evidence that we want to use pastness to explain. It does not seem merely contentious to question whether they use *went* to express pastness. Perhaps the difference between *go* and *went* is used to mark something else, like momentary happenings as opposed to persisting states (related to aspect), or wishes as opposed to facts (related to mood). The first puzzle, therefore, is how to determine whether a preinflectional child really understands pastness.

If we accept the claim that pastness is learned very early and so is available to support subsequent learning of Rule (1), then a second puzzle is why, if children understand *went* as incorporating pastness semantically, they redundantly add it again in *wented:*

(2)   *wented* = *went* + *ed* = *went* + pastness = (*go* + pastness) + pastness

Of course, children, not being logicians, may not note the double pastness of *wented* or, if they do, may see nothing wrong with such redundancy. On the other hand, if they did not understand *went* as incorporating a concept of pastness, then adding pastness with -*ed* would not seem redundant to them.

A third puzzle is how a child ever comes to link -ed with pastness. Indeed, in adult language there are so many exceptions to the rule that -ed expresses pastness that J. P. Thorne (personal communication) has concluded that it is not a rule of grammar at all. For example, in passive sentences like Breakfast is fixed by Mommy the -ed suffix on fixed does not express pastness. In sentences like I wish you liked spinach the -ed suffix on the subjunctive liked does not express pastness. In sentences like His nose is crooked or Keep your fingers crossed the -ed on the adjectives crooked and crossed does not express pastness. There are even denominal adjectives with -ed, as in his face was bearded or a blue-eyed baby, that do not express pastness. In short, the child must have heard many exceptions to Rule (1), and rules admitting many exceptions are usually the hardest to induce. Of course, the exceptions may not be noted by the child or, if they are, they may be incorrectly understood. On the other hand, it is at least conceivable that even when the -ed inflection begins to appear the child has still not understood correctly the adult notion of pastness.

None of these puzzles is sufficient to refute the semantic account that Lenneberg and others have given, but I do believe that some caution is indicated. It seems that we are entangled here with an inflectional version of the old question about which comes first, the symbol or the concept that the symbol expresses. The question is difficult because we are usually so uncertain about exactly what concept the symbol expresses when it is first used. One has an uneasy feeling that the concept may be changing as a consequence of increased experience in using the symbol that expresses it, and that the way the symbol is used may be changing as the concept changes. Moreover, all these uncertainties about the conceptual content of a symbol are heightened for concepts as abstract as temporal relations and for symbols as complex and contingent as those involved in the English tense system.

The fact of the matter is that we do not presently have any satisfactory theory of how temporal relations are expressed by verb forms in adult language. Lacking any clear notion of the syntactic–semantic system that a child is learning, we should be on guard against oversimplifications. At the very least, a theorist who gets his hypothetical child into this cul de sac should also get him out again. That is to say, he owes us some account of the subsequent learning of exceptions to Rule (1)—not merely of the obvious exceptions like goed and wented, but of the more complex exceptions in passives, subjunctives, and adjectives. It might turn out, when the learning of all the exceptions had been accounted for, that the complete theory of how a child learns to express pastness by verb forms would be unmanageably complicated, in which case a total revision of the theory might be called for.

The semantic puzzles I have noted in Lenneberg's account arise, I believe, as a consequence of speaking so simply about pastness as a semantic phenomenon. If so, the first step toward a less puzzling hypothesis would be to analyze the concept of pastness in adult language. Once we see more clearly what a child is learning to express, we may be able to formulate a more adequate hypothesis about the concept of pastness in child language.

REICHENBACH'S CONCEPT OF TENSE

I will, therefore, try to unravel a small part of the theoretical problems raised by pastness. Although a serious discussion of such a complex topic cannot avoid complexity, the central point I will try to make is that there are (at least) two components to the meanings of English tense markers. This idea is expressed by those linguists who describe the present perfect (*It has happened*) as "the past in the present" and the pluperfect (*It had happened*) as "the past in the past." It was made explicit by Reichenbach (1947), who extended it to the simple present (*It happens*) and the simple past (*It happened*). Reichenbach's formulation is given graphically in Figure 9.1, where the concept of time is represented as a horizontal line ordering successive moments from left to right and the states or events described by the tensed sentences are mapped onto that line in a particular order with respect to the moment of utterance.

According to Reichenbach, at least three times are required to specify truth conditions for the proposition expressed by any tensed sentence. There is, first of all, the time of speech, s, which we can take as the privileged moment *now*, or n. This point anchors the tense system deictically—the listener must know when the sentence was uttered in order to understand or evaluate it. Second, there is the time of the event or state of affairs that the main verb in the sentence denotes, e, which may be before or during (or after) the time of speech. This point in time, relative to the time of speech, represents the concept of past or present (or future) events. When people speak of a simple notion of pastness, it is presumably this relation—time of

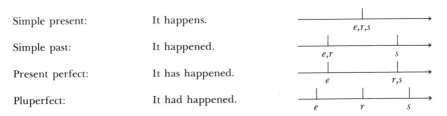

Simple present:	It happens.
Simple past:	It happened.
Present perfect:	It has happened.
Pluperfect:	It had happened.

Figure 9.1. Graphical representation of the relations between the time of speech s, the time of the event e, and the time of reference r. (Adapted from Reichenbach, 1947.)

event precedes time of speech—that they have in mind. Note, however, that in Figure 9.1 there are three ways to indicate that e precedes s, but only one way to indicate that e and s are simultaneous.

The need for a third time, which introduces a second component of the meaning of an English tense, is most obvious in the case of the pluperfect. As Katz (1972) points out, there seems to be an "undescribed event" in pluperfect indicative sentences like *He had earned the money*. Such sentences invite a further event description: *before he spent it*, perhaps. The undescribed event is thought of as occurring at a point in time between the time he earned the money, e, and the time of speech, s. Reichenbach calls this intermediate time the time of reference, r; its value must be determined from the general context provided by the text or discourse in which the sentence occurs. In order to introduce this point of reference between the time of the event and the time of speech, a second component of meaning is required for the tense system.

Reichenbach claims (but Katz does not) that all three of these times are required, not only for the pluperfect, but in order to represent the meanings of other tenses, where it is not possible to argue that there is some undescribed event that demands a third reference point. As illustrated in Figure 9.1, Reichenbach considers the time of reference to be the same as the time of speech in the simple present and the present perfect tenses, and to be the same as the time of the event in the simple past tense. Since Reichenbach's claim for three times when only two are different seems unparsimonious, I will try to provide arguments in its favor.

AN ARGUMENT FOR REFERENCE TIMES

An informal argument for reference times can be based on pragmatic rules of discourse. Out of context, a sentence in the simple past, like *He saw the boy*, has event and reference times that are indeterminately in the past. In a discourse context, however, there will be some phrase that introduces a reference time: *Yesterday*, or *When he walked in*, or *The third time he visited the house*, or *On March 21*, or whatever. Once a reference time is set by such a phrase, it can persist through many subsequent sentences until another phrase explicitly changes it; it may be necessary to look far back in the discourse or conversation to discover how the reference time was introduced. In the simple past, the event time is the same as the reference time; in the pluperfect, the event time precedes the reference time. The simple present and the present perfect, on the other hand, do not require such phrases to introduce a reference time, because, in the absence of any indication to the contrary, the reference time is understood to be the current time, not some previous (or subsequent) time. In particular, the present perfect enables a speaker to mention a past event without introducing a new reference time in the past. Thus, one component of the meaning of the English tense markers establishes the reference time and the second component signals whether the event time is before, during, or after that reference time.

A formal argument for reference times must be considerably more detailed, so it may be well to outline the argument in advance. First, it will be claimed that all four tenses in Figure 9.1 are semantically equivalent to expressions that have two syntactic surface markers of tense. Second, these two surface markers will be associated with two applications of logical operators. Since such operators are less familiar to psychologists than are, say, semantic markers, they will be explained in some detail. And, finally, it will be argued that two logical operations are required only if there are three times to be related; if only an event time and the time of speech were to be related, a single operation would suffice to locate the event as before or during (or after) the time of speech.

The first step, therefore, is to make the two surface markers of tense explicit. Since they are not explicit in the normal indicative mood, we will approach the problem from an unorthodox direction. There is a manner of speaking in English that is used when a speaker wishes to stress that what he has said is in fact the case. It results in emphasis on the auxiliary verb: *It **has** happened.* Let us call this the *emphatic mood.* The emphatic mood is useful for our present purposes because, in the simple present and past, the suppletive verb *do* can be introduced in order to carry the emphasis: *It **does** happen* or *It **did** happen.* In short, in the emphatic mood there can be an auxiliary verb to carry a tense marker, and so it is possible to see that both components of the meanings of English tenses are required. (Negative and interrogative sentences also introduce *do* in the simple present and past, but they introduce other complications not relevant to my argument.) The four emphatic cases of central interest to us can be displayed as:

(3) Simple present: It **does** happen.   Present, present
     Simple past: It **did** happen.   Past, present
     Present perfect: It **has** happened.   Present, past
     Pluperfect: It **had** happened.   Past, past

Note the pattern of tense markers on the auxiliary and main verbs, as indicated in the right column of (3). The simple present uses present tense for both; the simple past uses past for the auxiliary and present for the main verb; the present perfect uses present for the auxiliary and past for the main verb; the pluperfect uses past for both.

This pattern of tenses on the auxiliary and main verbs is related to Reichenbach's claim that three time points are required in order to specify all of these tenses, but in order to make the relation explicit we must introduce some elementary temporal logic. I will adopt the notation borrowed by Miller and Johnson-Laird (1976) from Rescher and Urquhart (1971), but will introduce only that fragment required for the present argument.

Let S represent a temporally indefinite proposition identifying or referring to an event or state of affairs whose temporal location on the time line is to be determined. Let R be an operator that takes a proposition as its argument and yields another proposition by specifying the time t at which it is realized. Thus, $R_t(S)$ is interpreted to mean that S is realized at time t. $R_t(S)$ makes this claim only for the moment t; it says nothing about other moments before or after t.

We will need five of the axioms of this system for the derivations to be considered:

(4)   a. $R_t(S \& S') = R_t(S) \& R_t(S')$
      b. $R_t((\exists t)S) = (\exists t)R_t(S)$
      c. $R_{t'}(R_t(S)) = R_t(S)$
      d. $R_t(n = t') = (t = t')$ and $R_t(t'' = t') = (t'' = t')$
      e. $R_t(n < t') = (t < t')$ and $R_t(t'' < t') = (t'' < t')$

(4a) says that the operator is distributive. Quantification is introduced in (b), which allows R to move in or out of the scope of quantifiers. In (c) there are multiple operators: first R_t is applied to the temporally indefinite S to give a temporally definite statement, then $R_{t'}$ is applied to that. According to (c), if S is a temporally definite proposition, then $R_{t'}(S)$ is taken as the equivalent of S—It was true at noon that it was true at dawn is taken as equivalent to It was true at dawn, for example. The exceptions to this rule involve now in any of its various disguises. When S is a temporally definite statement involving now, $R_t(R_n(S))$ is taken to be equivalent to $R_t(S)$, not $R_n(S)$. On this formulation, which is made explicit in (d) and (e), yesterday's today is not today, but yesterday. The equality signs in (d) represent the relation is the same time as and the inequality signs in (e) represent the relation is before. These five axioms, plus the first-order predicate calculus, are all that we will require.

Now we must define two tense operators in terms of R. I will introduce an operator N for the present and an operator P for the past:

(5) a. Present: $N_t (S) = (\exists t) [t = n \ \& \ R_t (S)]$
     b. Past: $P_t (S) = (\exists t) [t < n \ \& \ R_t (S)]$

In paraphrase, $N_t (S)$ is defined to mean that there is a time t that is now and S is realized at t; $P_t (S)$ is defined to mean that there is a time t that is before now and S was realized at that time. Semantically, the point is that pastness is defined in (5b) to mean *before now;* psychologically, the point is that pastness must be understood as contrasting with presentness, that *before now* in (5b) has meaning by virtue of its relation to *right now* in (5a). (A future operator F could be similarly defined in terms of $n < t$.)

The tenses sketched in (3) can now be represented by the application of two tense operators to a temporally indefinite S. Let us take first the pluperfect, since that is intuitively easiest to understand:

(6) $P_r (P_e (S)) = P_r ((\exists e) [e < n \ \& \ R_e (S)])$ by (5b)

$\qquad\qquad = (\exists r) [r < n \ \& \ R_r ((\exists e) [e < n \ \& \ R_e (S)])]$ by (5b)

$\qquad\qquad = (\exists r,e) [r < n \ \& \ R_r (e < n \ \& \ R_e (S))]$ by (4b)

$\qquad\qquad = (\exists r,e) [r < n \ \& \ R_r (e < n) \ \& \ R_r (R_e (S))]$ by (4a)

$\qquad\qquad = (\exists r,e) [r < n \ \& \ e < r \ \& \ R_r (R_e (S))]$ by (4e)

$\qquad\qquad = (\exists r,e) [e < r < n \ \& \ R_e (S)]$ by (4c)

As Rescher and Urquhart point out, applying the past tense operator twice yields the temporal description of the pluperfect, which Reichenbach described as $e < r < n$, or event time before reference time before speech time. Briefly stated, the event-time operator P_e moves e before r and the reference-time operator P_r moves r before n.

By appropriate substitutions into (6) it is a simple matter to work out the following results:

(7) Simple present: $N_r N_e (S) = (\exists e,r) [e = r = n \ \& \ R_e (S)]$
     Simple past: $P_r N_e (S) = (\exists e,r) [e = r < n \ \& \ R_e (S)]$
     Present perfect: $N_r P_e (S) = (\exists e,r) [e < r = n \ \& \ R_e (S)]$
     Pluperfect: $P_r P_e (S) = (\exists e,r) [e < r < n \ \& \ R_e (S)]$

Note that the application of these tense operators corresponds exactly to the pattern of tense markers on the auxiliary and main verbs in the emphatic mood, as shown in (3). In that mood, therefore, there is a particularly simple and direct relation between the syntactic tense markers and the semantic tense operators: the tense marker on the main verb corresponds to the application of the event-time operator and the tense marker on the auxiliary verb corresponds to the application of the reference-time operator. Moreover, the temporal order of e, r, and n in (7) corresponds exactly to Reichenbach's graphical representation of these four tenses in Figure 9.1.

In the emphatic mood, therefore, we find a remarkable correspondence between the syntactic and semantic analyses—between morphological indicators of tense at the linguistic level and the application of logical operators at the conceptual level. Since two operations would not be required unless there were three times to be related, I take this correspondence as an argument in support of Reichenbach's claim that reference times are involved in all four tenses, not merely in the case of the pluperfect.

If we accept this argument, of course, it means that there are two components to the meaning of pastness in English, even in the superficially single-component cases of the simple present and the simple past. I have made this argument, however, for the relatively unusual emphatic mood. It may be that this result is a consequence of the fact that there can be a suppletive *do* to take the emphasis and thus available to take the tense marker as well. In the more usual indicative mood (*It happens* and *It happened*) this tense marker is on the main verb. One might argue that *happen* in the emphatic sentences *It **does** happen* and *It **did** happen* is not really in the present tense at all—it is simply unmarked for tense because its tense marker has been usurped by *do*—in which case only a single conceptual operator should be required. (If I had used negative or interrogative sentences to display the pattern of double tense markers, this objection—that the main verb is really untensed—could still be pressed by a single-tense theorist.)

A decision concerning the need for two components in the indicative mood, therefore, must rest on one's opinion of the difference between the simple past and present perfect. Unfortunately, this distinction has baffled grammarians almost as much as laymen, and contradictory accounts of the semantic contrast between such pairs of sentences as *It happened* and *It has happened* are all too easy to find. The standard account is that the present perfect expresses a relevance to the present time that the simple past does not (see, for example, Twaddell, 1963; Palmer, 1965). "The present time," however, is vague; it is not to be defined in terms of minutes or hours, but can denote any length of time that includes the time of utterance. This can be illustrated by an example. If a speaker says *It happened in February for the first time,* he is usually understood to be speaking in some month subsequent to February, whereas if he says *It has happened in February for the first time,* he is usually understood to be speaking during February—it has present relevance because the time of reference is the month that includes the moment at which he is speaking. Perhaps a more perspicuous phrase would be "relevance to the present episode," where the episode that includes the act of speaking can be of indefinite length. There is, however, no objective definition of "relevance." The same past event can be introduced either in the simple past or present perfect: either *On April 15 we decided that . . .* or *We have decided that . . .* can introduce the same decision, regardless of its current relevance.[3] The real difference, therefore, is that the simple past establishes an antecedent reference time (*April 15,* in this example), whereas the present perfect establishes a current reference time. It would sound odd to say *On April 15 we have decided that . . . ,* unless the two reference times are the same, that is, unless the time of speech is April 15. (Even then it sounds odd to give the date instead of saying *today.*)

This distinction between *It happened* and *It has happened* is captured in the two-operator analysis, where the time of reference is in the past for the simple past, but in the present for the present perfect. With only a single operator to represent the meaning of pastness, no semantic account of this difference can be given. The difference is admittedly subtle and sentences uttered in the present perfect will often be remembered in the simple past (Clark & Stafford, 1969), perhaps because when they are recalled the original time of utterance is no longer considered in the scope of the present episode. But a subtle difference in meaning is still a difference, and a theory that accounts for it is to be preferred to one that does not.

Even in the indicative mood, therefore, where the morphology of the simple present and past gives no surface representation of two operators, Reichenbach's claim is defensible at a semantic level of analysis. Notice, however, that the syntactic expression of these conceptual relations is different for the indicative and emphatic moods. Whereas the emphatic mood provides a relatively clear marking for the two operators (perhaps because the emphatic mood is often used precisely to combat potential misunderstandings), the morphology of tense in the indicative is somewhat more complex, though shorter and more efficient:

(8)

Tense	Emphatic	Indicative	Operators
Simple present:	It **does** happen	It happens	$N_r N_e$
Simple past:	It **did** happen	It happened	$P_r N_e$
Present perfect:	It **has** happened	It has happened	$N_r P_e$
Pluperfect:	It **had** happened	It had happened	$P_r P_e$

In the simple present and past the *do* auxiliary is omitted and the tense marker it would have carried is shifted to the main verb.

[3] Roger Brown (personal communication) points out that, although the present perfect may signal that the speaker regards the past event as relevant to the present episode, its absence does not deny such relevance. It is not incorrect to use the simple past to introduce a past event of great current relevance.

THORNE'S CONCEPT OF TENSE

Since the past is ordinarily marked syntactically in English, whereas the present and future are unmarked, and since there seems to be a rule that prevents adding two past inflections to the same verb, it is necessary to have two verbs for the two pasts in the pluperfect—J. P. Thorne (personal communication) has suggested that we think of the *have* in the perfective tenses as suppletive, needed simply to carry the extra morphological marker of pastness. Since there is only one past operator to be represented syntactically in the simple past, it is a natural morphological simplification to represent it by adding the *-ed* onto the main verb. Conceptually, however, the *-ed* inflection in the simple past does not have the same meaning as the *-ed* inflection in the perfectives. In the simple past indicative, *-ed* represents the reference-time operator P_r, whereas in the perfective indicatives *-ed* represents the event-time operator P_e. (This difference is clearer with irregular verbs like *fall*, where *It fell* and *It has fallen* are differently marked.)

Thorne argues that much of the apparent variability in the syntactic representation of temporal relations in the English tense system is a consequence of an interaction of tense and mood. The same surface morphology expresses different meanings in different moods. We have already noted that in the subjunctive mood the *-ed* inflection on the verb does not express pastness at all. Since Thorne's analysis of the relations between tense and mood are unpublished at this time, I will not risk misrepresenting his views on subjunctive tenses. It is, however, a well-known fact that in sentences like *I believe he lived in Ithaca* the *-ed* inflection on the indicative *lived* does signal pastness, whereas in *I wish he lived in Ithaca* the *-ed* inflection on the subjunctive *lived* does not signal pastness.[4]

One part of Thorne's analysis of indicative tenses is particularly relevant to our present concerns, however, and therefore, with apologies for any unfaithfulness to his ultimate conclusions, I will present my understanding of his ideas. In brief, Thorne suggests that the reference-time operator (N_r or P_r) has the syntactic effect of attaching a tense marker to the mood of the sentence. Since mood is not represented explicitly by any morpheme in the sentence, this suggestion requires some development.

The contribution that the indicative mood makes to the meaning of a sentence can be pointed out (not defined or replaced, but simply pointed at) by prefixing to an indicative sentence the phrase *It is the case that*. If the sentence is the indicative *It happens*, then the synonymous sentence *It is the*

---

[4] The restriction of the tense of imperative mood verbs to present and future may be explicable on the pragmatic grounds that they are ordinarily used to make requests and give commands; it is useless to request or command past actions.

case that it happens calls our attention to its indicativeness. This indicative-indicating phrase can then support our intuitions if we use it to call attention to something than can take a second tense marker. Thus, Thorne suggests the following way to think about the indicative tenses (where *It be the case* is to be understood as a temporally indefinite representation of *It is the case*):

(9) Present indicative: *It be the case* **at this time** that S **at this time.**
Past indicative: *It be the case* **at some time before this time** that S **at that time.**
Present perfect indicative: *It be the case* **at this time** that S **at some time before this time.**
Pluperfect indicative: *It be the case* **at some time before this time** that S **at some time before that time.**

We have run through this quartet of tenses sufficiently often now that I trust it will be obvious that Thorne's analysis corresponds exactly to the four pairs of semantic operators: N_rN_e, P_rN_e, N_rP_e, and P_rP_e, respectively. The first operator assigns the tense to the indicative-indicating phrase and the second operator assigns a tense to the predicate phrase. The point in presenting it, however, is not merely to add another theorist to our team of two-component advocates, but rather for the light it throws on the reference time.

It is reasonably obvious what the time of utterance and the time of the event or state of affairs refer to, but, except for the pluperfect, we have had nothing obvious for the time of reference to refer to. Thorne's suggestion, that what we have been calling the reference time reflects the tense of a verb's mood, provides a clue as to why it seems so impalpable and unobvious in comparison with event and utterance times.

But what could it mean to assign a tense to the mood of a sentence? The pragmatic (or rhetorical) meaning is relatively clear. The moodal tense determines whether the person is talking about a present or a past episode; in the course of talking about that episode he can use the predicate tense to refer to events or states of affairs at that time or at some time before that time. That is what linguists have meant who have talked about present-in-the-present, present-in-the-past, past-in-the-present, and past-in-the-past.

The point might be clarified if we were to go Thorne one better and divide the indicative mood into two moods, which we could call the current indicative mood (current reference time) and the historical indicative mood (past reference time). Then our quartet would look like this:

(10) *It happens:* Present tense in the current indicative mood
It happened: Present tense in the historical indicative mood
It has happened: Past tense in the current indicative mood
It had happened: Past tense in the historical indicative mood

An introductory phrase *It is the case that* would serve to call our attention to the contribution that the current indicative mood makes to the meaning of a sentence, and an introductory phrase *It was the case that* would serve to call our attention to the contribution that the historical indicative mood makes to the meaning of a sentence. (Although I have systematically ignored futurity in this discussion of pastness, it should be noted that this strategy dictates what might be called an anticipatory indicative mood whose contribution to the meaning of the sentence would be suggested by the introductory phrase *It will be the case that*.)

Traditional ways of talking about tenses and moods are probably too ingrained for this formulation to attract many supporters, but whether one wishes to think of the operators N_r and P_r as determining reference times, or as attaching tenses to the mood of the verb, or as defining the semantic difference between two moods, the claim that there are two components to the meaning of pastness in English sentences provides the simplest account for a variety of semantic phenomena. I will take it to be established and return to the question with which I began, namely, how do children learn to talk about pastness?

DEVELOPMENT OF PASTNESS IN CHILD LANGUAGE

I will begin by disagreeing with Lenneberg on a point of fact. In the same paragraph from which I quoted earlier he says "At a later stage the past tense morpheme /ed/ appears but now is generalized also to those forms where it does not occur in the adult grammar; this may now result in forms such as *goed,* as well as *wented, gived, gaved,* etc. [p. 303]." Overgeneralization to the present forms of irregular verbs is certainly common enough (*drinked, eated, falled, gived, goed, teared, throwed,* and the like are easy to find) and suffices to make the important point about rule learning in child language. Overgeneralization to the preterit forms of irregular verbs, however, is far less common. Brown (1973, p. 325) lists all of the overgeneralizations of -*ed* that occurred in all of his transcripts of the speech of three children; overgeneralizations to present forms of irregular verbs outnumber those to preterit forms by 41/5. My own searches through protocols of slightly older children produced no instances of -*ed* added to a preterit.

If this point is correct, we can quickly dismiss one of the semantic puzzles I posed, namely, why a child would add a pastness marker to a verb form that is understood as already expressing pastness. The answer, very simply, is that there is no puzzle to explain because it very seldom happens.

Moreover, if it very seldom happens, then the case that children understand pastness in the meanings of past irregular forms is actually strengthened. That is to say, if it does not happen, children must have some basis for avoiding it; an obvious basis would be that they understand these forms as already expressing the concept that -ed would add. Therefore, by abandoning *dranked, gaved, wented,* and the like we also strengthen Lenneberg's conjecture that pastness is first learned as a semantic phenomenon. At least, something closely related to pastness seems to have been learned before the -ed inflections appear.

The empirical approach can also reduce the puzzlement associated with another question I raised, namely, how children come to associate -ed with pastness when they hear so many exceptions to the rule. Brown (1973) has tabulated the occurrence of various grammatical morphemes in the speech of parents to their children. The ratios of irregular pasts to regular pasts to present perfects in the speech of the parents of the three children he studied were 141/44/18, or 8/2.5/1. Brown does not report the frequency of pluperfects, but if his data are like transcripts I have collected, the reason is that pluperfects are seldom addressed to young children. In short, young children are not expected to cope with perfective constructions; mostly they hear pastness expressed by the simple past of irregular and regular verbs. On the basis of this corpus, the hypothesis that, for regular verbs, pastness is expressed by adding -ed is not implausible.

Moreover, Brown reports that these parents did not use any full passive sentences, in which case the child would be spared such counterexamples to the rule as *Breakfast is fixed by Mommy.* Brown does not report the frequency of subjunctives used by these parents, but I think it is safe to assume they are not frequent. Cromer (1968) reports that the kind of hypothetical meanings that subjunctives express do not occur in the speech of children until they are well beyond the first stages of using -ed to form the past. Some of the potential exceptions to the -ed rule, therefore, can be dismissed as not being part of a child's linguistic world at this stage.

One class of exceptions is rather common, however. It is not clear whether they should be called reduced passives or deverbal adjectives ending in -ed. Children at this age hear (and sometimes say) such things as *It isn't finished, What's this called?, It's cooked now, It hasta be hitched,* in contexts where -ed cannot easily be interpreted as expressing pastness. I do not have appropriate tabulations of frequencies of occurrence, but my impression is that the adjectival -ed is very much a part of the child's linguistic world. This much of the puzzle remains, therefore, and anyone who has serious doubts that children associate pastness with the -ed suffix might use it to strengthen his case.

The most I can make of it is that, if -ed is associated with pastness, it is usually not a very past pastness. Many students of child language have commented that children seldom introduce remarks about events outside of what might be called the time domain of the current episode. Their use of the past almost always has present relevance. I would speculate, therefore, that a child who uses the adjectival form in *It's finished* may not understand it very differently from the verbal form in *I finished it,* where -*ed* does add pastness to the verb. In both cases the child's -*ed* suffix extends the conceptual range from the present to a short way into the past.

In order to make this argument, of course, I must also argue that young children use their -*ed* forms to express a meaning very similar to that which adults can express in the present perfect. An adult who said *I finished it* would presumably be referring to an accomplishment in some earlier episode; he would probably use *I've finished it* as an announcement of a task just completed. The distinction is not obligatory, however, and the simple past enjoys greater latitude than the present perfect: *I finished yesterday* and *I just finished* are both acceptable, but *I've finished yesterday* is clearly inferior to *I've just finished.* This asymmetry helps to conceal the child's limited competence and, if it is germane at all, might be used to support the argument that the child's -*ed* constructions nearly always have current reference—no firm rule is broken thereby.

There is a weak and a strong form of this argument. The weak form would be that children initially use -*ed* to differentiate between events *right now* and events *before now;* the fact that their usage generally expresses a meaning that adults could express in the present perfect is merely an incidental consequence of the fact that children seldom talk about past events that do not have present relevance. The strong version would be that children do not know how to use the tense system to talk about past events that do not have present relevance—in order to shift the time of reference they must rely on time or place adverbials. According to this view, a young child who says *I finished* means *I have finished,* not some undifferentiated pastness that might be experienced disjunctively as *I finished* or *I have finished* or *I had finished.* The use of *have* as an auxiliary verb appears in child language much later than -*ed* (Brown, 1973, pp. 334–335); until it appears, the only way children can signal whether they mean an earlier episode or the present episode is by some adverbial phrase. Usually we must rely on our impression of the child's intent in the given situation of use; in nearly every case, that results in interpreting the child's simple past as meaning what an adult's present perfect would mean.

According to the weak form of the argument, children are able to talk about any remote past event by using the simple past construction, but the reason that they seldom do so is that it is difficult for them to "decenter" in time until about age 6 (Cromer, 1968, 1971). According to the strong form of the argument, children *are* able to remember past events that are not part of the current situation, but they seldom talk about them because they have not mastered the tense system well enough to use it to indicate an antecedent reference time. I tend to favor the strong version because I believe I can detect more reluctance and difficulty in children's accounts of remote past episodes than the weak version would predict. I do not have conclusive evidence to support my bias, but Harner's (1976) report that children between the ages of 2 and 4 years understand references to remote past events as well as they understand references to an action just completed is at least compatible with the argument that expressive, not conceptual, difficulties tend to confine their own references to the immediate past.

My picture of the child's tense system at this early stage, therefore, is that it is entirely in the current indicative mood (see [10] above) and might be represented as follows (where the hypothesized conceptual representations are associated with their respective linguistic expressions):

(11)

	Child	Adult
Simple present	N_e: It happen(s)	N_rN_e: It happens
Present perfect	P_e: It happened	N_rP_e: It has happened

At this age children seldom use *-ed* in the historical indicative mood because they seldom talk about episodes that are over and done with—either because they have not mastered the full tense system, or because they cannot decenter in time, or both. We can say this in different ways, as we saw earlier. In Reichenbach's terminology, we can say the child either does not use a reference time or that the child's reference time is always the present. Or, in Thorne's terminology, we can say the child does not attach a tense to the mood or that the child always attaches the present tense to the mood. My preference is to say that the child does not use the tense system to establish a reference time (or does not attach a tense to the mood). I believe that the child at this age uses a single tense operator and that the one learned first is the event–time operator, N_e and P_e. At this age children do not think of *-ed* as shifting the time of reference, which they can do only contextually, if at all.

However we say it, the hypothesis should be reasonably clear. The pastness that a child adds to a verb when he adds *-ed* is not the same pastness that an adult adds, but is rather a past-in-the-present, a pastness with present reference that the adult's *-ed* alone does not express. I think that this account helps to reduce the other puzzle I mentioned, namely, how a child, whose language is otherwise very concrete, comes to form such an abstract concept as pastness. If the present argument is right, a young child's expressions of pastness are not all that abstract—they are nearly always relevant to concrete events in the present episode, to the here and now.

Developmentally, one can argue that children first form a concept of past-in-the-present—that they begin to feel a need to make this distinction in their own speech—and discover the dental suffix as a way to express it. Other uses of -ed in adult speech do not interfere with this discovery; lacking the concepts these other uses express, the exceptions must seen to children as irrelevant to the -ed rule as would *bed, sled, hatred,* or *quadruped* to an adult. Children ignore them *because* they do not conform to the concept they are learning to express. That is to say, the rule must be that pastness implies -ed, not that -ed implies pastness. If a child starts with the concept, he can find a way to express it; if he started with -ed, he would never find the concept it expresses. Thus, as Lenneberg said, pastness is first learned as a semantic phenomenon.

This completes what I have to say about Lenneberg's comment on this aspect of child language. Given the occasion, I am glad that I have convinced myself—and the reader, I hope—that he was right, that the concept must come first. The story is incomplete, however, since nothing has been said about how children go on to master the perfectives or how their -ed verbs change in meaning from that of the adult's present perfect to the adult's simple past. That, to borrow a cliché, is a problem for further research (see, for example, Cromer, 1971; Nussbaum & Naremore, 1975). There is always something more to learn; I think Eric would have liked it that way.

ACKNOWLEDGMENTS

I am indebted to James P. Thorne and Roger Brown for very helpful comments on earlier drafts of this chapter.

REFERENCES

Berko, J. The child's learning of English morphology. *Word,* 1958, *14,* 150–177.
Brown, R. *A first language; the early stages.* Cambridge: Harvard University Press, 1973.
Clark, H. H., & Stafford, R. A. Memory for semantic features in the verb. *Journal of Experimental Psychology,* 1969, *80,* 326–334.
Cromer, R. F. *The development of temporal reference during the acquisition of language.* Ph.D. dissertation, Harvard University, 1968.
Cromer, R. F. The development of the ability to decenter in time. *British Journal of Psychology,* 1971, *62,* 353–365.
Harner, L. Children's understanding of linguistic reference to past and future. *Journal of Psycholinguistic Research,* 1976, *5,* 65–84.
Katz, J. J. *Semantic theory.* New York: Harper & Row, 1972.

Lenneberg, E. H. *Biological foundations of language*. New York: Wiley, 1967.

Miller, G. A., & Johnson-Laird, P. N. *Language and perception*. Cambridge: Harvard University Press, 1976.

Nussbaum, N. J., & Naremore, R. C. On the acquisition of present perfect *have* in normal children. *Language and Speech*, 1975, *18*, 219–226.

Palmer, F. R. *A linguistic study of the English verb*. London: Longmans, 1965.

Reichenbach, H. *Elements of symbolic logic*. New York: Macmillan, 1947.

Rescher, N., & Urquhart, A. *Temporal logic*. New York: Springer-Verlag, 1971.

Twaddell, W. F. *The English verb auxiliaries* (2nd ed.). Providence: Brown University Press, 1963.

chapter 10

Conflict and Progress[1]

HERMINE SINCLAIR

INTRODUCTION

Eric Lenneberg, like Jean Piaget, sought to discover the biological foundations of human capacities. Lenneberg's prime interest was in language, and biology is prominent in the title of his important work, *Biological Foundations of Language* (1967). Piaget has never studied language per se; his main interest is in the growth of knowledge, and one of his works is entitled *Biologie et Connaissance* (1967). Whereas Lenneberg combined neurology and psychology into a neurobiological approach to language, Piaget combines biology and epistemology into a biopsychology of knowledge. The different starting points explain a divergency of aims. Lenneberg's main interest was in the functioning of the human brain as a hierarchically organized system and, thence, in the structures that make such functioning

[1] The experimental work on which this paper is based was, in part, made possible by subventions from the Fonds National Suisse de la Recherche Scientifique, F.N. 1.133.69 and F.N. 1.190.75.

187

PSYCHOLOGY AND BIOLOGY OF LANGUAGE AND THOUGHT
Essays in Honor of Eric Lenneberg

possible. Piaget's search for biological continuity is focused on the biological mechanisms that are at work at all levels—from the cellular to the behavioral—of the organism's interaction with the environment. In his view, the continuity is to be found in the regulatory mechanisms, especially in those autoregulations that not only reestablish an existing equilibrium that has been perturbed, but transform it into a superior one. As to the phylogenetic levels where these transformations take place, Piaget (1970) did no more than speculate that they would be found in "the development of associative pathways in the brain (which are neither afferent nor efferent) [p. 70]." Our insight into what human language is, how it functions, and what makes it possible will certainly be greatly enhanced when, in the future, the two approaches—Lenneberg's and Piaget's—are combined.

Since my personal interest is mainly in young children's cognitive development and their acquisition of language, I will give two examples of the way Piaget's theory on cognitive processes throws light on modes of acquisition: One example concerns the concept of length, or more generally, measurement; the other concerns temporal relationships in language. By way of an introduction, I will try to give a general view of how Piaget conceives of the biological continuity between the organizational processes of all living organisms and the various forms of knowledge.

Instinctive behavior is the prototype of innate knowledge; the content and form of instinctive activities appear to be determined totally by genetic programming. However, regulatory processes are always present: Variations occur in the succession of activities, there is resumption of activity after interruption, there are correspondences between male and female action-sequences, etc. Moreover, in certain cases, the individual organism's instinctive behavior can be adjusted to unforeseen situations, although this capacity remains fairly limited, at least up to the level of the primates. In man, it is not that a totally new way of knowing, that is, intelligence, replaces the old, instinctive way of adaptation. It is rather that intelligence inherits this organic way of adaptation, but by means of a dissociation, that is, a liberation from specific context. The fundamental organizational principles of instinctual behavior become the basis for what Piaget calls "a new organ of deductive verification and of construction [1967, p. 420]"—intelligence. What disappears almost totally is the genetic preprogramming; what remain as a source for new constructions are the regulatory mechanisms and the phenotypic adjustments to new circumstances. Despite the hereditary character of the cerebralized nervous system, this constitutes a new departure; but it uses old ways of functioning that are deeply anchored in the organization of all living beings.

In human development, this detachment of a pattern or form of action from its specific content is an important aspect of the elaboration of cognitive structures. In Piaget's view, the preverbal, sensorimotor level of intelligence is characterized by the construction of action patterns ("*schèmes d'action*") that become liberated from particular actions on particular objects. Starting from a built-in grasping movement, for example, the infant will close his or her hand on many objects. After a while, he or she will acquire something like "the idea of grasping," and once this is acquired, it can be combined with "the idea of looking at." A new, more complex, possibility for action is created: grasping what one looks at and looking at what one grasps. This new activity will, in turn, be applied in many situations; and once again, a new pattern becomes detached from its content and is ready to be combined with yet other patterns. On the one hand, these forms of action become better and better adjusted to the properties of the objects; on the other hand, regulatory mechanisms ensure the efficacy of their combinations, thus creating more and more powerful capacities for action. The adjustment of the actions to the properties of the objects and situations is an extension of the phenotypic adjustments to unforeseen circumstances; the various forms of coordination needed for combining action patterns are extensions of the regulatory mechanisms affecting innate behavior.

With reference to the higher levels of intellectual functioning, it is possible to speak of an "awareness" of one's own actions and mental operations that leads to the construction of operations on operations and the development of formal logico-mathematical constructs. At the lower levels, during the preverbal period and until the age of 4 or 5, the term "awareness" cannot be used in the sense of conscious reflection on the subject's own reasoning procedures; it must be taken in the sense of a gradual interiorization of the action patterns in their general form, on the one hand, and a deeper apprehension of object properties, on the other. In a sense, "awareness" in the infant and the very young child can be seen as "intention" and "meaning." This awareness, or the reflection on one's own actions, is a psychological event; the genetic system determines, at all levels, the possibilities of reacting and acting, but this is not something that can be felt or thought about. It may be supposed that the nervous system forms a network of connections inside which neurons function in a way analogous to propositional logic or Boolean algebra (see Piaget's discussion [1967, p. 256] of the work of McCulloch and Pitt), but it does not follow that such neuronal organizations are cognitive mechanisms in themselves, and it appears impossible that we should become aware of their functioning and constitute our reasoning patterns through this awareness.

The terms "*action patterns*," "*operations*," and "*coordinations*" are all symptomatic of a conception in which living organisms are seen as complex epigenetic systems of interaction with the environment. Although genetic characteristics and innate modes of behavior differ from species to species, the most general processes at work in all interaction with the environment are the regulatory mechanisms that constitute the condition for hereditary transmission, reestablish the organism's equilibrium when a change in his interaction with the environment has created a disturbance, and, in the most interesting cases, transform an already attained equilibrium into a superior one.

In this way, Piaget justifies his view of cognitive functioning as a special case of biological adaptation. Intelligence is an extension of the organic and instinctive way of knowing, and cognitive mechanisms are specialized and differentiated organs of regulation in the subject's interactions with his environment. Disturbances should not be thought of as coming primarily from the environment; it should be emphasized that they occur in the interaction between the organism and its environment, and that they may, in many cases, be due mainly to a factor inherent in the organism, such as differences in rates of development of certain functions that modify its overall organization.

Early human development provides us with many examples of disequilibria that occur because a primitive overall organization falls apart into components that develop at different speeds; a later organization at a higher level will then recompose the parts into a new superior totality (Mounoud, 1976). In the first weeks after birth, the infant can easily put his hand into his mouth (due to a complex organization of postural reflexes), but by the age of 2 or 3 months he or she can no longer do so in certain positions; similarly, the baby can at first suckle and look at something at the same time, but later has to relearn the coordination between looking and other activities. At a more advanced level of development, good examples are provided by what happens in the acquisition of certain notions of conservation.

Conservation has been extensively studied in Geneva, first by Piaget, Szeminska, and Inhelder (Piaget & Szeminska, 1941; Piaget & Inhelder, 1941; Piaget, Inhelder, & Szeminska, 1948) and later by many of their collaborators. Quantitative properties, such as number, length, or area, remain invariant under certain transformations of objects: As long as nothing is added or taken away, folding a piece of paper changes its shape but not its size, bending a wire does not change its length, etc. To the very young child, such properties are inextricably bound up with all the other properties of the object, and he or she has no way of thinking about one or the other separately—in fact, questions on such problems have no sense for the child. When a red pipe cleaner is twisted in front of his eyes, he knows that it is still the same pipe cleaner—it is still red and a bit soft and, especially, the child can still play with it. Even when length, area, and surface have become properties the child can think about in relation to many different objects, certain changes in shape may be surprising, and he or she will be convinced that along with the shape, other properties have changed as well. This is the well-known phenomenon of nonconservation; the complex physical or geometrical systems that link mass, density, weight, and volume or length, area, and volume into coherent totalities fall apart into their components where cognitive elaboration proceeds at differing speeds, creating various internal disequilibria, before the components are recombined into a more powerful system of relations.

Let us look at one example in some detail. One of the first concepts of conservation to become established as an intellectual construct is that of numerosity. When number becomes something the child can think about as a particular property of any collection of objects, he will at first consider that a rearrangement of the objects so that they spatially "go beyond" the original arrangement has an effect on their number; they are thought to be more numerous. But quite soon (say, around the age of 5) the child will separate the spatial "going beyond" from number and realize that a gain in spaced-outness is compensated for by a loss in crowdedness; that "take away" or "add" bear on number, but that "space out" or "crowd together" do not. This is an important acquisition which precedes by several years a very similar construction of the concept of length. Until about the age of 5, number, length, and other properties are indissociable; comparisons of collections or objects with such properties will be solved by the "going beyond" principle (which, in many cases, works perfectly well). Later, number will be part of the full-fledged concept of measurement of length (at about age 7 or 8). But in between, the numerical component "splits off" and becomes accessible to a thought structure that then will incorporate the length concept.

In a series of learning experiments (Inhelder, Sinclair, & Bovet, 1974) many children made considerable progress in various conservation concepts during regular sessions over several weeks. These studies provide a better understanding of the different substages an individual child goes through, and they exemplify the working of the regulatory mechanisms.

In one of the studies (Inhelder et al., 1974, Chap. 6), toy houses glued on matchsticks (about 6 cm long) are used. When the sticks are set in a straight line, they form a row of villas along a straight road. When two such roads are set up, one directly beneath the other, children of about 5 will affirm that the roads are the same, that they are just as long, and that there are just as many houses along one road as along the other. When the disposition of one line of matchsticks plus houses is changed into a zigzag, so that the straight road goes beyond the zigzag road, they assert that the zigzag road is shorter, and that there are fewer houses along it (see Figure 10.1). Both properties, length and number, are judged by the same principle (which in this case is not opposite). In a subsequent phase of the learning sessions, a curious split

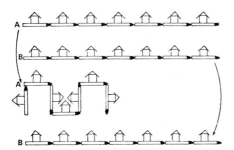

Figure 10.1. Line of matchsticks plus houses forming a straight road and a zig-zag road. (From Inhelder *et al.*, 1974. Reprinted by permission.)

appears. The children who have progressed, or those who at the start were slightly more advanced, tell us quite clearly that, of course, the number of houses has not changed; there are still exactly the same number as before we made the road into a zigzag—nothing was taken away, was it? and nothing was added. And anyway, you could put the zigzag road back into a straight line, and you'd see it.

> *Yes. And how about the length of the road?*
>
> *Oh well, obviously the straight road is longer. It goes farther, doesn't it?*
>
> *Yes, well how about the bits of wood, the sticks that make up the roads, they are the same, aren't they?*
>
> *Yes, of course. But the zigzag road is shorter; you don't have to go as far.*

Not only do these children apply different modes of reasoning to the number problem and to the length problem, but they are not disturbed by the discrepancy. In the next phase, in contrast, their equanimity is upset. When put to it, they may, reluctantly and without much conviction, admit the equality of the roads. But they may also go back to denying the equality of the number of houses. Notice that this conflict is not between a judgment and reality, as when a child predicts that a big wooden block will sink, and it turns out that it floats. In the number and length problem the conflict is between two patterns of thought.

The next phase is more clearly illustrated by what happens when the children are asked to construct straight roads equal in length to zigzag roads set up by the experimenter. The children are given shorter matchsticks than those used by the experimenter (proportion 5 to 7 cm), and they have to construct their roads in three different situations. At a certain level, situation 1 (see Figure 10.2) is solved by the not-going-beyond principle; the children use four sticks and are perfectly satisfied. In situation 2, they are again asked to construct a road of equal length to the experimenter's road in situation 1, but this time not directly underneath it. The not-going-beyond principle

Figure 10.2. Illustration of the not-going-beyond principle in situation 1. (From Inhelder *et al.*, 1974. Reprinted by permission.)

cannot be applied in this case; the children's idea of number (which neglects the difference in length of the sticks) comes into play, and they conclude that five sticks in a straight line is the right solution. Situation 3, where the experimenter's road is straight (see Figure 10.3), is once again solved by the not-going-beyond principle, correct in this case, with the use of seven sticks. No contradiction is felt, not even when the children are explicitly asked to count the sticks in the two roads of situation 3. But at a slightly higher level, when they are asked to count, conflict becomes very clear. The children will either doubt the numerical result ("I must have counted wrong") or they will give up and ask for different matchsticks ("with these, it can't be done"). Next the children go in for interesting compromise solutions, such as breaking sticks into bits, so as to be able to count five in situation 1 without "going beyond"; at this point they no longer doubt their own counting, nor the correct solution to situation 3, but situation 1 baffles them, and situation 2 (straight road made away from the zigzag model) does not benefit from transitivity reasoning; it is solved by using five sticks. Only in the last phase (reached after six or seven sessions, and not by all the subjects who took part in the experiment) is the problem solved by a perfect readjustment of the different thought patterns: The children understand the necessity of a double compensation (between number and length of the sticks, and between the extent to which the straight road goes beyond the other and the latter's zigzags), and the transitivity principle crowns the new organization. From situation 3, the answer to 1 and 2 is immediately deduced: seven sticks. This type of construction, which in cognitive development is the rule rather than the exception, does not resemble an acquisition process based on associationist, empiricist principles, nor does it represent the gradual unfolding of a program that is determined in its form as well as in its content.

In language acquisition, similar mechanisms seem to be at work. Let us take an example from Ferreiro's experiments on temporal relationships (1971). One of her studies concerned children's growing mastery of the means that speakers of French use to express the correct succession of two events *P* and *Q*, when starting their description with event *Q*. Several means can be used, either separately or in combination. In the utterance *He*

Figure 10.3. Illustration of the not-going-beyond principle in situation 3. (From Inhelder *et al.*, 1974. Reprinted by permission.)

ordered a sandwich; he had walked a long way, the tenses make the sequence clear. Tenses can be combined with subordination: *He drove away when he had eaten his sandwich; Before he drove away, he ate his sandwich.* Adverbs can perform this function as well: *He drove away, but first he ate his sandwich,* etc.

In Ferreiro's experiments, simple, noncausally linked actions were performed in front of the children; for example, in a dollhouse, a girl doll washed a boy doll's face, and then the boy doll went upstairs. This example will be used throughout, the first event being indicated by P, the second by Q, the agent of P by x, and the agent of Q by y. First the children were asked to describe in their own way what they had been shown (free-choice description). Then they were asked: "Tell me again what happened—look, I'll show you again—but I want you to start off with talking about the boy [y] (going upstairs)" (inverse-order description).[2] Questions were then asked about the temporal relationship, such as: "When did x . . . ?" "When did y . . . ?" If correctly answered, question plus response can provide a correct inverse-order description (e.g., "When did y go upstairs? When x had washed him" → "y went upstairs when x had washed him"). After these "when" questions, the children were once again asked for an inverse-order description. The total event was acted out as often as necessary.

Working with children between the ages of 4 and 10, Ferreiro found the following development in the ways children have of dealing with the different instructions and questions.

1. The youngest, least advanced children give their free-choice description most often, but not always, in the order P, Q. The two propositions are loosely linked by *and* or *and then* ("*et*" or "*et puis*"); the verbs are in the same tense, either present or past. Their inverse-order description is simply Q *and* P. Their answers to the "when" questions are: *now, right now,* or *just a moment ago.* In other words, two noncausally linked events are simply related as two things that happened; the order of the description is not felt as a necessary indication of the temporal sequence.[3] The "when" questions do receive a temporal answer (*now*), they are indeed understood as bearing on a temporal relation, but the answer simply relates P and Q, each in turn, to the moment of speaking—not to each other. The system works well, and no conflict is engendered by the instructions.

[2] This instruction was given in various ways. Its aim was simply to obtain a description of event Q before that of P. In some cases, as in the example given, agent y was patient x, and theoretically it would have been possible to use a passive form for the description of p. None of the younger children did this, however; if it was attempted, we specified our intention by adding "going upstairs."

[3] The use of "*et puis*" could therefore be interpreted as "and then there was another thing to tell you."

2. At the next level, all free-choice descriptions follow the sequence of events. The same tense is used for P and for Q. The "when" questions now begin to be understood as bearing upon the relation between the two events, and are often correctly answered, although the children seem to order the agents rather than the events: "When did the boy go upstairs?" Answer: *After the girl; He was second.* "When did the girl wash the boy?" Answer: *She was first; Before the boy.* The inverse-order description is still handled in the same way as at the first level; however, these children are very hesitant in their inverse-order descriptions—they do comply with the instruction, but in a rather doubting manner.

3. At a slightly higher level, the conflict arises in full-fledged form. At this stage, the order of the propositions becomes an absolute indication of the order of the events expressed: the first event, first; the second, second. These children feel that it is not possible to start the descriptions with event Q (or agent y): *It would come out wrong; It would be the wrong way around.* On the other hand, they answer the "when" questions, both on event P and on event Q, correctly: "When P?" *Before Q.* "When Q?" *After P.* Apparently they can place one event in temporal relation to another if one of them is given, as the experimenter does with the "when" questions. In other words, they can establish two separate relationships—P is anterior to Q, and Q is posterior to P—but these mappings are one-way and cannot be deduced one from the other. When the children themselves have to construct the temporal succession Q, P, they cannot manage it. They propose various solutions, often rejecting them immediately afterward. These solutions frequently have one of the following features:

a. There is curious inversion of the action performed by the agent of the second event; in the example given, "the boy goes upstairs" becomes "the boy goes downstairs." The total event is described as follows by a subject aged 5:10: *He goes downstairs again and the girl washes his hands.*

b. Another curious inversion occurs between the agents of events P and Q. The action performed in the second event is attributed to the agent of the first event and vice versa: *The boy goes and washes the girl's face and then it's she that goes upstairs* (subject aged 5:5).

c. A kind of neutral action is attributed to the agent of the second event. In this way the difficulty is avoided. It becomes possible to describe the events in their correct succession without having to introduce linguistic means that perform this function. In this solution, the children describe an action they invent themselves, and then continue with the events they have actually seen: *The boy came and waited a bit, the girl washed his face, and then he went upstairs* (subject aged 5:11).

These compromise solutions are highly interesting. The children seem to know that the inversion introduced by the instruction to start with event Q has to be compensated for by some other modification for the description to fit the observed sequence of events. However, they cannot yet hit on the right way of doing this, although all the verbal means (*before, after; later, but first; already*) are at their disposal, as is clear from their answers to the "when" questions.

4.   The most advanced subjects give correct answers to all problems. In many cases, subordinate temporal clauses are used in the free-choice description. The "when" questions receive immediate correct answers, and even if there are still many false starts and hesitations for the inverse-order description, the correct sequence is finally expressed through the use of conjunctions, adverbs, and tenses (though the latter sometimes receive rather unusual treatment). The most advanced subjects (generally around the age of 9) are capable of giving several formulations, such as: *The boy will go upstairs after the girl has washed him; The boy went upstairs after the girl had cleaned him up.*

A close parallelism seems to exist between the different substages the children go through in the temporal relationship problems and those that were observed during the experiments on the concept of length. A similar case can be made for children's gradual mastery of the production of passive sentences (Sinclair & Ferreiro, 1970).

In the development of the basic logico-mathematical and physical notions this mode of development, that is, the "falling apart" of an overall, primitive organization, followed by conflict and trials to compensate for the conflict, and ending in a higher order organization, is frequent. In language acquisition it has rarely been noted. One reason for this would seem to be that experiments in the production of a certain sentence pattern have not often been performed; experimentation usually bears on comprehension, whereas production is usually studied through analysis of spontaneous utterances. In comprehension experiments, however, "dips" in performance are often recorded in cross-sectional studies; one might hazard the guess that such dips correspond to the period of conflict. Another, more important reason may relate to the following fact. The basic logical and physical notions are necessary for consistency within one's own reasoning or for correspondence between one's judgment and what happens in reality. They are acquired in much the same way by children in very different cultural settings. The same is not true of linguistic structures, such as temporal subordinate clauses or passive sentences. These do not occur in all languages, and where they do occur, there does not seem to be any necessity to use them. Their function may be stylistic, or they may serve to indicate presuppositions and topicalizations, but there does not appear to be any class of events or mental constructs that demands a passive sentence or a temporal reversal for its expression. In fact, in order to obtain temporal inverse-order descriptions, Ferreiro had to use a rather artificial form of instruction, just as was necessary to obtain passive sentences. This constitutes a severe limitation on experimental techniques in production. A third, and last, reason for the present paucity of precise experimental examples of regulatory processes in language acquisition is to be sought in the fact that it is far more difficult to isolate components inside a linguistic structure than it is to do so in a cognitive construct such as conservation of length or measurement.

These cautionary remarks reflect the state of our relative ignorance about the constructive processes in language acquisition. Nevertheless, I think that the parallelism between the two examples is no mere superficial resemblance, and I would like to offer it as a detailed illustration of two theoretical statements, made by Piaget and Inhelder (1969) and Lenneberg (1967), respectively:

> There is the question of an overall equilibrium between structures: the conflicts between different sectors of knowledge can thus help to create a disequilibrium which in turn engenders new equilibration by means of reflexive abstractions and self-regulations [Piaget & Inhelder, 1969, p. 146].

> It might be more fruitful to think of maturation as the traversing of highly unstable states, the disequilibrium of one leading to rearrangements that bring about new disequilibria, producing further rearrangements, and so on until relative stability, known as *maturity* is reached [Lenneberg, 1967, p. 376].

REFERENCES

Ferreiro, E. *Les relations temporelles dans le langage de l'enfant.* Genève: Droz, 1971.

Inhelder, B., Sinclair, H., & Bovet, M. *Apprentissage et structures de la connaissance.* Paris: Presses Universitaires de France, 1974. [Translation: *Learning and the development of cognition.* Cambridge: Harvard University Press, 1975.]

Lenneberg, E. H. *Biological foundations of language.* New York: Wiley, 1967.

Mounoud, P. Les révolutions dans le développement du bébé. *Archives de Psychologie,* 1976, 171, 103–115.

Piaget, J. *Biologie et connaissance.* Paris: Gallimard, 1967. [Translation: *Biology and knowledge.* Chicago: University of Chicago Press, 1971.]

Piaget, J. *L'epistémologie génétique.* Paris: Presses Universitaires de France, 1970.

Piaget, J., & Inhelder, B. *Le développement des quantités physiques chez l'enfant.* Paris and Neuchâtel: Delachaux et Niestlé, 1941.

Piaget, J., & Inhelder, B. 1969. The gaps in empiricism. In A. Koestler & J. R. Smithies (Eds.), *Beyond reductionism.* Boston: Beacon Press, 1969.

Piaget, J., Inhelder, B., & Szeminska, A. *La géometrie spontanée de l'enfant*. Paris: Presses Universitaires de France, 1948. [Translation: *The child's conception of geometry*. New York: Basic Books, 1960.]

Piaget, J., & Szeminska, A. *La genèse du nombre chez l'enfant*. Paris and Neuchâtel: Delachaux et Niestlé, 1941. [Translation: *The child's conception of number*. London: Routledge and Kegan Paul, 1952.]

Sinclair, H., & Ferreiro, E. Etude génétique de la compréhension, production, et répétition des phrases au mode passif. *Archives de Psychologie*, 1970, 160, 1–42.

chapter 11

On the Biological Basis of Language Capacities[1]

NOAM CHOMSKY

The title of this chapter, of course, is taken from Eric Lenneberg's major study of language and biology (1967), now recognized as a classic in the field. He set himself the task of studying language as "an aspect of [man's] biological nature, to be studied in the same manner as, for instance, his anatomy."[2] The purpose of this study was "to reinstate the concept of the biological basis of language capacities and to make the specific assumptions so explicit that they may be subjected to empirical tests." Adopting this point of view, we may regard the language capacity virtually as we would a physical organ of the body and can investigate the principles of its organization, functioning, and development in the individual and the species. Personally, I feel that this is just the right way to approach the study of human language. I would like to make a few comments on the program that

---

[1] This chapter was first published in R. W. Rieber (Ed.), *The Neuropsychology of Language*, New York: Plenum Press, 1976. It is reprinted here with only minor revisions by permission of the author and publisher.

[2] This and the following quotations are from Lenneberg (1967), pp. 393–394.

Lenneberg outlined and developed, concentrating on two theses that seem to me of particular significance.

In his concluding discussion, Lenneberg (1967) presented two important observations on the nature of the inquiry into language and biology. He noted in the first place that

> The rules that underly syntax (which are the same for understanding and speaking) are of a very specific kind, and unless man or mechanical devices do their processing of incoming sentences in accordance with these rules, the logical, formal analysis of the input will be deficient, resulting in incorrect or random responses. When we say rules must have been built into the grammatical analyzer, we impute the existence of an apparatus with specific structural properties or, in other words, a specific internal organization.

He then observed that the fundamental question in the study of the biology of language is: "Just what is postulated to be innate in language behavior?" Evidently, "we must assume a biological matrix with specifiable characteristics that determines the outcome of any treatment to which the organism is subjected." The evidence, he argued, points "to great specificity of the underlying matrix." The "only thoroughly interesting problem" is to determine the range of possibilities that might be realized under given environmental conditions, this range is evidently determined by the biological matrix. It is, he emphasized correctly, "entirely an empirical question"; there is no room for dogmatic preconceptions or a priori argument. Biology, he observed,

> does no more than to discover how various forms are innately constituted, and this includes descriptions of a creature's reactions to environmental forces. Research into these reactions does not eventually free us from the postulation of innate features, but merely elucidates the exact nature of innate constitutions. The discovery and description of innate mechanisms is a thoroughly empirical procedure and is an integral part of modern scientific inquiry.

When I met Eric Lenneberg as a graduate student, just 25 years ago, these basic concerns were beginning to take shape in his mind. He wanted to see the study of language assimilated to the natural sciences, and he devoted his subsequent efforts to placing language in its biological matrix. From the point of view he was to adopt, the study of systems of grammar is concerned with the "specific internal organization" and "specific structural properties" of an "apparatus" to which we "impute existence" as one component in the system of cognitive structures developed in the course of individual growth. What many linguists call "universal grammar" may be regarded as a theory of innate mechanisms, an underlying biological matrix that provides a framework within which the growth of language proceeds. There is no reason for the linguist to refrain from imputing existence to this initial apparatus of mind as well. Proposed principles of universal grammar may be regarded as an abstract, partial specification of the genetic program that enables the child to interpret certain events as linguistic experience and to construct a system of rules and principles on the basis of this experience.

To put the matter in somewhat different but essentially equivalent terms, we may suppose that there is a fixed, genetically determined initial state of the mind, common to the species with at most minor variation apart from pathology. The mind passes through a sequence of states under the boundary conditions set by experience, achieving finally a "steady state" at a relatively fixed age, a state that then changes only in marginal ways. The basic property of this initial state is that, given experience, it develops to the steady state. Correspondingly, the initial state of the mind might be regarded as a function, characteristic of the species, that maps experience into the steady state. Universal grammar is a partial characterization of this function, of this initial state. The grammar of a language that has grown in the mind is a partial characterization of the steady state attained.

So viewed, linguistics is the abstract study of certain mechanisms, their growth and maturation. We may impute existence to the postulated structures at the initial, intermediate, and steady states in just the same sense as we impute existence to a program that we believe to be somehow represented in a computer or that we postulate to account for the mental representation of a three-dimensional object in the visual field. Evidence bearing on empirical hypotheses such as these might derive from many and varied sources. Ultimately, we hope to find evidence concerning the physical mechanisms that realize the program; it is reasonable to expect that results obtained in the abstract study of the program and its operation should contribute significantly to this end (and, in principle, conversely; that is, information regarding the mechanisms might contribute to understanding of the program).

In the case of the study of language, the question is complicated in practice by the obvious fact that the system of language is only one of a number of cognitive systems that interact in the most intimate way in the actual use of language. When we speak or interpret what we hear, we bring to bear a vast set of background assumptions about the participants in the discourse, the subject matter under discussion, laws of nature, human institutions, and the like. Continuing to think of the system of grammatical rules as a kind of "mental organ," interacting with other mental organs with other functions and properties, we face a rather typical problem of natural science, namely, the problem of appropriate idealization and abstraction. In an effort to determine the nature of one of these interacting systems, we must abstract away from the contribution of others to the actual performance that can be observed. Steps taken in this direction are not without their hazards;

they are also inescapable in rational inquiry. We therefore proceed to experiment with idealized systems, always bearing in mind the possibility that another approach might lead us closer to an understanding of the various systems that constitute the human mind.

There is much discussion in the literature of linguistics and psychology of the "psychological reality" of the linguist's constructions. I take it that the question at issue is whether it is legitimate to "impute existence" to the "apparatus," the properties of which are characterized by particular grammars or by universal grammar (which is, of course, not a grammar but rather a system of conditions on the range of possible grammars for possible human languages). The discussion of "psychological reality" sometimes seems to me to be rather misleading. Perhaps I can explain my misgivings by an analogy.[3]

Consider the problem of determining the nature of the thermonuclear reactions that take place deep in the interior of the sun. Suppose that available technique permits astronomers to study only the light emitted at the outermost layers of the sun. On the basis of the information thereby attained, they construct a theory of the hidden thermonuclear reactions, postulating that light elements are fused into heavier ones that convert mass into energy, thus producing the sun's heat. Suppose that an astronomer presents such a theory, citing the evidence that supports it. Suppose now that someone were to approach this astronomer with the following contention: "True, you have presented a theory that explains the available evidence, but how do you know that the constructions of your theory have physical reality—in short, how do you know that your theory is true?" The astronomer could respond only by repeating what he had already presented; here is the evidence available and here is the theory that I offer to explain it. The evidence derives from investigation of light emitted at the periphery. We might want to place a laboratory inside the sun to obtain more direct evidence, but being unable to do so, we must test and confirm our theory indirectly. One might argue that the evidence is inconclusive or that the theory is objectionable on some physical (or, conceivably, methodological) grounds. But it is senseless to ask for some other kind of justification for attributing physical reality to the constructions of the theory, apart from consideration of their adequacy in explaining the evidence and their conformity to the body of natural science as currently understood. There can be no other grounds for attributing physical reality to the scientist's constructions.

Suppose now that an ingenious experimenter hits upon a more direct method for studying events taking place at the interior of the sun: Namely, studying of the neutrinos that are released by the assumed thermonuclear

---

[3] The analogy is modeled on an account given by Bahcall and Davis (1976).

reactions in the solar interior and that escape into space. Using this new evidence, he may substantiate the old theory or construct a better one. Has this more "direct" investigation of events in the interior of the sun now answered the original objections? Are we now entitled to attribute "a higher order of physical reality" to the constructions that were only postulated before? Not really. No empirical evidence can be conclusive. Again, we can only say that with our more direct and more conclusive evidence, we may now be more confident than before that the entities and events postulated are physically real—that the theoretical statements in which reference is made to these entities, processes, and so on are, in fact, true. But again, there is little sense to the contention that we still do not know that what is postulated is physically real, as if there were some further standard that might be achieved in some qualitatively different way. The enterprise in question is empirical science, not mathematics; at best, we can settle on one of indefinitely many possible theories that account for crucial evidence, attributing physical reality to whatever is postulated in that theory.

Our investigation of the apparatus of the language faculty, whether in its initial or final steady state, bears some similarity to the investigation of thermonuclear reactions in the solar interior that is limited to evidence provided by light emitted at the periphery. We observe what people say and do, how they react and respond, often in situations contrived so that this behavior will provide some evidence (we hope) concerning the operative mechanisms. We then try, as best we can, to devise a theory of some depth and significance with regard to these mechanisms, testing our theory by its success in providing explanations for selected phenomena. Challenged to show that the constructions postulated in that theory have "psychological reality," we can do no more than repeat the evidence and the proposed explanations that involve these constructions. Or, like the astronomer dissatisfied with study of light emissions from the periphery of the sun, we can search for more conclusive evidence, always aware that in empirical inquiry we can, at best, support a theory against substantive alternatives and empirical challenge; we cannot prove it to be true. It would be quite reasonable to argue against a claim for psychological reality— that is, truth of a certain theory—on the grounds that the evidence is weak and susceptible to explanation in different terms; needless to say, the evidence that supports the linguist's constructions is incomparably less satisfying than that available to the physicist. But in essence the problems are the same, and the question of psychological reality is no more and no less sensible in principle than the question of the physical reality of the physicist's theoretical constructions.

The literature takes a rather different view. Certain types of evidence are held to relate to psychological reality, specifically, evidence deriving from studies of reaction time, recognition, recall, etc. Other kinds of evidence are held to be of an entirely different nature, specifically, evidence deriving from informant judgments as to what sentences mean, whether they are well formed, and so on. Theoretical explanations advanced to explain evidence of the latter sort, it is commonly argued, have no claim to psychological reality, no matter how far-reaching, extensive, or persuasive the explanations may be, and no matter how firmly founded the observations offered as evidence. To merit the attribution of "psychological reality," the entities, rules, processes, components, etc., postulated in these explanatory theories must be confronted with evidence of the former category. If these theoretical constructions can be shown to play a role in the study of reaction time, etc., then perhaps we may attribute to them psychological reality. Note that what is apparently claimed is that there is some conceptual distinction between two kinds of theories, a distinction based on the nature of the evidence advanced to support them, not on the reliability of the evidence or the depth of the theories.

Let me illustrate with a concrete example, much simplified for the purposes of exposition. Suppose that we are concerned with the process of sentence-formation in colloquial English and we note that while some questions are judged to be well formed, others are not. Consider the sentence

(1)   *Violins are easy to play sonatas on.*

This sentence might, for example, be the answer to the question

(2)   *What instruments are easy to play sonatas on?*

But sentence (1) is not a possible answer to question (3):

(3)   *What kinds of music are violins easy to play on?*

In fact, (3) is not a well-formed question at all. Corresponding to (1) we have such questions as

(4)   *What violins are easy to play sonatas on?*

but not

(5)   *What sonatas are violins easy to play on?*

The distinction between (4) and (5) has been repeatedly noted in recent discussion; let us assume that careful inquiry shows it to be well founded. Thus (5), like (3), is just not a well-formed question in colloquial English. The problem with (5) and (3) cannot be that the questioned term (*sonatas* in (1)) is too far toward the end of the sentence, or that it is within a verb phrase complement, or the like. Thus there is nothing wrong with question (6), which corresponds to sentence (7) as (5) corresponds to (1):

(6)   *What sonatas did John want Bill to play on the violin?*

(7)   *John wanted Bill to play sonatas on the violin.*

Evidently, (6) conforms to the rules of English grammar, as these are represented somehow in our minds, in a way in which (5) does not. Many facts of this sort have been noticed in the literature of linguistics. Clearly, they call for explanation. If an interesting explanation is forthcoming, then these observations will have been demonstrated to be significant for the insight they provide into mental representations and the computations involving them.

Suppose now that someone were to advance the following explanation for the facts noted.[4] We know that *wh*-clauses are "islands" in the sense of Ross (1967). We say that a phrase is an "island" if it is immune to the application of rules that relate its parts to a position outside of the island. Thus to say that a *wh*-clause is an island is to say, in particular, that the rule of *wh*-movement that forms questions and relatives by moving such expressions as *who, what, what sonatas,* etc., to the left of a clause cannot be applied in general to a *wh*-expression within a *wh*-clause. For example, given the sentences of (8), we cannot form the corresponding questions of (9), questioning *the book*:

(8)   a. *We wondered [to whom John gave the book].*
      b. *We found out [who wrote the book].*
      c. *We did [what you asked us to do about the book].*

(9)   a. *What book did we wonder to whom John gave?*
      b. *What book did we find out who wrote?*
      c. *What book did we do what you asked us to do about?*

In sentences comparable to (8) but without the bracketed *wh*-clause, the phrase *the book* is accessible to the *wh*-movement rule for forming questions; compare (9'):

(9')   a. *What book did we say that John gave to Bill?*
       b. *What book did we find out that John wrote?*
       c. *What book did we ask you to tell Bill to do something about?*

From such examples, we might conclude that expressions that lie within *wh*-clauses, such as those bracketed in (8), are not accessible to the rule of question-formation. More generally, *wh*-clauses are "islands," immune to such rules as *wh*-movement. The explanation for this and other island phenomena lies in still deeper properties of rules of grammar, I believe, but we may put this matter aside for now.

---

[4] I think, incidentally, that the explanation outlined is essentially correct, but that does not matter with respect to the point at issue. For discussion, see Chomsky (1977).

Returning to sentence (1), suppose that the expression *to play sonatas on* in (1) is the residue of a *wh*-clause in the mental computation by which (1) is formed—in particular, the same clause that appears as an infinitival relative in (10), analogous to the finite relative in (11):

(10)   I found [$_{NP}$ a violin [$_S$ to play sonatas on]]^5

(11)   I found [$_{NP}$ a violin [$_S$ that you can play sonatas on]]

Suppose, in other words, that we postulate that there really is a *wh*-clause, perhaps the clause represented as in (12), at the stage of computation at which *wh*-movement applies to give ultimately the sentence (5):

(12)   [$_S$ which for PRO to play sonatas on *t*]^6

Then the rule of question-formation cannot apply to the phrase *sonatas,* just as it cannot apply to the phrase *the book* in (8), and for the same reason: application is blocked by the *wh*-clause island constraint, and ultimately, by the deeper properties of grammar from which this constraint derives.

Tentatively accepting this explanation, we impute existence to certain mental representations and to the mental computations that apply in a specific way to these mental representations. In particular, we impute existence to a representation in which (12) appears as part of the structure underlying (5) at a particular stage of derivation, and to the mental computation that produces this derivation, and ultimately produces (5), identified now as ungrammatical because the computation violates the *wh*-island constraint when the rule of *wh*-movement applies to *sonatas* in (12). We attribute psychological reality to the postulated representations and mental computations. In short, we propose (tentatively, hesitantly, etc.) that our theory is true. Have we gone beyond the bonds of what is legitimate and proper, in so doing?

I think not. Granting the vast differences in the nature of the evidence, the depth and explanatory power of the postulated principles, etc., still the argument sketched seems to me analogous in relevant respects to that of the physicist postulating certain processes in the interior of the sun. Of course, there are differences; the physicist is actually postulating physical entities and processes, while we are keeping to abstract conditions that unknown

---

[5] Assume here a conventional representation of phrase-markers, with a string between paired brackets assigned to the category labelling the bracket. Thus in (10) the phrase *to play sonatas on* is categorized as an S (sentence); *a violin to play sonatas on* as an NP (noun phrase); etc. Other bracketing is omitted here and below for simplicity of exposition.

[6] Take *t* to be the "trace" left by movement of *which* from the position where *t* appears in (12), in accordance with the trace theory of movement rules; cf. Chomsky (1975a, 1976), and references cited here. Take PRO to be an abstract "pronominal" form, which can in fact be regarded as an "uncontrolled trace"; cf. Chomsky (1977) for discussion.

mechanisms must meet. We might go on to suggest actual mechanisms, but we know that it would be pointless to do so in the present stage of our ignorance concerning the functioning of the brain. This, however, is not a relevant difference of principle. If we were able to investigate humans as we study other, defenseless organisms, we might very well proceed to inquire into the operative mechanisms by intrusive experimentation, by constructing controlled conditions for language growth, and so on, thus perhaps narrowing the gap between the language example and the astronomical example. The barriers to this direct investigation are ethical. We must be satisfied with quite indirect evidence, but no particular philosophical problems arise from this contingency, just as no such problems arise in the case of the astronomer limited to investigation of light emissions from the sun's periphery as compared with the astronomer studying neutrinos escaping from the solar interior.

There are many questions that may legitimately be raised about the hypothetical explanation that I have briefly outlined. Thus, one might ask how firm is the evidence, and how well supported independently are the principles on which the evidence is based? Let us examine these questions.

Consider first the question of the nature of the evidence. There is no reason why we cannot proceed to test and refine the initial judgments of well-formedness for colloquial English. For example, we might devise experimental tests of acceptability, and if these tests met appropriate empirical conditions, we might decide to rely on them to determine the adequacy of the judgments to which we have appealed here, recognizing, however, that "well-formedness" is a theoretical concept for which we cannot expect to find a precise set of necessary and sufficient operational criteria (a fact of no great moment in itself). Notice that it is a trivial point, though one often overlooked, that any test of acceptability must itself meet certain empirical conditions, just as an explanatory theory must meet such conditions. (See Chomsky, 1964, for some comments.) Some linguists have been bemused by the fact that the conditions that test the test are themselves subject to doubt and revision, believing that they have discovered some hidden paradox or circularity of reasoning (cf. Botha, 1973; Ney, 1975). In fact, they have simply rediscovered the fact that linguistics is not mathematics but rather a branch of empirical inquiry. Even if we were to grant that there is some set of observation sentences that constitute the bedrock of inquiry and are immune to challenge, it nevertheless remains true that theory must be invoked to determine to what, if anything, these pure and perfect observations attest, and here there is no Cartesian ground of certainty. All of this is, or should be, obvious. Many argue that the problems of empirical uncertainty can be overcome by restricting attention to a corpus, and some (e.g., Ney) seem to believe that this has been the practice of traditional grammar. That is untrue.

A corpus may contain examples of deviant or ungrammatical sentences, and any rational linguist will recognize the problem and try to assign to observed examples their proper status. Furthermore, any serious work on language uses "elicited" material, often "self-elicited," as, for example, in Jespersen's classic works and other work that deserves serious attention. And insofar as a corpus is used as a source of illustrative examples, we rely on the same intuitive judgments to select examples as we do in devising relevant examples with the aid of an informant (or ourselves). Restriction of grammatical analysis to a real corpus would be about as sensible as restriction of physics or biology to motion pictures of events happening about us in our normal lives.[7]

To consider what appears to be a more productive (as well as intellectually far more interesting) approach, we may turn to the second of the two questions raised above and try to put the principles used in the explanation to independent empirical test. One way to approach this question is by trying to explain the wh-clause island constraint itself in terms of deeper principles of grammar that have other consequences, thus opening the proposed explanation to a broader empirical challenge. Or, we may try to find other evidence bearing on the postulated analysis of (1), with the underlying mental representation including (12) and the mental computation postulated (see Chomsky, 1977, for discussion).

Suppose that both of these approaches prove eminently successful. Thus we establish the reliability of the judgments and give substantial independent evidence for the theoretical constructions, showing that the postulated principles explain many other facts of a similar nature, withstand empirical tests in English and other languages, etc. Would we then have provided evidence for the psychological reality of the mental representations and mental computations postulated? If I read the literature correctly, many linguists would still reject this conclusion, arguing that something else is needed to carry us over that qualitative barrier of principle that distinguishes purely hypothetical constructions from others to which we may properly attribute "psychological reality."

Suppose now that someone were to devise an experiment to test for the presence of a wh-clause in underlying representations—let us say, a recogni-

---

[7] To avoid a possible confusion, recall here that we are considering the problem of discovery of linguistic theory and of particular grammar, two enterprises that go hand in hand. Given a linguistic theory, it should be possible for the grammar to be determined merely from the kind of primary linguistic data available to the child. If linguistic theory (universal grammar) is regarded along these lines, as a function mapping experience into the final state attained, then linguistic theory must provide a "discovery procedure" for grammar from a corpus (along with whatever else is essential for the language learner). Each child provides an existence proof. For discussion and an outline of a possible theory of this general sort, see Chomsky (1955).

tion or recall experiment. Or let us really let down the bars of imagination and suppose that someone were to discover a certain pattern of electrical activity in the brain that correlated in clear cases with the presence of *wh*-clauses, relative clauses (finite and infinitival), and *wh*-questions (direct and indirect). Suppose that this pattern of electrical activity is observed when a person speaks or understands (1). Would we now have evidence for the psychological reality of the postulated mental representations?

We would now have a new kind of "evidence," but I see no merit to the contention that this new evidence bears on psychological reality whereas the old evidence only relates to hypothetical constructions. The new evidence might or might not be more persuasive than the old; that would depend on its character and reliability, the degree to which the principles dealing with this evidence are tenable, intelligible, compelling, and so on. In the real world of actual research on language, it would be fair to say, I think, that principles based on evidence derived from informant judgment have proved to be deeper and more revealing than those based on evidence derived from experiments on processing and the like, although the future may be different in this regard. If we accept—as I do—Lenneberg's contention that the rules of grammar enter into the processing mechanisms, then evidence concerning production, recognition, recall, and language use in general can be expected (in principle) to have bearing on the investigation of rules of grammar, on what is sometimes called "linguistic competence" or "knowledge of language." But such evidence, where it is forthcoming, has no privileged character and does not bear on "psychological reality" in some unique way. Evidence is not subdivided into two categories: evidence that bears on reality and evidence that just confirms or refutes theories (about mental computation and mental representations, in this case). Some evidence may bear on process models that incorporate a characterization of linguistic competence, while other evidence seems to bear on competence more directly, in abstraction from conditions of language use. And, of course, one can try to use data in other ways. But just as a body of data does not come bearing its explanation on its sleeve, so it does not come marked "for confirming theories" or "for establishing reality."

It is not uncommon to draw a line separating the two disciplines, linguistics and psychology, in terms of the kinds of evidence they prefer to use and the specific focus of their attention. Thus, linguistics is the field that relies on informant judgments, elicited material, whatever limited use can be made of an actual corpus, and so on, to try to determine the nature of grammar and universal grammar. Its concern is competence, the system of rules and principles that we assume have, in some manner, been internally represented by the person who knows a language and that enable the speaker, in principle, to understand an arbitrary sentence and to produce a sentence expressing his thought; and universal grammar, the principles that specify the range of possible human grammars. Psychology, in contrast, is concerned with performance, not competence; its concern is the processes of production, interpretation, and the like, which make use of the knowledge attained, and the processes by which transition takes place from the initial to the final state.

To me, this distinction has always seemed quite senseless. Delineation of disciplines may be useful for administering universities or organizing professional societies, but apart from that, it is an undertaking of limited merit. A person who happens to be interested in underlying competence will naturally be delighted to exploit whatever understanding may be forthcoming about process models that incorporates one or another set of assumptions about linguistic knowledge. Furthermore, it seems evident that investigation of performance will rely, to whatever extent it can, on what is learned about the systems of knowledge that are put to use. The theory of particular and universal grammar, so far as I can see, can be sensibly regarded only as that aspect of theoretical psychology that is primarily concerned with the genetically determined program that specifies the range of possible grammars for human languages and the particular realizations of this schematism that arise under given conditions. One may perfectly well choose to study language and grammar with other purposes in mind and without concern for these questions, but any significant results obtained will nevertheless be a contribution to this branch of psychology. I take it that this is one major point that Lenneberg was putting forth in his work. It seems to me entirely correct.

Not everyone agrees, or so a literal reading might suggest. It is illuminating to see how opposing views are put in the literature. In Chapter 1 of their text on cognitive psychology, Kintsch and associates (1974) argue that the "strict separation" between competence and performance

> permits the linguist to deal with convenient abstractions, uninhibited by psychological reality, and it provides the psychologist with the facetious argument that linguistic theories have nothing to do with processes anyway. As long as linguistic theory is strictly a competence theory, it is of no interest to the psychologist. Indeed I doubt that it should be of much interest to linguists either, but that is for them to decide.

These remarks, which are not untypical, reflect deep-seated confusions. The approach that Kintsch criticizes, as his references make clear, is the one outlined above: the approach based on the assumption that a person's knowledge of language can properly be represented as a system of rules of grammar, and that process models concerned with language use will incorporate such representations of linguistic competence. On this assumption, which is of course not God-given but must be evaluated in terms of its empirical consequences, the goal of the investigator will be to determine the nature of the competence system that expresses what it is that the mature speaker knows, and to develop process models that show how this knowledge is put to use.

Kintsch asserts that study of the abstracted competence system is "uninhibited by psychological reality"; only processes have "reality." But plainly we can have no special insight into what is real apart from normal scientific practice. Adhering to these reasonable norms, we impute existence, subject to verification and test, to whatever structures and processes are postulated in the effort to explain significant facts. The enterprise is not "uninhibited by psychological reality," but is rather concerned with specific aspects of psychological reality. Kintsch's psychologist has "no interest" in explanatory theories, no matter how far-reaching and well-confirmed, dealing with these aspects of knowledge of language and the basis for its acquisition (particular and universal grammar). In short, fundamental questions of cognitive psychology are to be excluded from the concern of the psychologist (or for Kintsch, the concern of anyone). Note that these positions are taken on purely a priori grounds, not on the basis of alleged empirical or conceptual inadequacies of the approach he rejects as compared with some alternative. It is difficult to imagine comparable dogmatism in the natural sciences.

Kintsch's psychologist not only declares his lack of interest in this central domain of human psychology; furthermore, he decides, a priori, that a characterization of the system of knowledge attained can be of no relevance for investigation of the process models to which he limits his attention. Note that this is what a literal reading of Kintsch's remarks implies, for if indeed the study of competence models along the lines he rejects (namely, those I have just outlined) were to bring to light a system embedded in processing models in the way that Lenneberg (and others) propose, then clearly results attained in this study would be of great relevance for the investigation of process models. Again, such astonishing dogmatism about matters so poorly understood can hardly be imagined in the natural sciences. One might put forth a rational hypothesis that perhaps expresses what Kintsch has in mind: Namely, one might propose that once process models are developed we will find that all relevant facts are explained without any abstraction to a rule system that articulates the speaker–hearer's knowledge of his language. This thesis might prove correct. To reject it out of hand would be as irrational as Kintsch's dogmatic stand. But the dogmatic insistence that it must be correct and that alternatives must be discarded on a priori grounds, as a literal reading of Kintsch's remarks implies, is simply a reflection of the irrationality that has hampered investigation in the human sciences for many, many years.

Note that the "strict separation" between competence and performance that Kintsch deplores is a conceptual distinction; knowledge of language is distinguished from behavior (use of this knowledge). This conceptual distinction is surely quite "strict," though one might argue that a different conceptual framework would be preferable. In fact, Kintsch adopts throughout the conceptual distinction that he believes he rejects, where his discussion is coherent.[8] The main concern of his book is "the study of the properties" of a certain "level of representation in memory, both theoretically and empirically," namely, representation of a sentence "conceptually in terms of its meaning," which he takes to be a "propositional" representation. This is the study of a certain aspect of linguistic competence. Kintsch simply presupposes some system of rules that generates the representations he postulates, in particular cases. And like everyone else, Kintsch tries to gain some understanding of this "level of representation" through the study of performance and tries to show how it figures in process models. In short, while Kintsch believes that his approach "has no use at all for the competence–performance distinction," in fact, he invokes it in pretty much the conventional way. This is not surprising, given that no coherent alternative framework of concepts has been proposed in this domain, to my knowledge.

My comments so far have been directed to the first of the two conclusions cited from Lenneberg's study of the biology of language. Let me now turn to the second, namely, his conclusion that "the discovery and description of innate mechanisms is a thoroughly empirical procedure and is an integral part of modern scientific inquiry." The study of innate mechanisms leads us to universal grammar, but also, of course, to investigation of the biologically determined principles that underlie language use, what has sometimes been called "pragmatic competence," and cognitive structures of other sorts that enter into the actual use of language.

In drawing his conclusions concerning the investigation of innate mechanisms, Lenneberg felt that it was necessary to emphasize the empirical nature of this research because "there was a time when 'innateness' was on the index of forbidden concepts," and "there are still many scientists who regard the postulation of anything innate as a clever parlor trick that alleviates the proponent from performing 'truly scientific' investigations," a position, he noted, that "is odd to say the least," but one that has had and in fact still retains quite a grip on the modern imagination.

---

[8] There are, however, many problems with his account; for example, the discussion of definite and indefinite description on p. 48, or the account of quantificational structure a few pages later. But where the discussion is coherent, it makes use of representations of the sort assumed in one or another competence model, and develops the kinds of arguments that might be used in connection with representation of linguistic competence and the process systems in which they find their place.

It is easy to illustrate the persistence, to this day, of serious qualms concerning explanations that rely on postualted innate mechanisms, though I agree entirely with Lenneberg that these reservations are "odd to say the least." Of course, specific proposals may be open to all sorts of legitimate objections. But I am referring now rather to the commonly expressed belief that there is some objection in principle to such an approach. Such objections have been expressed in an extreme form by a number of philosophers. I have argued elsewhere that their objections are groundless, and will have nothing to say about this here.[9] Similar doctrines sometimes appear in the linguistic literature as well (see, for example, Peizer & Olmsted, 1969, Note 1), also, to my knowledge, without valid supporting argument.

Appeal to innate mechanisms is also regarded with great suspicion by many psychologists, and not—contrary to widespread belief—only by those who regard themselves as "behaviorists," whatever that designation may mean today, if anything. Consider, for example, the objections raised by Piaget and his colleagues. Piaget (1975) argues that the postualted innate mechanisms are "biologically inexplicable" and that what can be explained on the assumption of fixed innate structures can be explained as well as "the 'necessary' results of constructions of sensory-motor intelligence." However, he offers no argument at all that the postulated mechanisms are any more "inexplicable" than mechanisms postulated to account for physical development; indeed, even the most radical "innatists" have suggested mechanisms that would add only a small increment to what any rational biologist would assume must be genetically determined. Piaget's complaint would be correct if he had said "biologically unexplained" instead of "biologically inexplicable," but then the same might be said about the current theory of development of physical organs of the body. As for Piaget's further claim that the facts for which an explanation has been offered in terms of a postulated genetically determined universal grammar can also be explained as the "necessary" result of constructions of sensorimotor intelligence, I will only say the obvious: The literature contains no evidence or argument to support this remarkable factual claim, nor even any explanation of what sense it might have. Again, we see here an instance of the unfortunate but rather common insistence on dogmatic and unsupported factual doctrines in the human sciences.

The same doctrine is advanced by Piaget's colleagues. Consider, for example, the discussion of this point by Inhelder, Sinclair, and Bovet (1974). Citing Piaget, they put forth "the basic hypothesis of developmental constructivism," which "postulates that no human knowledge, with the obvious

---

[9] For detailed discussion of the views of several contemporary philosophers, see Chomsky (1968, 1975a), and references cited therein.

exception of the very elementary hereditary forms, is performed in the structures of either the subject or the object." In particular, they reject the hypothesis that certain principles of language structure (and other cognitive structures) are "not only present at an extremely early age, but hereditary [p. 8]."[10] The postulated principles, they insist, are not "preformed" (i.e., governed by genetically determined factors) but rather arise through the child's activity, and are explained by "regulatory or autoregulatory mechanisms." These are, however, described in terms so vague that it is hard to know what is intended. Taking the hypothesis of "developmental constructivism" literally, they are claiming that such principles as the wh-island constraint, or the deeper principles from which it derives, must arise on the basis of the same kinds of principles that account for the child's early sensorimotor constructions and the like. While one cannot dismiss this contention out of hand, it seems a most astonishing claim.

The persistence of such empirical claims in the absence of any argument or even an intelligible formulation can perhaps be explained in terms of another doctrine of the Geneva school. Thus, Inhelder et al. "agree with Piaget" that the approach they attribute to neonativists "does not help to solve any problem; all it does is to transfer the question from the psychological to the biological level by formulating it in terms of biological development [p. 10]." If this argument had any merit, it would apply as well to standard accounts of physical development. Suppose that someone postulates that binocular vision or the fact that we grow arms instead of wings is genetically determined. By the argument of the Geneva school, this assumption "does not help to solve any problem," but only transfers the question from the psychological to the biological level.

Plainly, no one would take this argument seriously, nor would the Geneva psychologists advance it in the case of physical development. If the general structure of binocular vision is genetically determined, then naturally we must seek to explain its origin in terms of biological (evolutionary) development rather than in terms of learning. In short, we must "transfer the question [of development] from the psychological to the biological level." Exactly the same is true when we turn to cognitive structures or the (unknown) physical mechanisms that underlie them. If, say, we find extensive evidence that the wh-island constraint or the principles that underlie it belong to universal grammar and are available to the language learner

---

[10] Inhelder et al. (1974) attribute to "rationalist psycho-linguists" the view that "linguistic competence" and "cognitive structure" are hereditary. Presumably by "linguistic competence" they mean what these psycholinguists call "universal grammar." Surely no one holds "linguistic competence"—for example, knowledge of English—to be hereditary. Similar remarks may be made about cognitive structure. What has been proposed is that specific properties or conditions on cognitive structures attained are hereditary.

without relevant experience, then it would only be rational to suppose that these mechanisms are genetically determined and to search for a further account in terms of biological development. The Geneva school doctrine seems to be that no matter how substantial the evidence in favor of such a thesis may be, and no matter how weak the argument for ontogenetic development, nevertheless we must maintain the thesis that the principles in question are derived by "regulatory or autoregulatory mechanisms" in accordance with the hypothesis of "developmental constructivism." At least, I see no other way to read their proposals, since the arguments they put forth are in no way empirical but rather purely a priori. All of this again simply seems to constitute another chapter in the history of dogmatism.

Notice that I do not suggest that the Piagetians cannot be correct in their contentions. Rather, I ask why they insist that they must be right, whatever the evidence seems to show, and why they propose arguments in the case of mental development of a sort that they would never accept in the case of physical growth of organs? Why, in short, must the normal procedures and assumptions of scientific inquiry—in particular, its open-mindedness—be abandoned, when we turn to cognitive structures and their development?

To mention one last case, consider the critique of "nativist" linguistics and psycholinguistics by the distinguished Russian neuropsychologist A. R. Luria (1975). He insists that the natural place to seek the origin of principles of universal grammar[11]—say, the wh-island constraint, to make the discussion concrete—is "in the history of our society and in the active forms of man's relations with reality." Just how the principles of universal grammar might arise in this way, Luria does not tell us, even in the most vague and hypothetical way. Rather, like Piaget and others he offers a purely methodological argument. The assumption that certain principles of universal grammar are genetically determined, he asserts, "makes a postulate out of a problem and this in itself means that all further study in the area can lead us nowhere."

Once again, if this a priori argument were valid, then it would hold as well for the development of physical organs; that is, it would show that the hypothesis that the growth of arms rather than wings is genetically determined makes a postulate out of a problem and guarantees that further inquiry will lead us nowhere. Since Luria would obviously not accept this conclusion, we are left with only one way of interpreting his argument: Cognitive development must, on a priori grounds, be fundamentally different from physical development in that it has no genetic component. It is an

---

[11] Throughout the discussion, Luria mistakenly identifies "universal grammar" and "deep structure." There are other misinterpretations of this sort, but they are easily corrected. The point he is making is clear.

a priori truth that cognitive development is "decoupled" from biology in this basic respect. Luria goes on to make a series of empirical claims about what "we must" assume and where "we must look" for an account of the origin of linguistic universals: namely, "in the relations between the active subject and reality and not in the mind itself." Note that no argument is advanced to show that this *is* true, or even any hint of an argument. Rather, it *must* be true; argument is therefore superfluous. If, indeed, investigation shows that the *wh*-island constraint derives from principles of universal grammar and is available to the language learner without relevant experience, we must, nevertheless, insist that this constraint (or the underlying principles) is acquired by the child through "the active relationship between the subject and the world" or "active reflection on the objective world." Note that the reference to "the history of our society" is entirely beside the point, since however language has evolved, a given child must acquire it on the basis of the evidence available. What is most curious of all, perhaps, is that all of this is offered as the "genuinely scientific" approach, the "scientifically philosophical manner" of studying the question at hand. One can imagine how comparable dogmatism would be regarded in the natural sciences.

Perhaps these citations suffice to show that Lenneberg (1967) was quite right to take the trouble to emphasize that "the discovery and description of innate mechanisms is a thoroughly empirical procedure and is an integral part of modern scientific inquiry," and to insist that there is no room here for dogmatism or a priori doctrine. It is significant that this simple observation seems so difficult for many researchers to accept. Rather, the normal canons of scientific method and procedure have met with great resistance in the study of mind and cognition, and there has been a compulsion to adhere to a priori theses, whether they are those of associationism, S–R psychology, developmental constructivism, etc. The belief expressed by Luria, that "all patterns present in the human mind are simply a reflection of the interaction between the subject and the outside world," can be traced directly back to scholastic doctrine, and is often attributed, probably erroneously, to Aristotle. It is interesting to ask why this docrine is regarded as so sacrosanct. I think that a history of the study of these questions in the modern period will show that such doctrines have been proposed not as bold empirical hypotheses, to be developed and tested—but rather as necessary truths that it would somehow be dangerous to abandon, whatever inquiry may reveal. It seems evident that no science can advance unless it frees itself from intellectual shackles of this nature.

It is interesting to note, in this connection, that the approach that Lenneberg and others recommend—the approach often designated by its opponents as "nativism," though "open-mindedness" would seem a more accurate term—has not met with comparable objections from natural scientists, to my knowledge. Conclusions that have been tentatively advanced by "neonativists" seem to be regarded as unexceptionable in principle, though perhaps incorrect as formulated, by many biologists speculating on questions of language and mind.[12] Furthermore, assumptions similar to those of the "neonativist" psychologists and linguists are proposed without special comment by neurophysiologists quite regularly. To cite one case, in a review of research on vision two neurophysiologists (Grobstein & Chow, 1975) formulate what they call the "principle of restricted potential" in the following terms:

> By this we mean to emphasize that the developing nervous system is not a tabula rasa, free to reflect whatever individual experience dictates. Rather, the development of the nervous system is a process sharply constrained by a genetic program. At certain points, the genetic program permits a range of possible realizations, and individual experience acts only to specify the outcome within this range.

In particular, they suggest, "there appears to be a small range within which individual experience operates to assure proper binocular fusion," though the general character of binocular vision in cat and monkey is genetically determined; and "there is some genetically determined range of possible orientation specificities for an individual neuron within which the actual orientation specificity is realized by experience." I have no independent judgment as to whether these suggestions are correct. My point, rather, is that no one would argue that by thus attributing some general restrictive principles to the genetic program they are violating some methodological canon, turning a problem into a postulate, aborting further inquiry, etc. Why then should we take a different stance when it is proposed that universal grammar, genetically determined, permits "a range of possible realizations" and individual experience acts only to specify the outcome—namely, as a particular grammar and performance system—within this range?

The answer is: We should not. Specific arguments with regard to native endowment should be assessed on their merits, without intrusion of a priori doctrine as to the nature of legitimate idealization, the structure of mind, the character of mental representations and mental computation, the role of history and experience, etc. There is, in short, no reason to adopt the common view that the human mind is unique among the systems known to us in the biological world in that, it its higher cognitive functions, it is unstructured apart from some minimal "hereditary forms" or "quality space."

One might be disinclined to suppose that a principle such as the *wh*-island constraint, assuming it to be a principle of universal grammar, is

---

[12] See, for example, Monod (1970). For references and comment, see Chomsky (1971, pp. 11f.); Jacob (1973, p. 322); Luria (1973, pp. 137f.); Stent (1975).

genetically programmed as such. Perhaps such a principle, if indeed it is genetically determined, arises from the interaction of other more basic properties of the language faculty. I think that this is in fact the case, as noted earlier. I have suggested elsewhere that the *wh*-island constraint follows from quite general properties of rule systems that have many other consequences as well. Suppose that we can show that these or other principles of comparable generality are well confirmed in human language and suffice to explain such principles as the *wh*-island constraint and, thus, to explain why the sentences described earlier are interpreted as they are. We might then ask whether these deeper principles are specific to the language faculty or apply to the operation of other "mental organs" as well. Thus, these deeper principles might result from some sort of organism–environment interaction, difficult as it is to imagine at present how this might come about, or more plausibly they might be characteristic of a broad class of cognitive processes, reflected in various ways in particular cognitive domains. Lenneberg (1967) has some interesting speculations along these lines. In discussing the general principles of organization of grammar, he suggests that phrase structure and transformational systems may be "simply special applications of general modes of organization, modes that are common to the organization of the behavior of all higher animals [p. 302]," though these systems must be "highly adapted biologically" in humans. It remains an open question, and an interesting one, to determine whether there really are significant analogies between the principles of mental representation and computation that seem to be well motivated in the study of language, and other mental operations, in other domains. Personally, I am rather skeptical; I see no interesting analogies in other cognitive domains, but so little is known that we can really say very little.

In this connection too, it seems to me that one must deplore the common tendency to insist that the mechanisms of language must be special cases of "generalized learning strategies" or general cognitive mechanisms of some sort. Perhaps this will prove true, but there is, for the moment, little reason to suppose that it is. I see nothing surprising in the conclusion, if it proves correct, that the principles of rule organization that underlie the *wh*-island constraint are special properties of the language faculty, just as distribution of orientation specificities is a special property of the visual cortex. Similarly, it would not come as a great surprise to find that, in some respects, the human auditory system is specifically adapted to speech or that general principles of semantic structure and organization derive from the language faculty. At the level of cellular biology, we hope that there will be some account of the properties of all organs, physical and mental. There seems little reason to suppose, for the moment, that there are general principles of cognitive structure, or even of human cognition, expressible at some higher level, from which the particular properties of particular "mental organs," such as the language faculty, can be deduced, or even that there are illuminating analogies among these various systems. Of course, we do expect to find that some systems—say, the systems of memory—enter into a variety of cognitive processes, but that is another matter altogether.

There are many barriers to progress in the study of the biological basis for human language capacities, among them, the impossibility of direct experimentation on humans to answer the many questions that arise. In the case of some systems, such as the visual system, investigation of other higher animals helps to overcome this limitation, but the lack of significant analogues to the language faculty in other species, which, I suspect, will become clearer and better understood as research with language-like symbolic systems in apes advances, appears to foreclose this option in the case of language. The abstract study of competence systems and the study of process models offers a great deal of promise, I believe, and can place significant conditions on the biological mechanisms that enter into the language capacities. Eric Lenneberg, in his very productive work, developed a range of other approaches that seem very promising, as have other researchers in several related disciplines. The study of the biological basis for human language capacities may prove to be one of the most exciting frontiers of science in coming years.

REFERENCES

Bahcall, John N., & Davis, Jr., Raymond. Solar neutrinos: a scientific puzzle. *Science*, 1976, *191*, 254–257.

Botha, Rudolf P. *The justification of linguistic hypotheses: a study of nondemonstrative inference in transformational grammar.* The Hague: Mouton, 1973.

Chomsky, Noam. *The logical structure of linguistic theory.* New York: Plenum, 1955.

Chomsky, Noam. *Current issues in linguistic theory.* The Hague: Mouton, 1964.

Chomsky, Noam. *Language and mind.* New York: Harcourt, 1968.

Chomsky, Noam. *Problems of knowledge and freedom.* New York: Pantheon, 1971.

Chomsky, Noam. *Reflections on language.* New York: Pantheon, 1975. (a)

Chomsky, Noam. On cognitive structures and their development. *Proceedings of the Royaumont Conference on Phylogenetic and Ontogenetic Models of Development,* 1975. (b)

Chomsky, Noam. *Conditions on rules.* New York: American Elsevier, 1976.

Chomsky, Noam. On *wh*-movement. In P. W. Culicover, T. Wasow, & A. Akmajian (Eds.), *Formal syntax.* New York: Academic Press, 1977.

Grobstein, Paul, & Chow, Kao Liang. Receptive field development and individual experience. *Science,* 1975, *190*, 352–358.

Inhelder, Bärbel, Sinclair, Hermine, & Bovet, Magali. *Learning and the development of cognition.* Cambridge: Harvard University Press, 1974.

Jacob, Francois. *The logic of life.* New York: Pantheon, 1973.

Kintsch, Walter, with Crothers, E. J., Glass, G., Keenan, J. M., McKoon, G., & Monk, D. *The representation of meaning in memory.* New York: Wiley, 1974.

Lenneberg, Eric H. *Biological foundations of language.* New York: Wiley, 1967.

Luria, A. R. Scientific perspectives and philosophical dead ends in modern linguistics. *Cognition,* 1975, *3.*

Luria, S. E. *Life: the unfinished experiment.* New York: Scribners, 1973.

Monod, Jacques. *Le hasard et la nécessité.* Paris: Editions du Seuil, 1970.

Ney, James W. The decade of private knowledge: linguistics from the early 60's to the early 70's. *Historiographia Linguistica,* 1975, *II.*

Peizer, David B., & Olmsted, David L. Modules of grammar acquisition. *Language,* 1969, *45.*

Piaget, Jean. La psychogenèse des connaissances et sa signification epistémologique. *Proceedings of the Royaumont Conference on Phylogenetic and Ontogenetic Models of Development,* 1975.

Ross, John R. *Constraints on variables in syntax.* Ph.D. dissertation, Massachusetts Institute of Technology, 1967.

Stent, Gunther. Limits to the scientific understanding of man. *Science,* 1975, *187,* 1052–1057.

Can an Inquiry into the Foundations of Mathematics Tell Us Anything Interesting about Mind?[1]

GABRIEL STOLZENBERG

INTRODUCTION

I must ask you to disregard, temporarily, the title question of this chapter. At the end, I shall return to it and explain how the body of my remarks may be regarded as constituting an affirmative answer, albeit one of a nontraditional sort.

Several years ago, Eric Lenneberg and I had some long and, for me, very enjoyable conversations about an unpublished essay of his entitled "Knowledge of Grammar and Grammar of Knowledge." These conversations with Eric stimulated me to think more seriously than I had before about the fundamental role of language use in the construction of the pure mathematician's world view. In this chapter, I shall attempt to share some of these thoughts with you. Although I am not going to discuss the content of Eric's essay, I do wish it to be known that the main methodological issues are, at

---

[1] This is a greatly revised and expanded version of the original talk.

PSYCHOLOGY AND BIOLOGY OF LANGUAGE AND THOUGHT
Essays in Honor of Eric Lenneberg

least in my own mind, closely related to ones that troubled Eric too and with which he tried to deal in that work.

THE VIEW THAT PURE MATHEMATICS
HAS FALLEN INTO A TRAP

It is my view, a view that I share with the rest of the so-called "constructivist" mathematical community, that during the latter part of the nineteenth century, in the course of an attempt to rigorize itself and establish proper foundations, the science of pure mathematics fell into a certain intellectual trap; and that, since that time, mathematicians, with the help of logicians, have been going along digging themselves in deeper and deeper. In this chapter, I want to show you what this trap is like: how it is built up out of certain structures of logic and language, why it is so easy to fall into it, and what happens when one does. As a mathematician, I also would like to do something to get my discipline out of this trap. But that is another matter. Also, it should be understood that what I am calling here "a trap" is seen by most other pure mathematicians, who look at it only from within, as more like an intellectual paradise; and, really, there is no contradiction. But so much already has been said elsewhere about mathematics as paradise; here I shall talk about traps. Why? In part, it is simply because I find the subject intellectually fascinating. But it is also because I believe that there is a significant piece of practical knowledge to be gained by other scientists who familiarize themselves with the case of contemporary pure mathematics. For, what is at issue here are certain fundamental questions about the proper form of scientific inquiry. And an understanding of what went wrong in the case of pure mathematics may help other scientists to avoid making the same kind of mistakes elsewhere.

What then did go wrong in the case of pure mathematics? What is the trap into which it has fallen?

In order to answer these questions I first have to explain, in reasonably general terms, what I mean here by "a trap" or by "being trapped." In addition, I must specify those particular institutionalized attitudes, beliefs, and habits of thought of contemporary pure mathematics that I claim constitute such a trap. And, finally, I must give my reasons for making this claim. In my view, the case that can be made on the basis of a careful examination of existing mathematical theory and practice is far stronger than it is possible to indicate here. But I believe also that even in this nontechnical discussion I can make out a prima facie case that is strong enough to leave a substantial burden of explanation on those who may wish to dispute it.

Use of the Term *Trap*;
Considerations of Standpoint

The conditions I impose upon the use of the term *trap* are very stringent: in order to justify its use in the case at hand one must show, for the institutionalized attitudes, beliefs, and habits of thought referred to above, not merely that they constitute a closed system but also, and more significantly, (a) that certain of these beliefs are demonstrably incorrect; and (b) that certain of the fixed attitudes and habits of thought prevent this from being recognized. And in order to carry out such a demonstration, or merely to recognize one when it is presented, one first must establish a standpoint from which those givens of contemporary mathematics that are to be called into question are no longer givens but merely hypotheses or proposals which, as it stands, are neither accepted nor rejected.

This raises the crucial question of how such a standpoint may be established. Although I shall discuss this question later in this chapter, the value of what I shall have to say there is limited by the consideration that any adequate answer must take into account the particular position from which one begins; and that may vary significantly from person to person. Also, if one's starting point is inside the system, then what is required is a procedure for getting out; and that will entail the "undoing" of certain seemingly fundamental beliefs and habits of thought.[2] While such procedures are available, it takes considerable discipline to follow them correctly.

Having said this much, and having already observed that what I am calling here "a trap" is seen from within as something completely different, it should not be too surprising that I say also that the basic methodological errors that landed pure mathematics into this trap and that, even now, contribute to keeping it there, consist chiefly in ignoring basic considerations of standpoint. What we have, in case after case, is a failure to take into account how certain of the givens of one's particular standpoint may be contributing both to the way in which a question is construed (e.g., by construing it as being equivalent to some other question) and, also, to the way in which certain answers to it are judged. In some cases, the relevant givens are beliefs or hidden assumptions, including "nonfactual" assumptions about the meaningfulness of certain modes of discourse; but they may also be attitudes, habits of thought, as well as other social and psychological phenomena.[3]

---

[2] In particular, the belief that one possesses a concept of "truth independent of knowledge" of the sort that is needed to support the practice of "excluded middle" type reasoning.

[3] For example, in certain cases, a relevant given is that one simply is unable to take seriously a particular answer to some question, even though it may be seen "from without" that, in fact, the answer is correct. There is an amusing instance of this in Imre Lakatos's "Proofs and

I hope it is quite clear that, when I stress the importance of taking into account considerations of standpoint, I am not preaching any brand of relativism. I do not say that there is your truth and my truth and never the twain shall meet. On the contrary, what I do say is that, in order to be truly objective—in order to give one's answer to some question an objective basis—it often is necessary to pay attention to how the givens of one's particular standpoint may be influencing the way in which the question is being answered. And, sometimes, the result of paying such attention will be to recognize the need, for the sake of really answering the question adequately, to give up one's own standpoint temporarily and adopt a completely different one. However, when psychological factors are involved (and they very often are), when some of the givens that have to be relinquished, at least for a while, are beliefs and habits of thought, then carrying this through in practice may be extremely difficult. On the other hand, nobody ever promised us that doing science would be easy.

The Process of Entrapment: A Brief Description in General Terms

Thus far, I have characterized a trap as a closed system of attitudes, beliefs, and habits of thought for which one can give an objective demonstration that certain of the beliefs are incorrect and that certain of the attitudes and habits of thought prevent this from being recognized.[4] In this formulation, the "methodological errors" are those failures to take into account considerations of standpoint that have the effect of *maintaining* the system. But nothing is said of its *origin;* of how such a trap may be formed. So I now would like to give a very brief description of what might be termed "the process of entrapment," still in very general terms but mindful of some of the distinctive features of the case of pure mathematics.

Refutations" (1976). One of the characters in this play about pure mathematicians at "work" has what in fact is a perfectly good counterexample to the conjectures that the others are continually putting forward. However, even though there are many other counterexamples that they do take seriously, to this one they invariably respond, "Quit kidding around!"

   [4] However, in significant respects (some, not all) it would not make much difference if, instead, it were possible to give an objective demonstration that the beliefs *are* correct, but that the fixed attitudes and habits of thought prevent *that* demonstration from being recognized as such. If this were the case for pure mathematics, which it is not, then we might have the mathematicians producing correct results but without themselves truly participating in the knowledge that they are correct. And, on general scientific grounds, this too would be an intolerable situation.

The process of entrapment. Insofar as its general form is concerned, it consists, first, *in being taken in (a)* by certain uses of language that have the appearance, but only that, of being meaningful; and (b) by certain modes of reasoning that have the appearance, but only that, of being self-evidently correct; second, *in being locked in* as a result of the psychological act, or process, of accepting these appearances as being "really so." Somehow, by a process that may be quite complex, they become so thoroughly woven into the very fabric of what we take to be our web of reality that it no longer seems possible to adopt a standpoint from which the question of their correctness may be entertained seriously as a "mere" hypothesis. What were, originally, assumptions have now become givens and the idea of calling them into question is no longer intelligible.

Notes

i.   For the case of contemporary pure mathematics, when I speak about being taken in by certain uses of language and modes of reasoning, I have in mind specifically (a) the use of a "present tense" language "of objects and their properties" in a manner that presupposes a literal interpretation of it; and (b) the practice of reasoning according to the so-called "law of excluded middle."

ii. In the introduction to this chapter, I said that the science of pure mathematics has fallen into a trap. However, the term "process of entrapment," as I am using it here, may be taken to refer either to something that the entire discipline of pure mathematics went through from about 1870 to 1930 in the course of an attempt to "do itself over right" after producing a literal confusion of riches over the preceding 200 years or, with equal validity, to a process that each new student of pure mathematics goes through, even today, in the course of what nowadays is called "learning to think like a pure mathematician."

iii. What I have presented here as an account of the process of entrapment actually is a description of a somewhat more general kind of process, one which may, but need not, result in a trap. The last line of the account reads, "What were, originally, assumptions have now become givens and the idea of calling them into question is no longer intelligible." Now, if it is in the nature of these givens to determine the shape of further inquiry, then the effect of accepting them may be to block off precisely those directions that if followed would reveal these givens to be not merely unfounded but, in fact, false. And, if that is the case, then what we have is a trap. Moreover, I claim and shall, later on, endeavor to demonstrate that this *is* the case for the acceptance of "excluded middle" type reasoning as a given for pure mathematics. However, in general, even if we arrive at a state in which the idea of questioning certain givens is no longer intelligible to us, it does not follow that we must, or will, remain in that state. It may well be that, as a result of pursuing other lines of investigation within the system, we unexpectedly find ourselves in a position where we can, once again, question these givens. Thus, even though the process does include a phenomenon of acceptance that is not, in any *trivial* sense, reversible, it does not necessarily produce a closed system, much less a trap. However, any such system that is not closed has to contain the wherewithal to overcome the deep resistance to change that is produced by an act of accepting something in this way—and by current standards any such system would be pretty exceptional.

One might suppose that such an "opening up" is unavoidable whenever the system that has been created is found to contain "the seeds of its own destruction" in the form of an internal inconsistency. Several such givens are accepted and, for each, the idea of calling it into question appears to be unintelligible. But then an internal inconsistency is generated: a contradiction. However, it really is not so clear what will happen in such a situation. When just such a "crisis" arose during an early phase of the formation of the system in which contemporary pure mathematics is practiced—I am referring here to the discovery of the so-called "paradoxes of set theory"—it was "resolved" without undoing the basic psychological act of acceptance that had produced it. That was the act of accepting that talk "about sets" does have a meaning of the sort that traditionally it is supposed to have. Really all that happened was that the account was modified in a merely technical way so as to remove the appearance of a contradiction. Nevertheless, the shock of arriving at the contradiction did have an effect upon the system as a whole, basically by throwing it permanently into a new, and much more problematical, state.

I am now going to elaborate upon the ideas just presented and attempt to present a single coherent account of what I mean, in the context of a scientific inquiry, by "falling into a trap." After that, until the concluding remarks, I shall devote myself exclusively to the particular case of contemporary pure mathematics.

Falling into a trap is something that can happen in the course of scientific activity. But, *in* science, what sort of things *happen*? What acts are performed in the activity of science? Certainly, a part of the answer is that questions are raised and investigations are carried out. But there also are those acts by means of which, intentionally or not, there is "built up" the "structure" of the very system (of beliefs, practices, habits of thought, attitudes, language use, etc.) within which the activity of a science is carried out (including the activity of building up the structure of the system within which the activity is carried out). And these are not merely acts "of construction" but, also, "of acceptance." Or, rather, I should say, "of acceptance as such." Let me elaborate on this very important point.

THE CONCEPT OF AN ACT OF
ACCEPTANCE AS SUCH

In general, to "accept" something—an experience or an object—"as such" consists in taking it for what it appears, or is purported, to be, *and proceeding on that basis*. (In other words, it consists in treating the object or experience—for example, the experience of waking up in the morning and "seeing that the sun is shining"—as being what it appears to be and operating accordingly.) Despite a certain superficial similarity, there is all the difference in the world between (a) *accepting* something as being what it appears to be and proceeding (in life, as an experiencing being) on that basis; and (b) merely exploring the consequences of *the assumption* that some thing is what it appears to be. When I wake up in the morning and "find" that the sun is shining, it is not that I have a certain sensory experience and, on the basis of it, make the assumption that "the sun is shining." Of course, there *are* mornings when I do that; but I am talking about ones for which, when I wake up, I simply see that the sun is shining. I do so because that is how my experience is constituted for me. Now, my waking up in the morning and finding that the sun is shining is a typical instance of what I am calling here "an act of acceptance as such." Notice: It is not deliberate and, in fact, from the standpoint of the "performer," there is no such act. On the contrary, it is only if I had chosen to question the authenticity of my "seeing that the sun is shining" that there would be, from my standpoint, any recognizable act. Nevertheless, with hindsight or from the standpoint of an outside observer, it does make sense to say that an act of acceptance as such has been, or is being, performed. This may be seen in various ways. For example, the observer may have conned me by setting up some artificial source of light that makes it appear, from my standpoint, that the sun is shining. Then, from this observer's standpoint, what I experience as "seeing that the sun is shining" consists in my *accepting* what appears to be "seeing that the sun is shining" *as such*. From that standpoint, but not my own, I am being taken in by certain appearances. Falling into a trap is something that can happen in the course of a scientific activity as a result of being taken in by appearances; in other words, it is something that can happen as the result of certain acts of acceptance as such.

Therefore, let me now demonstrate the ubiquity of such acts of acceptance as such in the activity of building up the structure of the system in which the activity of a science is carried out. I think the following example should suffice. The structure of the system in which pure mathematicians operate is, in part, built up by acts which are accepted as establishing a new theorem or introducing a new concept; and the qualification "which are accepted as" is an essential part of the account. For, how is a new theorem established? From within the system, the answer is simply: by constructing a proof. But, from the standpoint of an outside observer, any such act "of constructing a proof" may be recognized as that of constructing what appears to be a proof—that is, what, so far as one sees, is a proof—and accepting it as such. Let us examine the matter a little more closely. The experience of constructing a proof is basically this: A mathematical argument is made which is then checked out step by step and found to be correct. However, the experience of checking out a mathematical argument and "finding it to be correct" is not different in kind from the experience of waking up in the morning and "finding that the sun is shining." In each case, there is an implicit act of acceptance as such that may be recognized only with hindsight or from the standpoint of an outside observer. In the case of checking out a mathematical argument, this may be shown by the following.

Suppose that a "great authority" announces that there is something wrong with the argument. In that case, my experience upon checking over the argument may be quite different from what it was before this announcement was made. Instead of having the experience of "seeing that the argument is correct, that it checks out," my experience may now be that of "finding that I cannot see what, if anything, is wrong with it." (And, if I truly accept the "authority's" authority, we may also delete the "if anything.") Just as before, I find that the argument *appears to be* correct; only this time I do not accept it *as being* correct. And there we have the difference between the two situations; in the first, there is an act of acceptance as such while, in the second, there is instead an act of questioning something that appears to be correct. If I do find the argument to be correct, then the theorem is established and may then be used to do other things, for example, to establish other theorems or to disprove certain conjectures. But, so long as I am trying to see what is wrong with the argument, my energies are engaged otherwise. I may recheck the argument again and again, looking for an error or a gap. Am I overlooking something? Or, am I, perhaps, reading into the argument something that is not there? It may happen that the "great authority" publishes an explanation of what is wrong with the argument. That ought to help; however, I may find that, as it stands, I am unable to follow this explanation. (To pursue this fantasy just a little bit further, here are three possible "outcomes:" 1. I finally manage to grasp the "great authority's" explanation and can see what is wrong with the argument. 2. The situation remains unresolved. 3. I decide that the "great authority" is not such a great authority after all and that, in fact, the argument is "obviously" correct.)

I believe that this single example makes it abundantly clear how, in general, acts of acceptance as such enter into each and every step of the building up of the structure of the system in which the activity of any science is carried out. I remarked earlier that the presence of such acts may be recognized by an outside observer or sometimes, with hindsight, by the performer himself. And, indeed, for the case of acts "of mathematical proof," mathematicians themselves often discover with hindsight that some act of acceptance as such has been made. And, within the limitations imposed by their unquestioning acceptance of what they take to count as a proof, they are open both in principle and in practice to doing whatever may be required in order to attempt to eliminate any errors which may have resulted from such acts. By contrast, for those more fundamental acts of acceptance as such of the kind that landed mathematics into its trap, there is no such tradition of critical reexamination; nor is there any provision for introducing one. On the contrary, the accepted attitude is that *these* issues need not be reconsidered and that, although a mathematician is free to carry out his own private investigation into such matters, any substantive claims he puts foward can simply be ignored. I shall return to this subject later on when I get into the specifics of the case of contemporary pure mathematics.

For us, the three most important facts about acts of acceptance as such are

1. From the standpoint of the "performer," there is no recognizable act at all, only an absence of questioning.
2. Such acts are potential sources of error; that such an error is being made may sometimes be seen from the standpoint of an outside observer.
3. The significance of accepting something as such is that one then treats it, and everything else, accordingly.

Thus, in any given case, accepting and not accepting may lead one down very different roads. By accepting something as such and integrating this belief into how one then sees the world, one may, in some cases, effectively lose the capacity for going back and calling it into question. And, by not accepting it as such but instead choosing to question it, one may be led eventually to the recognition that it, as well as certain of its consequences, is in fact incorrect.

Acts of Acceptance as Such in the Domain of Language Use

But, also, acts of acceptance as such are ubiquitous; unavoidable. That simply is how things are.[5] Therefore, it is evident that the proper question to be considered is not how such acts may be avoided but, rather, how the knowledge that they can and do occur needs to be taken into account in the conduct of science. My own answer to this question is that we need to adopt an activist policy concerning the invention and following of procedures that entail the undoing of accepted beliefs and habits of thought; and we ought to regard the invention of such procedures as one of the fundamental means by which scientific knowledge may be increased.

I say this for two reasons; first, because, as scientists, our interest is in the world, not merely in the world as seen from within one particular system of beliefs; and second, because, for any of the particular beliefs or habits of thought that we ourselves now possess, we have to allow for the possibility

---

[5] Indeed, even the recognition that some thing is "in fact incorrect" quite obviously entails its own act of acceptance as such; and so it too might be "found to be incorrect."

that it is held by us not for the reasons we suppose but, rather, on account of our having performed, unwittingly, certain seemingly innocuous acts of acceptance as such in a domain that, conceptually, is far removed from that of the belief or habit of thought.[6] I have in mind, particularly, acts of acceptance as such that take place strictly in the domain of language use and yet produce beliefs about matters "of fact." Indeed, I believe it is a matter of common experience that people sometimes come to "see" certain things, for example, some "fundamental truth about the nature of reality," solely as a result of having been taken in by some use of language that has the appearance, but only that, of making sense. Moreover, it seems clear that the main reason such things can and do occur is that we all are taught, when we learn to use language, to attribute both to ourselves and others much more of a command of language use than actually has been established. In ordinary language use we almost never look for more than an appearance of sense.

To make these ideas more concrete let us consider for a moment one particular belief about a matter "of fact" that is produced by an act of acceptance as such, performed unwittingly in the domain of language use. This also will provide an opportunity to consider, in a very simple case, conditions of the sort that may result in a trap.

Story of a Definition That Was Too Good To Be True

Some people "learn" in high school that "π is, by definition, the ratio of the circumference of a circle to its diameter." I have found that if you ask such a person how one might prove that, for any two circles, the ratios of circumference to diameter are equal, you are likely to be told that "of course they are equal; they are both equal to π." Many years ago, I had the interesting experience of attempting, without success, to convince a group of such people that it simply is not obvious that if you take a big circle, measure its circumference and diameter, form the ratio, and then do the same for a small circle, that (to within the accuracy of the measurements) the results will be equal. To them, it *was* obvious because what they "saw" is that "both are measurements of π." I tried to instill some doubt in them by pointing out that what they were telling me was really remarkable: that through a mere act "of learning a definition," an act that takes place strictly in the domain of language use, they had come into possession of a nontrivial piece of "factual" knowledge. And they agreed that it *was* rather remark-

---

[6] I claim that we have no difficulty in observing this to be the case for beliefs that *other* people hold; it remains only to learn how to apply the lesson of these observations to ourselves.

able; but, instead of this arousing their suspicions, it merely confirmed their opinion of what a "good" definition it was.

My own position was that they did not know what they were talking about and, more specifically, that what they mistakenly took to be "a definition of π" depended for its validity upon it first being established that, in fact, the ratio of the circumference to the diameter *is* the same for all circles. To me, it was obvious that such a proof had to precede the definition (and I was prepared to show them the beautiful demonstration based on inscribed polygons and the proportionality theorem for similar triangles). But, to them, their "definition" was obvious. As they saw it, they knew "what definitions are" and could recognize one when they saw one.[7] I questioned this. They saw no need to do so. And we left it at that.

In this particular case, what would it have taken to arrive at a mutual understanding? Certainly, if we had been operating in a system with accepted canons of definition, we could have settled the matter simply by checking whether their purported definition was, in fact, correct. But obviously we were not operating in such a system; they had their canons and I had mine. We might have settled the matter anyway if I had managed, somehow, to show them on their own terms that their ideas about "definition" were, in fact, defective; and with hindsight I see how this might have been accomplished. But, in the absence of these alternatives, it seems to me that mutual understanding could have been achieved only if, for the sake of attempting to achieve mutual understanding, those within the group had been willing to do something that they otherwise saw no need to do: namely, to refrain, at least temporarily, from taking their purported "knowledge of definitions" as a given.

In this example, we have a very transparent case of standpoint-dependent reasoning that is seen as being "objective." Without its being realized, the conclusion is, in effect, built in to the standpoint from which the question is being considered. But notice how it is built in. It is *not* that the people in the group were *assuming* the conclusion to be true. That might have been the case if what they had been told in high school was that mathematicians had proven that, for any two circles, the ratios of circumference to diameter are equal; and the definition of π had been presented on that basis. However, in that case they would have understood that the conclusion is not obvious; that it requires proof. And this is precisely what they could not see. The problem was not that certain assumptions had been

---

[7] Very likely, this belief was reinforced throughout their mathematical education. At a more advanced level, the pseudo-definition for π does get corrected; but much worse ones, such as those given for "the square root of 2" and "real number," do not.

made but, rather, that certain acts of acceptance as such had been performed.

USE OF THE TERM *TRAP*:
THREE CONDITIONS THAT
MUST BE FULFILLED

The situation just described exhibits some, but not all, of the features of a trap. The two main reasons it would not be correct to call it a *trap* are, first, that it was an isolated encounter; so, despite the students' unwillingness at that time to reconsider their apparent grasp of "what definitions are," there is no reason to suppose that they really were wedded to this position. Second, even though they did believe their position to be secure and were not threatened by what I said (they took me to be a crank), in fact, their position was not secure. For example, by using their own "acceptance criterion" for definitions, I could have introduced a new "number," Π, as "the ratio of the area of a circle to its diameter" and, on the basis of what else they knew, they would have been forced to the conclusion "that Π is not constant." But then they would have been open to the question, "How do you know that π is constant?"

This leads me to an important point. For an observer of a system to be in a position to conclude that "the system is a trap," there are three conditions that must be fulfilled. One is that he must possess an objective demonstration that certain of the accepted beliefs are incorrect. I use the word "objective" to emphasize that the demonstration must be one that can be grasped by anyone within the system, provided only that he is willing to follow certain procedures which may, however, take him outside the system. The other two conditions, taken together, entitle the observer to conclude that the system has features that prevent someone who is inside it from recognizing the incorrectness of the accepted beliefs. One is a matter of attitude: the observer must see that, within the system, the only legitimate procedures for undoing an accepted belief are those that are provided by the methodology of the system itself. The third and final condition is that the observer must see that, for the beliefs in question, there is no procedure for undoing them within the system itself. It is this last condition that was not fulfilled in the case discussed above.

Another way to say all this is that, for someone to fall into a trap, each of the following conditions must obtain.

1. One must make an error (as a result of some act of acceptance as such) and acquire certain incorrect beliefs.

2. One must be attached to these beliefs so that one will not give them up unless one is compelled to do so.[8]
3. One's position must be irrefutable, in the sense that although it need not be maintained, so long as one desires to do so there is nothing to prevent it.

BELIEF SYSTEMS; ATTITUDES ABOUT UNDOING ACCEPTED BELIEFS

It should now be quite clear that the question of whether one might *ever* fall into a trap depends fundamentally on what attitude one adopts toward the idea of undoing accepted beliefs and habits of thought. Thus, once again, we find ourselves having to confront this basic issue. It is true that acts of acceptance as such are unavoidable; and there also is no avoiding the possibility that as a result of such acts we may come to hold certain beliefs that someone else is in a position to see are incorrect. However, what can be avoided and what, on strictly scientific grounds, should be avoided is the adoption of a methodology that effectively prevents one from coming to share in this knowledge. From one standpoint, it is obvious that no scientist would knowingly adopt such a methodology; the idea of being locked into a belief that someone else is in a position to see is incorrect is, for the scientist, intolerable. Nevertheless, such methodologies *are* adopted and sometimes the resulting system does become a trap.

The underlying attitude that gives rise to such a methodology is the desire for a system, a world-view, that can be maintained and that one will want to maintain. This is what Maturana likes to call "the sin of certainty." Any system that is informed by such an attitude will be called here a "belief system." And any belief system that, in fact, can be maintained will be called a "self-justifying," or "irrefutable," belief system.

A belief system may be like a genuinely scientific system in every other respect, but it has this one distinguishing feature: All acts of observation, judgment, etc., are performed solely from the particular standpoint of the system itself. Therefore, once any belief or operating principle has been accepted, that is, is seen as "being so," any argument for not accepting it will be rejected unless it can be shown that there is something "wrong" with it from the standpoint of the system itself.[9] Thus, it may be the case that, from

---

[8] However, I do not say that the desire to hold these beliefs precedes the state of believing; on the contrary, for some beliefs, it may be that the very holding of them produces the desire to hang onto them.

[9] In particular, the only way that one could show that there is something wrong with the

the standpoint of not having already accepted a certain principle, say the law of excluded middle, a very good reason for not accepting it is simply that one sees no reason *to* accept it; whereas, if this is an accepted principle within a belief system, such a consideration will have no force at all.

This way of operating does not, by itself, provide a system with any principles or procedures governing the acceptance of beliefs; that is, with procedures for coming to see that something "is so"; that is, with canons of "proof." However, it does suggest accepting, as a fundamental methodological principle, that the "acceptance criterion" for any other belief or methodological principle is that it can be shown that once it is accepted and incorporated into the system it cannot be shown to be incorrect on the terms of the system itself.[10] This is essentially the approach that the pure mathematicians took in establishing the canons of "proof" for the belief system in which contemporary pure mathematics is practiced; and it is what they are referring to in their well-known slogan that "in pure mathematics, the only criterion for correctness is consistency—the consistency of the system itself."

Unfortunately, because scientists have not yet gotten around to making a scientific study of the experiences of being inside a belief system, or stepping outside one, or being outside one and looking in, they have failed to make the very important observation that even an irrefutable belief system may be based upon principles that are demonstrably incorrect. Had this been generally recognized, the pure mathematicians' desire for "certainty" notwithstanding, it would never have been possible for them to institutionalize, as a basic methodological principle, the view that in pure

---

accepted methodology of the system would be by using that very same methodology. And any such demonstration would collapse as soon as it had been given because its force would depend upon the correctness of the very methodology that had just been found to be incorrect. Of course, the entire system would also collapse.

[10] A word of caution is called for here. What I have just "stated" is something that, at least to some people, has the appearance of being a fundamental methodological principle. In my view, it has the appearance but only that. Nevertheless, in certain situations, for example, in the practice of contemporary pure mathematics, it has been possible for people to accept it as such and operate accordingly. But, in fact, as soon as one adopts a critical attitude it becomes obvious that for this so-called "fundamental methodological principle" to have any functional significance we must first establish the methodological principles that govern "it can be shown that . . . it cannot be 'shown to be incorrect.'" That is, we are faced here with the need to first understand what it means "to prove" a "negative" assertion about the system itself. And since we want to use our purported prior to understanding of this to introduce one of the system's fundamental methodological principles, that is, to create part of the basic structure of the system, we seem to be caught in a circle. An equally major difficulty is that the operation of negating a statement (whenever it is defined) inevitably depends upon one's already accepted methodology. Generally one ignores this issue by pretending, or perhaps actually believing, that "not" and "is false" are primitive terms that we somehow already understand.

mathematics there is nothing more to correctness than "logical consistency." For it would have been understood that such a view is at best nothing more than a *thesis* about mathematics: a subject for investigation. And then it would have been possible to carry out the epistemological analysis that L. E. J. Brouwer did, in 1908, which showed that this thesis is in fact incorrect. However, by the time Brouwer accomplished this, in a memorable essay entitled "The Unreliability of the Logical Principles" (Brouwer, 1975), it was too late. The equation of "consistency" with correctness had already been accepted; and, from the standpoint of the new system, Brouwer's demonstration, which was based upon a straightforward analysis of the nature of mathematical knowledge, no longer had any force.

Descriptive Fallacies Produced by a Failure to Respect Considerations of Standpoint

It is important to bear in mind that being inside a belief system means seeing things a certain way, for example, that "the sun is shining," or that "π is, by definition, the ratio of the circumference of a circle to its diameter," or that "every mathematical statement is either true or false," but without any awareness of how this way of seeing things is standpoint dependent. One simply takes for granted that everyone else sees things this way too; and, because of this, one is almost guaranteed to get a seriously mistaken understanding of the beliefs and experiences of others who, in fact, do not see things that way.

For example, the chapter entitled "Deviant Logics" in W. V. Quine's "Philosophy of Logic" (1970) is marred by errors of this kind, and they result in factually incorrect conclusions about matters to which the author attaches considerable significance. Quine's position is interesting in that, at least in one respect, he would appear to be a counterexample to a claim I made above; for, even though he operates only from within a particular belief system (classical logic and the world-view it produces), he does not regard it as being "God given." In fact, he agrees that it is something that is acquired as a result of (or, along with) acquiring what we take to be "a mastery" of language use. Furthermore, Quine emphasizes that the test of a good system is in how it functions as a way of "seeing the world" and, most importantly, as a way for scientists to "see the world." He lists convenience, simplicity, and also beauty among the criteria that are to be used in comparing competing systems. On the basis of this account it seems quite clear what needs to be done in order to carry out such a comparison in any particular case: namely, each of the competing systems must be tried out in order to see how well it works. However, this is not what Quine does. Instead, he remains squarely inside his own system as he attempts to see what it is like to operate within a different one. It is no wonder that he finds it confusing to try to do this. Moreover, he treats this experience as if it shows, somehow, that actually operating in the other system is confusing, even though, of course, it shows nothing of the sort. Nevertheless, on the basis of such "evidence," Quine draws the significant conclusions that what he calls "our logic" is simpler, more convenient, and even more beautiful; none of which is correct. Note that my objection is not that these are value judgments and, therefore, are subjective. My point is that Quine himself cannot know which "logic" he would find to be simpler, more convenient, or more beautiful because he has failed to do what is necessary to really find out.

The basic error in Quine's methodology is revealed most clearly by his talk about the price of having to think in what he calls "a deviant logic." One might as well talk about the price that a Chinese has to pay for using a "foreign" language. Throughout Quine's entire discussion, there is no sign of awareness that, for "the deviant," the "deviant" logic is not deviant.

On strictly scientific grounds, what Quine does is inexcusable. However, the conclusions that he draws are ones that have long been generally accepted as being "obviously so." And the errors he makes are bound to be made by anyone who attempts to treat such an issue without first doing what is necessary in order to take into account the way in which the givens of one's own standpoint may be entering into what appear to be objective judgments.

To sum up, a belief system is a system in which all acts of observation and judgment are made solely from within and in which all other considerations are subordinated to the maintenance of the system itself. When an outside observer is in a position to see that such a system contains an incorrect belief and also that no proof of its incorrectness can be given on the terms of the system itself, then he is in a position to say that this system has become a trap. In such a situation, the outside observer will see those within as being dogmatic while those on the inside will see the observer as someone who refuses to accept what is "obviously so." And, in fact, both will be right.

THE CASE OF PURE MATHEMATICS

The Contemporary Mathematician's Attachment to His Beliefs

One point not in dispute is that the system in which the contemporary mathematician operates is, indeed, a belief system. We know that the contemporary mathematician does have a fixed way of "seeing" mathematics; for example, he sees that, given any "set" and any "mathematical object," that object either does or does not "belong to" that set (and he sees also that whichever of these is the case will remain so). Moreover, we know from the mathematician's own account that he is deeply attached to this particular way of seeing mathematics, that he has no experience of seeing it any other way, and that he belongs to a community of fellow practitioners who participate with him in the experience of seeing it this way. And, finally, we know how the contemporary mathematician responds to the idea of being, perhaps only temporarily, in a state of not seeing mathematics in this way—of undoing the basic givens of his particular mathematical world-view. He finds it disturbing—in fact, disruptive—and the occasional suggestions that, for strictly scientific reasons, one ought to do so anyway have been responded to with such epithets as "utterly destructive" and "the Bolshevist menace."

The contemporary mathematician is very impressed by the "reality" of his mathematical experience; and the fact that it is a shared experience—shared by a world-wide community of mathematicians—greatly reinforces his belief in its "objectivity." But in what does this objectivity really consist? First, in the use of an objective mode of discourse and, second, in there being a well-known and widely employed "learning process" by means of which apparently anyone can come to "see" mathematics in this particular way. The latter fact is not without interest. However, because the contemporary mathematician has no experience, not even in the imagination, of standing outside the system and looking in, he attributes far more significance to what is "seen" from inside than what actually is warranted on the basis of more objective considerations. This is true both with respect to the *mathematical* significance he attaches to certain of his "findings," for example, that some mathematical structure is what he calls "finite dimensional" or that some equation has the property that he calls "having a solution," and also with respect to what is perceived to be the significant *methodological* advantages of doing things this way, for example, that it is "simpler" and that "you can do more." There is absolutely no awareness of the extent to which these perceptions and value judgments are merely by-products of the same acts of acceptance as such (in the domain of language use) out of which the system itself is created.

In particular, there has been no end to the talk about how much more "complicated" mathematical reasoning becomes when one does not accept the law of excluded middle as a given. It also is said that when one refrains from accepting this "law" one limits what can be accomplished. David Hilbert merely was expressing the general sentiment when he said that it would be like denying the astronomer his telescope or the boxer the use of his fists. It is remarkable how obvious this appears to be when one is standing inside the contemporary mathematician's belief system and yet how utterly naive and wrongheaded it is seen to be when one steps outside and checks.

From within the system, there is no recognition of *how* the acceptance of the law of excluded middle as a given contributes to the construction of that very same "mathematical reality" about which one then "discovers truths" by using, among other things, the law of excluded middle. Instead, the contemporary mathematician imagines his task of proving theorems to be rather like that of a lawyer whose job is to attempt to establish things in court. On this view of the matter, by "disallowing" appeals to the law of excluded middle one is, in effect, restricting the "legal" means by which a case can be made; that is, the means by which a mathematical theorem can be proved. Hence, one expects that, in general, there will be fewer successes and that what ones there are will be always no easier and in some cases much harder to achieve. But this is an incredibly naive conception of mathematics; it simply takes for granted that, when one undoes one's acceptance of excluded middle reasoning for mathematics, the "reality" of mathematics remains the same while the "allowable" methods of proof are reduced in number. In fact, nothing could be further from the truth.[11]

A VIEW FROM THE EDGE OF THE SYSTEM: THE TUG OF LANGUAGE THAT PULLS ONE INSIDE

Let me now try to present to you, as plainly as I can manage, what I take to be some of the defining characteristics of the belief system in which the contemporary mathematician operates. To this end, instead of starting off either with a picture of mathematics as seen from *inside* the system, or with a view of the system itself as seen from the *outside* looking in, I shall take the unorthodox approach of heading directly for what might be regarded as "the edge." This strikes me as being as good a way as any of gaining an understanding of the system's "defining" features. Furthermore, from such a position, it will be relatively easy for us to shift a little bit in either direction and thus acquire some firsthand experience at doing and undoing the basic

[11] On the contrary, when one views mathematics from a standpoint that does not have excluded middle reasoning "built in," one finds that the effect of introducing it is to make it impossible to maintain certain important discriminations. As a result, the structure of mathematics is "flattened" and much of its pattern and internal organization is rendered opaque.

acts of acceptance as such by means of which the "reality" of the contemporary pure mathematician's system is actually constructed.

To get to the edge of the system, we can follow a route that Michael Dummett took several years ago and which he reported upon in a brilliant essay entitled "The Philosophical Basis of Intuitionistic Logic" (Dummett, 1975). The discussion that follows is based upon the latter part of that work. Dummett was investigating the force of various arguments that someone in my position might offer to a mathematician inside the system to get him to see that certain of his accepted beliefs about mathematics are, in fact, incorrect. And, while developing a complex line of reasoning designed to show why a certain approach would not necessarily succeed, Dummett was led to focus his attention upon the following question.

Suppose that we have two mathematical assertions, S and T, and also a computational procedure, P, which has the property that by carrying it out either S or T (and possibly both) is established. (Example: S is the assertion that more than a million terms of the sequence $s(n) \equiv$ the fractional part of $(3/2)^n$ lie in the interval from 0 to $\frac{1}{2}$; T is the corresponding assertion for the interval from $\frac{1}{2}$ to 1; and P is the procedure of computing two million and one terms of the sequence, keeping count of how many fall into each of the two intervals.) Suppose also that the procedure has not been carried out. Question: In such a case, is it correct to say that what we possess is either a procedure for establishing S or a procedure for establishing T (and possibly both)? When T is the negation of S, the question being asked is whether, without having carried out the procedure, we are nevertheless in a position to say that we now possess either a way of proving S or a way of disproving S, although we are not in a position to say which.

Now, one reaction to such a question might be that it has only to do with terminology; that all the facts were laid out before the question was posed and that we can "say" whatever we like so long as it is understood that by so doing we are merely introducing a paraphrase of what we said in the beginning. If that is your reaction then you are standing outside the system at this point. However, at the time he wrote that essay, Dummett was clearly standing a bit inside the system; and, as a result, for him the matter was not nearly so simple as I have just made it out to be. Indeed, the position I have just stated is one that he continually refers to as "hard-headed"; and he suggests that it takes a significant act of will to be so hard-headed. (In fact, as he told me later, at the time he wrote the essay he did not believe that anyone was actually capable of holding such a position.) Why? Because, so we are told, "It is very difficult for us to resist the temptation to suppose that there is already, unknown to us, a determinate answer to the question of which of the two disjuncts we should obtain a proof of, were we to apply the decision procedure [p. 36]." Thus, from where Dummett stood at the time he wrote these lines, there is a certain temptation that is difficult to resist. This temptation is part of the "reality" of that standpoint; let us now attempt to find out where it comes from.

Note

> In the discussion that follows, it is important to try to keep in mind what one's own position is at any given point. My aim is to shift back and forth so as to give one the experience of what it is that creates the "reality" of the contemporary mathematician's system along this particular part of its "edge." This means, on the one hand, being completely on the "outside" so as to feel no temptations of the sort to which Dummett refers and, on the other hand, also allowing ourselves to experience the tug that pulls one "inside." In addition, we shall have to attempt to act as observers of ourselves in the course of having these experiences.

Anyone who experiences the temptation to which Dummett refers must, first of all, attribute to himself an understanding of the expression "there is already, unknown to us, a determinate answer" to a certain question. In other words, such a person must suppose of himself, correctly or not, that he has participated in an establishment of language use that specifies, at least implicitly, what is entailed in "supposing that there is already, unknown to us, a determinate answer" to a certain question. I contend that this is the fundamental act "of acceptance as such"—one taking place strictly in the domain of language use—that creates the conditions that produce the temptation. Let me now attempt to support this contention as best I can.

Consider first my own position. When I take Dummett's statement in the straightforward way that it is presented in his essay, my response to it is this: Let him first explain to me what he means by it and then I might have something more to say. No matter that the expression "there is already, unknown to us, a determinate answer" is suggestive; that I have a number of associations to it; and that I find myself thinking that I understand what sort of things prompt Dummett to say what he does. All of this is relevant. But let us recall the context in which we are operating; it is a scientific context, the science being pure mathematics. And we have focused our attention upon a class of cases whose description has been given with admirable clarity: Two mathematical statements and a procedure by means of which at least one and possibly both can be established. Therefore, however suggestive one may find the language use, "there is already, unknown to us, a determinate answer to the question of which of the two statements we should obtain a proof of, were we to carry the procedure out," unless we have provided a clear account of what we mean by "supposing" that "this is so," we would simply be mucking up our scientific discourse and also our conceptual framework to "accept" such a "supposition" without any further ado. As I see it, on this ground alone, the temptation is highly resistible.[12]

Let us take this as a sign that one who finds the temptation difficult to resist feels that the meaning of the expression *is* quite clear; and let us attempt to figure out in what this meaning might consist. We could of course take the meaning of "there is already, unknown to us, a determinate answer" to be "there is already, known to us, a determinate procedure for getting the answer but the procedure has not been carried out." In fact, this is the meaning I myself assign it, and I believe that many other people do too. But if one takes this approach, then there is no temptation, no resistance; there is merely a paraphrase of what has already been said. Therefore, someone who feels such a temptation must mean, or believe that he means, something more than this. What could that possibly be? Perhaps what is meant is that, although the answer is unknown to us, it is known to someone else. This way of attaching a meaning to the expression does go beyond the data; however, it clearly is not what is intended in the case at hand. When Dummett says "unknown to us," he means to all of us. Of course, someone else *might have* carried out the procedure and determined the answer; it is just that in most cases there is no particular temptation to suppose that this is the case.

By the way, it also is clear that, whatever the expression "there is already, unknown to us, a determinate answer" is supposed to mean, it is not going to be something that we are capable of knowing, only of supposing. (This is true even in the case where what we mean is that somebody else has determined the answer.) Therefore, what we need an account of is not what is required in order to know such a thing but rather of what is entailed in supposing it; that is, in accepting it "as so."

Dummett's own discussion of this matter is based on a consideration of the adjective "determinate." He asks: Is this a case in which it is correct to say that there is a "determinate" answer? And he argues, quite successfully in my opinion, that it is. As he sees it, the situation we are considering is of the following sort: we know that if an act of type A is performed, then the outcome will be either of type B or type C. But, in many such cases, the answer to the question of which of the two outcomes we would get, were the act to be performed, is "indeterminate" in the sense that it may depend upon other factors. For example, we know that if the Red Sox and the Yankees play a complete game, then either the Red Sox or the Yankees will win; but

---

[12] However, it would be quite proper for anyone who feels so inclined to attempt to produce an account of the required sort. Should one be produced, it might then be possible to discuss these matters in a very different way. Also, by attempting to provide such an account and not succeeding one might be led to reconsider one's position.

on different occasions it may be one team or the other. However, the mathematical case is definitely not of this kind; the answer to the question of which of the two statements would be established if the procedure were to be carried out cannot vary from one act of carrying it out to another.[13] In this sense, it is not "indeterminate." As Dummett says, "since at each step the outcome of the procedure is determined, how can we deny that the overall outcome is determinate also?"

Dummett's point is well taken. And yet, notice that if we accept it, it still does not take us beyond the level of a mere paraphrase of "we have a determinate procedure that has not been carried out." So there is no temptation and no resistance. Therefore, we still have to look elsewhere.

I believe that I know where to look. "There is already . . . an answer." Certainly, if we were to carry the procedure out, we would come to know the answer and we would be able to say either "The answer is S" or "The answer is T." Also, even before the procedure has been carried out, we may wonder: Is the answer S? Is it T? Or both? Hence, it may appear that what we are talking about is a certain "thing," the answer; that is, that "there is," at least in the realm of potentiality, this "thing," the answer, about which we would acquire a certain piece of information were we to carry out the procedure. Similarly, when we discuss the case that T is the negation of S and remark that by carrying out the procedure we would establish either that S is true or that it is false, it again may appear that we are talking about a certain "thing," the statement S. In this case, what is at issue is whether this "thing," the statement S, "already" possesses a certain property. What property? Answer: That one of the two properties, "being true" and "being false," that we would discover it to possess, were we to carry out the procedure.

As soon as we allow ourselves to accept that talk "about answers" and "about statements" is, in some literal sense, about "things" that stand in some relationship to us—more specifically, to accept that, in the cases under consideration, being in a state of "knowing the answer" (as a result of having carried out the procedure) constitutes a recognition of "its" existence—it also appears to make sense to ask whether "knowledge of the answer" is a *necessary* condition for "the existence of the answer." And it is precisely here that we may feel an irresistible temptation to say "No, it is not." By accepting that at least *after* we have carried out the procedure there is a "thing," the answer, that we then confront, we find ourselves faced with the question of whether the act of carrying out the procedure is one of "creation" or "discovery." By carrying out the procedure, do we actually "make"

---

[13] Why? Answer: because we do not allow it. Thus, were we to perform two acts, each of which we accept as an instance of "carrying out the procedure," and find afterwards that they yield two different answers, we would say "An error must have been made."

either *S* or *T* (or both) "be" the answer or do we merely "find out" which of them "is" the answer? Is there already, unknown to us, a determinate answer or does it only come into being by the act of carrying out the procedure? In a case that *T* is the negation of *S*, by carrying out the procedure do we actually "make" *S* have the property of "being true" or of "being false," or do we rather "find out" either that *S* "is" true or "is" false?

Once we have, unwittingly, committed those acts "of acceptance as such" concerning language use that make these pseudoquestions appear to be genuine ones, it does indeed seem to be hard-headed, and perhaps even solipsistic, to refuse to accept that the act of carrying out the procedure is one of discovery and not of creation. Why? One reason is that, whereas the act of carrying out the procedure is obviously repeatable, that "thing" we call "the answer" is unique. If the act of carrying out the procedure literally produced the answer, then by carrying it out twice we would get two answers; and we see this as being plainly counterfactual. By contrast, the explanation that we "find" the answer seems to fit the situation very well because an act of finding some thing is one that can be repeated again and again, and by different people.

Also, to someone who has already accepted this much, the thought of somebody maintaining that the act of carrying out the procedure is what "makes" there be an answer is likely to conjure up other images of an apparently similar sort; for example, that of someone insisting that his act of finding an old pair of shoes in the closet is what "made" those shoes "be" in the closet. We are conditioned to find this position repugnant.[14] We can see that it is incorrect but it also seems to be irrefutable. Why is it incorrect? We might say that it is because the shoes were already in the closet before we found them there; however, that would not be right because, for all we know, the shoes were *not* in the closet before we found them there. It is rather that, however and whenever the shoes did get into the closet, it was not by an act of perception. In case you are playing the devil's advocate here and asking "But how do you know that?" let me take the trouble to put this in the proper way. I am not pretending that we can literally *rule out* the possibility of it being established that, at least in some cases, an act of perception "makes" that which is perceived "be." I am merely observing that, as it stands, we have no grounds for supposing this to be so. All we know is that the position of maintaining that it is so appears to be irrefutable. But it certainly is not something that we "see" to be so; our experience is not constituted for us that way.

In other words, the reason it is incorrect to insist that an act of percep-

---

[14] And, unfortunately, this repugnance tends to spill over onto other positions which, when looked at superficially, seem to be close to this one.

tion "makes" that which is perceived "exist" is simply that, as it stands, we have no knowledge that this is the case. This does not rule out the possibility that in the future someone might provide us with such knowledge. But, in the meantime, it is just talk.

ON NOT BEING TAKEN IN BY LANGUAGE

The question of why we find the idea of solipsism so repugnant is an interesting one; however, it does not need to be answered here. For us, it is enough to recognize that it is a position that need not be maintained. And, likewise, we need not maintain the position that "the answer did not exist until the procedure was carried out." On the other hand, we also need not maintain the position that "the answer did exist before the procedure was carried out." So long as we do not allow ourselves to be taken in by language, we do not have to maintain either position; and, as I shall argue, there are very good reasons why we should not.

Thus far I have presented my account of what it is that creates the temptation to which Dummett refers in his essay. In the course of doing this, I have tried to use language in a way that allows one to experience the tug that pulls one "inside" the system at this point. It is a way of using language that seems to force us to choose between what in fact are two metaphorical descriptions of the manner in which pure mathematical knowledge is acquired: discovery or creation. And it strongly compels us to accept that the "correct" answer is "discovery" and not "creation." If one yields to this compulsion—or temptation, call it what you will—then, in the absence of any pull in the opposite direction, one will be drawn almost immediately to a completely Platonistic conception both of mathematical statements and also of the activity of mathematics; that is, of the relationship between the mathematician and his domain of inquiry. However, we have seen that the source of this tug is to be found in certain unexamined acts of acceptance as such that take place strictly in the domain of language use. So long as we do not fall for the idea that talk "about statements" and "about answers" must be taken literally as being about "things" that stand in a certain relationship to us, there is no temptation and no choice to be made. Nor does this way of talking have to be abandoned; on the contrary, by providing a strictly operational account of what constitutes correct usage, it can be made into an extremely precise and efficient means for the expression of pure mathematical knowledge. Let me now elaborate on this point of view.

Statements as Signals: Using Language to Make Knowledge Sharable

I begin from the position that, in a science, the chief function of language is to make knowledge sharable. For example, if I know that no square of a rational number can be equal to 2, then by an appropriate use of language I may be able to "share" this knowledge with you; I may be able to "prove it" to you. Of course, in order for us to be able to participate in such a "sharing" of an experience of knowing something, we must already share an understanding as to how language is to be used for such a purpose; we have to be able to "read" each other's signals. But the conventions of language use are something that we ourselves have to establish; and, among these conventions, there must be ones that specify the conditions under which it is correct to assert such and such. In a scientific context, the conditions under which it is correct to assert such and such are precisely those that constitute being in a state of knowing that such and such; for example, of knowing that no square of a rational number can be equal to 2 or that some odd numbers are prime. Thus, a "statement," or "assertion," is nothing more (nor less) than an announcement, or signal, that one is in possession of a certain piece of knowledge. Also, at least in the case of pure mathematics, it is understood that this is knowledge that one is in a position to share; for example, by using language to specify certain procedures that are to be followed in order to attain this knowledge.

From this standpoint, to inquire about some statement whether "it might be true, independent of our knowing it" is merely idle talk, devoid of substance. For there are not literally such "things" as "statements"; only acts "of stating." And, in a scientific context, the idea that one "might be" speaking "the truth" without knowing it is at best a confused way of attempting to pose a question.

In other words, what is called for here is not an attempt to define some notion of a statement S "being true" or "being correct" but rather an account of what one has to know, as an observer of one's own states of knowing, in order that it be correct to assert S; or, equivalently, that it be correct to assert that "S is true." Since such an assertion is supposed to be a signal that one knows that S is true, it is correct to assert it when one does know that S is true and it is incorrect when one does not. In the same spirit, a question of the form "Is S true?" ought to be construed as signaling, literally, a quest: a quest after knowledge that S; for example, a quest after knowledge that no square of a rational number equals 2. And such a quest is successful when it results in the attainment of the desired state of knowledge; in a state that one recognizes as "knowing that S."

Note

One might object to this last remark on the grounds that attaining a state of "knowing that S is false" should also be counted as a successful resolution of the quest. In other words, a question of the form "Is S true?" may be answered either "yes" or "no." Fine, but there is an important proviso. In order to give this more than an appearance of making sense, we need to establish the conditions under which it is correct to say of a statement that "it is false." Equivalently, we need to give an account of "negation."

This is a very interesting subject. One might wish to say that a statement S "is false" unless it is backed up by knowledge that S. But in doing that one really is thinking of "a statement" as a particular act of saying something; and in calling it "false" or "hollow" we are saying that it is "just talk." In other words, we are remarking that this is a case in which it it incorrect to assert S; however, the intended meaning of "not S" is such that being in a state of knowing that not S is supposed to entail considerably more than merely not knowing that S. It is supposed to entail knowing that "it is impossible" to get into a state of knowing that S. But it still remains to say in what knowledge of that is supposed to consist. (Also, at least in pure mathematics, it is traditional to reserve the expression "S is false" to be a signal for knowledge that not S; let us agree to maintain this convention here.)

I realize that, in both ordinary and scientific discourse, we nearly always attribute to ourselves (and others) a remarkably broad command of the use of the term "not," one that certainly extends far beyond the particular context in which such a command actually has been established. It is evident that our use of "negation" lies very deep and also that it is ubiquitous both in discourse and in thought. We try to explain "negation" in other terms and, most often, we find ourselves talking once again in terms of "negation." Should this be taken as a sign that we possess tacit knowledge of "the operation of negation," knowledge that we are as yet unable to articulate? My answer to this question is: knowledge of what?

From observation of actual language use, it is possible to specify some of the characteristic properties that we require any operation answering to the name "negation" to possess. For example, we require $not\ S$ to imply, for each T, if $(S\ or\ T)$ then T. In other words, we require "knowing that $not\ S$" to entail knowing also that, for any other statement T, knowledge of a procedure for coming to know either S or T is, in fact, knowledge of a procedure for coming to know T. One slightly unorthodox approach to negation would be simply to declare that a statement U "is of type $not\ S$" provided that "knowing that U" possesses the above mentioned property that we demanded of "knowing that $not\ S$." That is, that U implies, for each T, if $(S\ or\ T)$ then T. The difficulty is then in establishing, for some particular statement S and some other statement U, that U is indeed of type $not\ S$. For example, if S is the statement "some square of a rational number is equal to 2," we might wish to show that "there is a procedure by means of which, for each rational number r, it can be established either that $r^2 < 2$ or else that $r^2 > 2$" is of type $not\ S$. I do believe that results of this kind can be established; however, in practice, the complete epistemological analysis that is required to do so is rarely carried out. (In this respect, and also in many others, the as yet unpublished foundational work of Alexander Volpin is quite exceptional.) One way or another, such an analysis has to reduce the problem of showing that some S "cannot possibly be known" to a question of whether, after certain procedures have been carried out, certain other statements S_1, S_2, etc., are or are not known. And the "not" that here modifies "known" has to be explained as part of a general account "of knowing."

I myself do not know how to do a fully adequate job of introducing an operation "not" on general statements, even in the context of pure mathematics. At this moment the best I can do is to offer the following sketch of one possible account: The condition under which it is correct to assert "not S" or "S is false" is that one is in a position to see that if anyone else should be found to see himself as being in a state "of knowing that S" then one would be able to point to a certain distinction that this person was failing to make; that is, one would be able to discern two things that this other person was treating as being "the same." I should add that, despite the sketchiness of this account, in practice even sketchier versions have proved fairly serviceable for some mathematical purposes. See, for example, the book *Foundations of Constructive Analysis* by my colleague Errett Bishop (1967).

Considering how heavy a burden the undefined, but supposedly well understood, "operation of negation" is required to bear in contemporary pure mathematics,[15] it would make good sense for the mathematicians to investigate whether they do indeed possess the knowledge they attribute to themselves of such an operation on statements. However, that would entail calling into question one of the fundamental acts of acceptance as such upon which the contemporary mathematician's belief system is based; and within that system this cannot be done. Besides, contemporary pure mathematicians are quite content with their finding that "not" *can* be seen as being "completely understood" and that one can operate with the term formally in a way that has a striking appearance of making sense. Furthermore, these formal "linguistic" rules can be made very precise, giving the entire enterprise an overall appearance of great exactness; and the question of whether it all is built on anything *but* appearance need never be considered. And even if it is considered, it need not be taken seriously.

Two Mathematical Statements and a Procedure for Getting into a Position to Make at Least One of Them

Now let us reconsider the type of situation in which it was said to be "very difficult for us to resist the temptation to suppose that there is already, unknown to us, a determinate answer to the question of which of the two disjuncts we should obtain a proof of, were we to apply the decision procedure." We have a computational procedure P and we know that by carrying it out either S or T, and possibly both, would be established. This is a type of situation in which what we possess knowledge of is a means for acquiring other knowledge of a particular sort; more specifically, we are in a state of knowing that if we were to carry out the procedure we would get either into a state of "knowing that S" or else into a state of "knowing that T," and possibly into both.

But so far we have been talking only about a hypothetical situation; therefore, let us now consider a specific case of this type, the one that was mentioned earlier parenthetically. S is the assertion that more than a million terms of the sequence $s(n) \equiv$ fractional part of $(3/2)^n$ lie in the interval from 0 to $\frac{1}{2}$; T is the corresponding assertion for the interval from $\frac{1}{2}$ to 1; and P is

---

[15] Try stating without it either the law of contradiction or the law of excluded middle.

the procedure of computing the first two million and one terms of the sequence, keeping count of how many fall into each of the two intervals and noting at each stage of the procedure whether at least one of the two counts exceeds a million. We know that, were the procedure to be carried out, the sum of the two totals would (be found to) exceed 2 million and also that each individual total either would or would not (be found to) exceed 1 million. But we know also that if neither of the two totals were (found) to exceed 1 million, then their sum would not (be found to) exceed 2 million. So we now know that, were the procedure to be carried out, at least one of the two totals would (be found to) exceed 1 million. Hence, this is a particular case in which we now know that, were we to carry the procedure through to completion, we would be either in a state of "knowing that S" or else in a state of "knowing that T." And there is nothing more to it than that.

We saw earlier that when we allow ourselves to be taken in by superficial characteristics of language use, we may find ourselves forced to choose between two metaphorical descriptions of the act of carrying out the procedure P: "discovery" or "creation." Now, from the present standpoint, S and T serve as signals to be made when one is in a certain state of knowing; and the function of the procedure P is to get one either into one state or the other. Therefore, in the absence of any other way of getting into one of these states, it is definitely *not* correct to assert either S or T *before* the procedure has been carried out. In this sense, the actual state of affairs is operationally, if not conceptually, more accurately captured by the "creation" metaphor than by the "discovery" one; note that this is exactly the opposite of what we found when we allowed ourselves to be taken in by the metaphorical use of a language "of things." From a scientific standpoint, what counts is knowledge not talk. Thus, in the present case, what would constitute something significant would be to get either into a state of knowing that S or else into a state of knowing that T.[16] And, as it stands, we know only one way of doing this: namely, by carrying out the procedure P.

In this case, we may say that the act of carrying out the procedure "creates" or "produces" a certain state of knowledge: either knowledge that S or knowledge that T. However, it does not follow that it produces any thing called "the answer to the question of which of these two states of knowledge would be produced, were the procedure to be carried out." If we want to continue to talk metaphorically about things called "answers," then we still do better to speak about "finding" the answer, rather than "making it," by

---

[16] So far as I have been able to determine, neither S nor T has been established. To anyone who enjoys tackling such questions I recommend the following policy: Attempt to establish both statements by proving more generally that for each positive integer k there is a $N \geq 2k$ with the property that among the first N terms of the sequence "fractional part of $(3/2)^n$" there are at least k in each half of the interval from 0 to 1.

carrying out the procedure. But if we are going to maintain such a metaphorical use of language in a scientific context, we at least ought to recognize it as such.

UNDERSTANDING MATHEMATICAL STATEMENTS[5]

Notice that, in using language the way we did in the preceding illustrative example, the seemingly "present tense" statement "more than a million terms of the sequence 'fractional part of $(3/2)^n$' lie in the interval from 0 to $\frac{1}{2}$" is not presumed to refer to anything that, literally, "is now the case." What we have to bear in mind is that, from the present point of view, being in a state of what would be called "understanding this statement" consists in nothing more nor less than understanding, in strictly experiential terms, the conditions under which, according to the conventions that we have established, it is correct for someone to perform the act of making this statement in order to signal a certain state in which he finds himself. However, we really have not yet explained just what these conditions are. And anyone who still is inclined to think that the expression "terms of the sequence" *must* somehow refer to "things" that are "already there" in the interval may suppose also that these conditions must consist in "finding out" something that "is already the case."

Thus, in a sense, we are back in a situation in which we found ourselves earlier; only now, instead of talking "about answers" and "about statements," we are talking about what certain of these statements are about. By carrying out the appropriate computation, do we "find" that a certain term of the sequence lies in the interval between 0 and $\frac{1}{2}$? Or do we "make it" be there? When I compute $(3/2)^5 = 243/32 = 7 + 19/32$ and thereby come to know that the fifth term of the sequence equals 19/32, which is between $\frac{1}{2}$ and 1, am I "finding out" something that "was already the case" or am I "making it be so"? As before, once we allow ourselves to accept that there really is such a choice to be made, we feel compelled to accept also that the correct answer is "find" and not "make."

Fortunately, there is no need to repeat, in this new context, the discussion presented earlier. Our previous remarks about the use of a language "of things" for talk "about answers" and "about statements" apply equally well to its use within the statements of mathematics themselves: to talk "about numbers," "about functions," "about sets," etc. It is true that, when we approach this way of using language uncritically, it does indeed exert a powerful influence upon us; and we do find ourselves feeling compelled to suppose that, in some unexplained (and apparently unexplainable) way, such statements as "7 is odd," "19/32 is between ½ and 1" and "more than a million terms of the sequence 'fractional part of $(3/2)^n$' lie in the interval between 0 and ½" are, in some literal sense, "present tense" assertions "about objects and their properties." Therefore, this way of using language should *not* be approached uncritically; for, as scientists, we simply have no business playing guessing games about "the meaning" of our scientific language, which in this case is the language of pure mathematics.

On the contrary, if we want mathematical language to function as a vehicle for signaling, recording, and communicating mathematical *knowledge*,[17] then we must take the position that an "understanding" of mathematical language, that is, an understanding of "what the statements of mathematics are about," can consist in nothing more nor less than an understanding of the conventions that do, in fact, govern the use of mathematical language for precisely those purposes. But, as I have already remarked, these conventions must be established by *us;* and until we have done so they do not exist.

Now it may and, indeed, does appear to us that some conventions of this kind already have been established and that we know (well enough) what they are; the evidence for this is simply that we find ourselves accepting certain particular mathematical statements, for example, "19/32 is between ½ and 1," as being already understood. That is, we accept that conventions governing their use have been established (though without necessarily being written down anywhere) and that we possess an adequate working knowledge of them. But any particular belief of this sort can be put to the test; and, on strictly scientific grounds, it ought to be.

Note

It cannot be emphasized too strongly that I am writing here about conventions governing the use of language for the purpose of signaling, recording, communicating, etc. certain experiences *of knowing,* those that we label "mathematical," and not (or, more precisely, not only) about rules of some formal "language game" in which one is allowed to make certain utterances, or marks on paper, on the condition that certain other ones already have been made. We are concerned here with mathematics as knowledge acquired by acts of mathematical proof and with mathematical language as a means of communicating that knowledge.[18]

[17] And, moreover, in such a way that those acts of mathematical language use that we call "proofs" are precisely the acts of acquiring such knowledge.

[18] In contemporary mathematics, there are precise definitions stipulating the form that a succession of utterances or marks on paper must display to be a "formal proof" of a "formal mathematical statement" S. Since mathematicians sometimes work for years, even decades, attempting to produce either a formal "proof" or "disproof" of some particular "statement," obviously the construction of such formal entities does, in this one sense, provide us with new and often highly nontrivial knowledge. But in and of itself the construction of such formal entities does not—and cannot—provide us with any knowledge of the sort that is traditionally taken to be

Furthermore, in keeping with this concern, I shall not leave this part of the discussion without explaining, in the most concrete way that I can, exactly how mathematical language can be, and to some extent already has been, made to function in just such a way. However, before I do this, I want to describe in more general terms the kind of understanding of mathematics that a systematic operational account of mathematical language use provides.

First, one gets a clear understanding of the very special role that language acts (of a certain kind) play in pure mathematics; I have discussed using mathematical language as a "vehicle" for communicating pure mathematical knowledge. But in fact, pure mathematical knowledge is knowledge *about* pure mathematical language use.

Also, in contrast to every other science with which I am familiar, pure mathematics is "epistemologically closed." In pure mathematics, the means by which one seeks and sometimes acquires knowledge (that is, the procedures that one carries out to get into certain states of knowing) are themselves among the very "objects" about which one seeks and sometimes acquires knowledge (by means that are themselves among the very "objects" about which one seeks and sometimes acquires knowledge). In the main, this is what gives pure mathematics its complex "hierarchical" structure that we often perceive as "levels of abstraction."

One Way of Making Mathematical Language Work

Let me now give substance to the preceding discussion by showing how the traditional language "of counting numbers," including statements "about the operations of addition and multiplication," can be and to a considerable extent already is used for the purpose of signaling, recording, communicating, etc., knowledge about acts "of counting." In fact, more will be shown; for we shall see how this language is used also for the purpose of *acquiring* mathematical knowledge, and not only knowledge about acts of counting (which are themselves acts of mathematical language use) but also about acts of mathematical language use that provide us with knowledge about acts of counting; for example, acts "of performing a computation." (And not only knowledge about acts of mathematical language use of that sort but also about acts of mathematical language use that provide us with knowledge about acts of mathematical language use of that sort, etc.)

To begin, we must distinguish between "recitational" counting, say in base 10 notation, and what, for want of a better term, will be called here "real" counting; for example, tallying a vote or counting the number of

---

"mathematical": knowledge of the laws of arithmetic that we use in daily life, of the theory of proportions, elementary geometry, and so on. In particular, it does not and cannot provide us with any knowledge about the results of performing arithmetic (or any other) computations—for example, that if one adds a column of figures from the top down or from the bottom up the results will be equal. (So that if we find that "they are not equal" an error must have been made.) Knowledge of this sort *can* be acquired by acts of mathematical proof, but not within the context of a strictly "formal game" approach to mathematics.

primes less than 100. We do not have to attempt to explain what, in general, constitutes an act "of real counting" because in pure mathematics we carefully prescribe the context in which such acts are performed; and this permits us to give an account of them that is special to that context.

Once we have learned how to recognize and perform acts of recitational counting (which consist in making one after another, in a specified order, certain distinguishable utterances or marks on paper), and have learned the general rule of formation, we may also learn how to recognize and perform acts of the type "counting B numbers after A." For example, counting five numbers after 7 is done as follows: 8 is 1, 9 is 2, 10 is 3, 11 is 4, and 12 is 5. In this context, we make the convention that a statement of the form "$A + B = C$" is to be used to signal being in a state of knowing that were one to count B numbers after A one would end up with "C is B." Thus, with apologies to Kant, on the basis of our just having counted five numbers after 7 and having ended up with "12 is 5" we are now in a position of knowing that $7 + 5 = 12$.

In addition to the "standard" base 10 system for recitational counting, 1, 2, 3, 4, 5, 6, etc., we may also introduce ones of the type "counting in blocks of B;" for example, counting in blocks of three could be taken to be 1, 2, 3, 1, 2, 3, 1, 2, 3, etc., except that in this notation the marks (or utterances) are not all distinct. So we correct for this by using instead some notation like (1,1), (1,2), (1,3), (2,1), (2,2), (2,3), (3,1), (3,2), (3,3), (4,1), etc. Once such systems have been introduced, one is in a position to perform (and to talk about) acts of the type "counting up to A in blocks of B"; for example, counting up to 7 in blocks of 3 is done as follows: 1 is (1,1), 2 is (1,2), 3 is (1,3), 4 is (2,1), 5 is (2,2), 6 is (2,3), 7 is (3,1). And we make the general convention that a statement of the form "$A = C \cdot B$" is to be a signal for knowing that were one to count up to A in blocks of B one would end up with "A is (C,B)." Thus, by what we have done above, we are in a position to make the assertion that $6 = 2 \cdot 3$.

Note

It is easy to see that, in general, by counting up to A in blocks of B one can establish a relationship of the form $A = CB + R$ with R less than B (and possibly equal to 0). Talk "about division," which will not be discussed here, is talk of a particular kind about acts of establishing relationships of this general type.

By continuing in this manner, we may readily establish conventions of a similar sort governing all the rest of the traditional language of arithmetic (and, for that matter, analysis, algebra, etc.). This includes notation like "N^k"; statements of the form "$A = B$" and "$A < B$ "; talk "about negative numbers," "about integers," "about rational numbers," "about real numbers"; the use of predicates, as in statements of the form "*A* is odd" or "*A* is prime"; and so forth.

Note

Talk "about rational numbers" is merely a paraphrase for talk of a particular kind "about integers" and, more specifically, "about ordered pairs of integers *A/B* with *B* different from 0"; for example, the convention governing the use of statements of the form "*A/B* = *C/D*" is that the conditions under which it is correct to assert "*A/B* = *C/D*" are precisely those under which it is correct to assert "*AD* = *BC*."

Talk "about real numbers" is somewhat more complicated. An act "of defining a real number *R*" entails (1) an act of specifying a type of interval [*a,b*] with rational endpoints; that is, establishing a convention governing the use of statements of the form "[*a,b*] is an *R*-interval" (2) an act of establishing that each two *R*-intervals intersect[19] and (3) an act of providing a means whereby for any particular positive rational value of ϵ one can determine an *R*-interval [*a*(ϵ),*b*(ϵ)] of length less than ϵ. Talk "about real numbers" is talk about acts of the sort just described; this includes talk "about the operations of addition and multiplication of real numbers," statements of the form "*R* = *S*," "*R* < *S*," and so on. For example, we make the convention that a statement of the type "*R* = *S*" is to be used to signal knowledge that each *R*-interval has a point in common with each *S*-interval; that is, to signal knowledge that were we, for any *R*-interval [*a*(*R*),*b*(*R*)] and any *S*-interval [*a*(*S*),*b*(*S*)], to compare *a*(*R*) with *b*(*S*) and *a*(*S*) with *b*(*R*) we would get that *a*(*R*) $\leq$ *b*(*S*) and *a*(*S*) $\leq$ *b*(*R*).

Statements involving predicates have the superficial appearance of being "present tense" assertions "about objects and their properties"; consider, for example, "7 is prime," "There is a number greater than a million that is prime," "For every positive integer, there is a number greater than it that is prime," and "Every positive integer is either prime or composite." However, according to the conventions that we establish in order to use such statements for signaling knowledge about acts of counting, acts of acquiring knowledge about acts of counting, and so on, this mode of expression is strictly metaphorical. (Nor do we know of any other way of establishing conventions governing its use according to which it is otherwise.) For example, a statement of the form "*A* is prime" is, by convention, a signal for being in a state of knowing that were one to perform certain acts of mathematical language use, that is, certain "computations," they would display a certain specified form. The computations are these: For each value of *B* that is greater than 1 and less than *A*, count up to *A* in blocks of *B*, ending up in each case with an utterance (or mark on paper) of the form "*A* is (*D,E*)." Then check whether *E* is less than *B* or equal to *B*. We use the statement "*A* is prime" to signal knowledge that were one to carry out these computations one would get in each case that *E* is less than *B*. We also make the convention that "*A* is composite" is to be used to signal knowledge that

[19] That is, that were we, for any two *R*-intervals [a_1, b_1] and [a_a, b_2], to compare a_1 with b_2 and a_2 with b_1 we would get that $a_1 \leq b_2$ and $a_2 \leq b_1$.

were one to perform these same computations, one would get some value of B for which E is equal to B (in which case $A = D \cdot B$). Evidently, by carrying out these computations for any particular value of A we get into one of the following two states: knowing that A is prime; knowing that A is composite. And we signal our knowing this by the statement "Every positive integer is either prime or composite."

Note

We make it a general convention that a statement of the form "Every x is either of type A or type B" is to be used to signal knowledge of a procedure by means of which, for any particular value of x, one can get into one of the following two states: knowing that x is of type A; knowing that x is of type B. But it should be noted that a statement of the form "x is of type T" may itself be used to signal knowledge of a procedure which, were one to perform it for the particular value x, would display a certain specified form. In some cases, for example, "A is prime," the procedure too is specified in advance. But not all cases are of that sort; for example, for a statement of the type "N has the property that there is a number K that is greater than N and is prime," the convention governing its use is only that one must know of some procedure (requiring the performance of various language acts) which, were it to be performed, would get one into a position of being able to make an assertion of the form "K_0 is greater than N and is prime."

Our general convention governing the use of statements of the form "Every x is of type T" is that such a statement is to signal knowledge of a procedure by means of which for any particular value of x one can get into a state of being able to assert "x is of type T." And a statement of the form "There is an x of type T" is to be used to signal knowledge of a procedure which, were it to be performed, would get one into a state of being able to make some particular assertion of the type "x_0 is of type T."

For the purpose of the present discussion, I have now said enough (and perhaps somewhat more than that) about how "present tense" talk "about mathematical objects and their properties" can be made to function as a vehicle for signaling, recording, communicating—and acquiring—knowledge of a particular kind. However, it is important to remember that mathematical knowledge does not consist solely in knowledge of conventions governing mathematical language use. Thus, it is one thing to know what are the conditions under which it is correct to assert "For all positive integers m and n, $m + n = n + m$" and it is quite another to be in a position to make this assertion; that is, to be in a state of knowing that, for all positive integers m and n, $m + n = n + m$. This means knowing in advance that were one, for any particular values of m and n, to count n numbers after m, m numbers after n, and compare the results one would find that they were equal.[20] This is typical of the kind of "predictive" knowledge that one obtains in pure mathematics and it is this quality of "prediction" that, in

---

[20] For example, that were we to count seven numbers after 5 we would get the same result, 12, that we did when we counted five numbers after 7.

practice, makes pure mathematical knowledge of value. Unfortunately, this not being a course in pure mathematics, I have not been able to demonstrate in any significant case how mathematical language acts can be used to acquire such "predictive" knowledge. Therefore, let me now conclude this section by presenting a very brief sketch of how, in one important case, it actually is done.

Example. I shall indicate, without actually doing it, how one can get into a state of knowing that, for all m and n, $m + n = n + m$.

1. Get into a state of knowing that, for all a, b, and c, $(a + b) + c = a + (b + c)$. This can be done by comparing the form of the notation to be used in counting, respectively, c numbers after $(a + b)$ and $(b + c)$ numbers after a.
2. Get into a state of knowing that, for all m, $m + 1 = 1 + m$. This can be accomplished by using a procedure similar to that to be described in Step 3.
3. Using the preceding steps, I shall establish a procedure by means of which, were one for any particular values of m and i in a state of knowing that $m + i = i + m$, one could get into a state of knowing also that $m + j = j + m$ for $j = i + 1$. The procedure consists (essentially) in performing the following computation for those particular values of m, i, and j: $m + j = m + (i + 1) = (m + i) + 1 = (i + m) + 1 = i + (m + 1) = i + (1 + m) = (i + 1) + m = j + m$. For any particular values of m and n, the act of successively performing this procedure for the values $i = 1, \ldots, n - 1$ constitutes a procedure for getting from a state of knowing that $m + 1 = 1 + m$ (Step 2) into one of knowing also that $m + n = n + m$.

Note

Before I proceed, a word of explanation may be in order. It may appear that in the course of the preceding discussion I have lost sight of the main business of this chapter, which is to describe the trap into which I claim that pure mathematics has fallen. However, in reality, my task here is twofold: It is to identify those particular beliefs, attitudes, and habits of thought of contemporary pure mathematics that I claim constitute a trap *and also* to provide at least some indication of the kind of work that has to be done in order to establish a standpoint from which a rigorous and objective demonstration of this claim can be carried out. My sketch of an operational account of mathematical language use falls into the second category.

For the particular demonstration that I have in mind, one requires an understanding not only of the particular conventions of mathematical language use that I have sketched out earlier, but also, and more importantly, an understanding of what in general has to be done to establish *any* such conventions; however, I do not claim that the preceding discussion provides anything more than an indication of what the latter entails.

One needs such a general understanding in order to be able to see why certain particular attempts to establish conventions of mathematical language use have the appearance, but only that, of being successful. I have in mind specifically those standard "explanations" of mathematical language use—of talk "about sets," "about axioms," "about primitive terms," "about mathematical reasoning," and so on—the acceptance of which constitutes the first and most important step in the process of entering into the contemporary mathematician's belief system. A general method for revealing the inadequacy of such an "explanation" is to show that in order for it to work we must already know certain other things of a sort that we demonstrably do not.

I now wish to turn back to a consideration of the contemporary mathematician's belief system and use the groundwork that has just been established to provide support for my claim that this system is a trap. There are two general points that I wish to make and each has to do, in one way or another, with matters of language use of the kind discussed above.

THE CONTEMPORARY MATHEMATICIAN'S UNFULFILLED TASK: MAKING MATHEMATICAL LANGUAGE FUNCTION THE WAY HE WANTS IT TO

Whether or not one happens to "like" the particular conventions of mathematical language use that I sketched out in the preceding sections, the fact remains that they do the job that is required of them. Namely, once they are adopted, pure mathematics does become a genuine scientific discipline in which acts of mathematical proof are, in the traditional sense, acts of acquiring knowledge; in other words, the proofs really do prove something and we can say just what that something is. By contrast, despite appearances, the contemporary pure mathematician's way of "using" mathematical language is not governed by *any* set of conventions that make it function in such a way. To my mind, this is a devastating criticism of contemporary mathematical practice. On the other hand, from within the system, this particular criticism has no force whatsoever. It takes the form of a question that the contemporary mathematician has learned he does not have to answer.

That the contemporary mathematician does not accept the particular conventions I have outlined in the preceding sections is, in itself, no criticism of his position. He may prefer to establish conventions according to which the statements of pure mathematics will be about something *other* than acts of counting, acts of acquiring knowledge about acts of counting, etc. Indeed, we know that he does have such a preference and we also know why. He feels that to say that pure mathematics is about such acts as counting is as wrongheaded as saying that astronomy is about acts of looking through a telescope rather than about "what one sees" when one looks through a telescope. And, in this spirit, he wishes to insist that a statement such as "$7 + 5 = 12$" is not about acts of counting but rather about "a relationship among numbers" that may be discovered by means of certain acts of counting. Fine; but in that case he faces the task of establishing conventions of mathematical language use that will make mathematical language function that way. However, no such thing has ever been done; nor is there the slightest reason to suppose that it ever could be done.

Notes

i. During the nineteenth century, the founders of the contemporary system attached great importance to the task of establishing the requisite conventions of mathematical language use; and, for a good while, they believed that they had in fact accomplished this by explaining all pure mathematical discourse as being "about sets." One fundamental error that they made was to allow themselves to be taken in by the notion that talk "about sets" is, in some literal sense, talk about certain things called "sets." It is instructive to reread, with a critical eye, those traditional (and also contemporary) accounts that are supposed to produce in us knowledge of "what sets are" and, in particular, of referents for such terms as "the set of all odd positive integers less than 10," "the set of all primes," and so on. One finds that, so long as one does not accept in advance that the author of the account is already in possession of such knowledge (even though he may believe that he is), the account does not succeed in providing the reader with any such knowledge either. Furthermore, despite appearances, these accounts do not succeed even in establishing what *sort* of thing a set is supposed to be; that is, in telling us what special properties a thing must possess in order to be a set. And the chief reason for this is that we lack any sufficiently general account of "what things are" of a sort that would enable us to make the traditional pseudoaccounts of "what sets are" into genuine accounts of specific conditions that must be fulfilled for "a thing" to be "a set."[21] For the same reason, attempts to establish such a language use by axiomatics do not work any better than the "informal" attempts.

ii. In the preceding remarks I am not criticizing talk "about sets" as such but only attempts to construe it as being talk about certain "things" (conceptual or otherwise) called "sets." Talk "about sets" has a straightforward operational interpretation in terms of acts of declaring type and, as such, has a proper and very significant role in pure mathematical discourse.

iii. Eventually the inadequacy of the purported accounts of "what sets are" was recognized even within the contemporary mathematician's system; but the attitude that was taken had the effect of leaving the situation basically unchanged. Thus, the contemporary mathematician still feels that he has some intuition of "what sets are" but, since he finds himself unable to make it precise, when pressed he will take the position that his mathematical language use is strictly formal, that his mathematical statements are not *really* about anything but that the structure of his formal language is intended to "model" (whatever that means) his "intuitive idea of set." However unsatisfactory such a response may appear to an outside observer, for the contemporary mathematician it serves the important purpose of enabling him

[21] We are told that a set is "made up" out of its elements; however, as it stands, this use of language is strictly metaphorical.

to stay inside his system. And he can rationalize what he describes as his inability to make precise his "intuition of what sets are" by attributing it to the inherent imperfection of the human mind as "an organ" for "seeing into" the realm of pure mathematics.

iv. An even more fundamental error that the nineteenth-century founders of the contemporary system made was to take for granted that making mathematical language use precise necessitates taking talk "about mathematical objects" literally; so that, for example, talk "about the square root of 2" must be explained as being about some thing, "a real number" having a certain specified property. Why is it that in pure mathematics the use of a language "of objects" can exert such a tug upon us, a tug to take it literally, whereas in so many other regions of discourse we use such a mode of expression to communicate complex pieces of information precisely and efficiently but without feeling any such tug whatsoever? Certainly, had the founders of the contemporary system given the matter any thought, they would have seen from the most trivial considerations that talk "about objects" can be completely precise without being, in any literal sense, about objects. And had they done so, they might also have recognized that a rigorization of mathematical language use need not, and perhaps should not, entail giving "present tense" talk "about objects and their properties" a meaning that is in accord with its surface form.

A Pseudomystery About the Nature of Mathematical Knowledge and the Manner in Which It Is Acquired

Thus, one manifestation of the trapped state into which I claim that pure mathematics has gotten itself is that, although it is supposed to be and appears to be a scientific activity, that is, a discipline in which research is conducted and knowledge is acquired, it is committed to a position for which there is no intelligible account of what, if anything, the statements of pure mathematics are about (and hence of what, if anything, one is acquiring knowledge about when one conducts pure mathematical research). Moreover, this is the case even for such seemingly well-understood statements as "Every positive integer is a sum of four squares" or "π is between 3 and 4." Of course, these statements may be understood operationally, that is, according to the particular conventions that were sketched out before. But, as I have pointed out, the contemporary mathematician explicitly rejects the operational account even though he is not in a position to replace it with any other. He knows what he wants and if he cannot have it he is prepared to do without.

Hence, for the contemporary mathematician, the nature of mathematical knowledge—what it is knowledge of and by what "faculty of mind" one obtains it—is a great and apparently unresolvable mystery. And yet, from the standpoint of an outside observer, there is no mystery as to how this pseudomystery is created. The basic acts of acceptance as such by means of which one enters into the system, that is, by means of which one learns to think "like a pure mathematician," consist chiefly in attributing to oneself (and others) knowledge (that one does not possess) of conventions (that do not exist) according to which "present tense" talk "about the truth or falsity of unproven statements" and "about mathematical objects and their properties" does have a meaning that is in accord with its surface form. Therefore, it really is not surprising that afterwards, when the contemporary mathematician attempts to locate this knowledge that he "knows" that he possesses, he discovers that it is, or at least appears to be, inaccessible to him. But instead of taking this as evidence that he might do well to review the grounds on which he attributes to himself such knowledge, he prefers to treat it as evidence of certain inherent limitations to human understanding. And, in this fashion, by building up fantasy upon fantasy, the contemporary mathematician's world view is expanded to encompass not only mathematics but also the human mind.

Note

Furthermore, as is well known, certain technical results in the theory of formal systems are interpreted as providing more rigorous proof of such limitations to human understanding. The principle is very simple. Suppose that, in the basis of an analysis of possible ways of making proofs, one is able to give a reasonably convincing argument that, for a particular mathematical statement S, both S and its negation are unprovable. From a strictly operational point of view, this is no more evidence of any limitation upon our "capacity" for acquiring knowledge than is, say, our manifest inability to acquire knowledge that $2 + 2 = 3$. However, if one attributes to oneself a mastery of conventions governing the use of "true" and "false" according to which it is correct to say that every mathematical statement is "either true or false, independent of our knowledge of which," then it will indeed appear to be the case that, of the two statements S and not S, at least one is a "truth" that is unknowable to us. But if one recognizes that, despite appearances, no such conventions have been established, then the entire picture collapses and one is left only with an empty piece of phraseology, "true or false, independent of our knowledge of which," and a technical result in the theory of formal systems.

THE DECISIVE INFLUENCE OF LANGUAGE USE ON THE CONDUCT OF MATHEMATICAL RESEARCH

Thus far I have talked mainly about how, by certain acts of acceptance as such taking place in the domain of language use, the contemporary mathematician acquires certain beliefs that may be described as beliefs "about mathematics."[22] I have criticized these beliefs, the grounds upon

[22] If I did not use quotation marks here it might appear that I am accepting that a statement like "I believe that mathematical objects are discovered and not created" expresses a belief about the nature of certain things called "mathematical objects." But it is rather the belief that it does express such a belief that I am calling here a belief "about mathematics."

which they are based, and also the inability of the contemporary mathematician to reconsider the process by which they are acquired. But I have not yet established any connection between the holding of these beliefs and the day to day conduct of mathematical research; and, because of this, one may be tempted to dismiss what I have said so far by contending that my criticism is directed not against the activity of contemporary mathematical research, nor against the product of that activity, but only against certain admittedly metaphysical beliefs about the nature of that activity and its product.

On this view, that body of "theorems and proofs" that is to be found in contemporary mathematical textbooks and journals has a significance, an intellectual value, that somehow manages to be above the criticism I have presented here. It is easy to see why this may appear to be so, especially from the standpoint of someone who holds the beliefs that have been criticized.[23] Nevertheless, to take such a position is to overlook completely the fact that much, perhaps most, of what the contemporary mathematician takes to be the activity of "acquiring mathematical knowledge"—that is, knowledge about continuous functions or partial differential equations—is seen by him as such *only* because of his holding these beliefs. In performing this activity, the contemporary mathematician relies on certain "principles of reasoning" that appear to him to be self-evidently correct. But this perception is completely standpoint dependent; the principles will appear to be self-evident to anyone who has been taken in by the use of a "present tense" language "of objects and properties" and they will not appear that way to anyone who has not. A brief consideration of what Errett Bishop has called "the principle of mathematical omniscience" should suffice to make this point clear.

The principle is that, whenever one is in a position to make an assertion of the form "Every x is either of type A or type B," one is also in a position to assert "Either every x is of type A or some x is of type B." In other words:

If every x is either of type A or type B, then
either every x is of type A or some x is of type B.

Notice how the use of a "present tense" language "of objects" makes this appear to be, somehow, true "by definition."[24] It is therefore no wonder that the contemporary mathematician accepts it as such and operates with it

---

[23] Thus, the contemporary mathematician knows well enough that his account of what mathematics is about is somewhat incoherent. But the lesson he learns from "the reality" of his everyday mathematical experience is that it simply does not matter. Also, even when one takes contemporary mathematical research to be "only a formal game," there is no gainsaying the extraordinary technical virtuosity that sometimes is displayed in the construction of a formal "proof" or "disproof" of a formal mathematical "statement."

[24] One almost is tempted to say that it must be by definition of "true."

accordingly; nor is it any wonder that by means of it he is able to "obtain" a great many "significant results" that he would not otherwise be able to establish. To the contemporary mathematician, the principle of omni-science[25] is a self-evidently correct principle of mathematical reasoning. He sees it this way because in fact the principle *would* be true "by definition" if one *were* able to establish conventions of mathematical language use ac-cording to which "present tense" statements "about mathematical objects and their properties" do have a meaning of the sort that the contemporary mathematician *anyway* attributes to them.

On the other hand, no such conventions have been established; nor, as the very name of the principle suggests, is there any reason to expect that they ever could be.[26] Furthermore, according to the only set of conventions that *have* been established, those described in my sketch of an operational account of mathematical language use, the principle of omniscience is demonstrably incorrect; for, in particular cases, one can see by inspection that one *is* in a position to make an assertion of the form "Every x is either of type A or type B" and yet one *is not* in a position to assert "Either every x is of type A or some x is of type B."[27]

Note

However, it does not follow from this that all the "significant results" that are based upon the principle of omniscience also are incorrect. Some are; others are not.[28] As a matter of fact, despite the widespread use of the principle of omniscience (and others like it), contemporary mathematical theories do contain a good deal of significant operational content. On the other

[25] Which he does not call by that, or any other, name.

[26] The name "principle of omniscience" is suggested by a consideration of those cases in which the range of the variable x is a potentially infinite domain such as the domain of positive integers. In case the range of the variable is finite, we do have a procedure—namely, checking for each value of x whether it is of type A or type B—which, were we to perform it, would put us either into a state of knowing that every x is of type A or that some x is of type B. But we do not have any such general procedure for those cases in which the domain is potentially infinite. There is a much quoted remark by Bertrand Russell to the effect that the lack of such a procedure—in particular, the inability to complete an unending step-by-step process—should be regarded by the pure mathematician, and by the mathematical logician, as a "merely medical" impossibility that he should feel free to disregard. To me, this witty remark of Russell exhibits one of the distinctive features of contemporary pure mathematics: Namely, a failure of "that feeling for reality" that Russell himself declared "ought to be preserved even in the most abstract studies [Russell, 1919, p. 169]."

[27] For example, I am in a position to make the assertion "For each positive integer k, either no more than a million of the first k terms of the sequence 'fractional part of $(3/2)^n$' lie between 0 and ½ or more than a million of them do" but I am not in a position to assert "Either for all k no more than a million of the first k terms lie between 0 and ½ or for some k more than a million of them do."

[28] And, of those that are, some are only "a little bit" wrong while others are almost entirely so.

hand, even though much of it can be extracted fairly mechanically, the overall job of digging it out has proved to be fundamentally a salvage operation. Thus, direct experience has shown it to be only a myth that the contemporary system is, in any sense, a convenient framework for producing mathematics that is operationally significant. On the contrary, it is a handicap: a very serious one. Not only are so many of the "theorems" of contemporary mathematics operationally incorrect; it is the theories themselves that are, almost always, fundamentally off-base from an operational point of view. What may appear to be the main result or a key concept from one standpoint need not be anything of the sort from the other.

The Influence of Talk "About Statements Being True"

In the preceding illustrative example, I showed how the use of a "present tense" language "of mathematical objects and their properties" can make the principle of omniscience appear to be true "by definition." However, in the essay by Michael Dummett (1975) to which I referred earlier, the point is made that it is possible to separate the contemporary mathematician's beliefs about what constitutes correct mathematical reasoning from his belief that the statements of mathematics are in some literal sense about certain things called "mathematical objects." To see how this can be so, consider the following reformulation of the principle of omniscience wherein talk "about mathematical objects and their properties" is eliminated (or, rather, suppressed).

If, for each x, either statement $A(x)$ or $B(x)$ is true, then either all the statements $A(x)$ are true or some statement $B(x)$ is true.

Notice that, as before, it is the use of a "present tense" language "of objects and their properties" that makes the purported principle appear to be true "by virtue of its meaning." However, this time the objects are "statements" and the purported property is "being true." In a similar manner, all the rest of the contemporary mathematician's "principles of correct reasoning"—his laws of logic—can be framed in such a way that all talk "about mathematical objects" is eliminated and it is only his beliefs about the meaning of talk "about statements being true" that make him see these purported principles as being self-evidently correct.

By acts of acceptance as such in the domain of language use the contemporary mathematician acquires the belief that he knows "what it is like" for a mathematical statement "to be true without anyone knowing or being able to know that it is true."[29] As a consequence, he sees himself as being in a position to regard talk "about mathematical statements" not merely as talk about signals that we agree to use (according to conventions

---

[29] See Note ii at the end of this section.

that we establish) to announce that we are in a certain kind of state "of knowing" but, more fundamentally, as being about things that stand in the following kind of relationship to us[30]: there is a property called "being true" that each of these things, unchangingly, either does or does not possess and it does so irrespective of whether any of us knows or is capable of knowing that it does.[31]

This is the "present tense" aspect of mathematical talk and we experience it most vividly at those moments in which we find ourselves wondering about some mathematical statement,[32] not whether we can prove it, or disprove it, but "whether is it true." For the contemporary mathematician, it is experiences like these—ones in which he sees himself as being in possession of a concept of "truth independent of knowledge"—that constitute the unstated justification for the practice of excluded middle reasoning: that practice that the contemporary mathematician would describe as "reasoning according to the principle that every mathematical statement either is or is not true, independent of our knowledge of which."

At bottom, it is this one belief "about mathematics"—a belief that one possesses a concept of "truth independent of knowledge" of a sort that makes the principle of excluded middle be "true by definition"—that makes all the rest of the contemporary mathematician's operationally incorrect "principles of reasoning" seem to be self-evidently correct. And, however innocuous the holding of this belief may appear to someone who does already hold it, it nevertheless is fair to say that no other belief "about mathematics" occupies nearly so central a role either in the construction or in the maintenance of the contemporary mathematical world view.[33]

[30] Who, on this account, also are things: ones constructed in such a way as to be capable of "acquiring knowledge about" other things.

[31] It is interesting to observe how this conception of mathematical statements, each residing permanently in one of the two categories "true" or "false," leads the contemporary mathematician to adopt a "definition" of "S implies T" that does not entail T in any sense "following from" S. From an operational standpoint, it is appropriate to use "S implies T" or "If S then T" to signal possession of a procedure for *getting from* a state of knowing that S *into* a state of knowing that T. By contrast, the contemporary mathematician "sees" four possibilities: S and T both true; S and T both false; S false and T true; S true and T false. And he "defines" the expression "S implies T" to "mean" that one of the first three cases "holds," which for him is equivalent to the fourth case "not holding."

[32] For example, the statement that for every value of N, no matter how large, each half of the interval from 0 to 1 contains at least N terms of the sequence "fractional part of $(3/2)^n$."

[33] Its role in maintaining this world view is manifested most clearly by the manner in which the contemporary mathematician, or logician, comprehends and responds to criticism of the sort that has been presented here: criticism that has no force unless one *first* undoes the basic belief that is being called into question. He responds to it with the observation that when one considers this belief only from the standpoint of holding it, there does not appear to be any good reason for rejecting it. And since he is operating within a belief system, to him this is an entirely

Notes

i. From the standpoint of an outside observer, one of the most significant consequences of adopting the practice of excluded middle reasoning is an inversion of the natural relationship between "truth" and "proof." Instead of "S is true" being a signal to announce a state of knowing which one has attained by means of an act of proof, the very notion of an act of proof is to be explained in terms of a prior notion of "truth independent of knowledge" which may then be appealed to in the course of performing such an act. On this account, an act of proof is an act of reasoning about things called "statements," each of which "is already" either true or false, in order to discovery *for a particular one of them* either that it is true or that it is false. But this is a description of an activity that is radically different from anything that would constitute an act of proof on *any* operational account of conventions of language use.

ii. In my earlier account of what I referred to as "the edge" of the system I described how, by certain acts of acceptance as such taking place in the domain of language use, one may acquire a belief that an act of mathematical proof consists in finding out something that "is already the case"—in other words, that any mathematical statement that can be proved "is already true"—and in this way come to hold a belief that one knows "what it is like" for a mathematical statement "to be true without anyone yet knowing it." But a belief of this sort *may be* entirely compatible with the view that "is true" means nothing more than "is provable," and if it is then it does not support either the practice of excluded middle reasoning or the use of any of the other operationally incorrect "principles of mathematical reasoning" that the contemporary mathematician finds self-evident. The holder of such a belief will find it correct to assert that a mathematical statement "either is or is not true independent of our knowledge of which" provided that he has a procedure by means of which the statement can be either proved or disproved. But for him to see no need to have such a procedure in order to make the assertion, to see himself as being in a position to say that *every* mathematical statement "either is or is not true independent of our knowledge of which," it is necessary that he hold the more obscure belief that he knows "what it is like" for a mathematical statement "to be true without anyone being able to know it."

No account has been given here of how this "stronger" belief is acquired, but I claim that, in fact, it is a product of the same acts of acceptance as such that, in my earlier discussion, were shown to produce the more modest, if also unwarranted, belief that one knows "what it is like" for a mathematical statement "to be true without anyone yet knowing it." Recall that these are acts of acceptance as such that are performed not in the course of actually having an experience of "seeing that some mathematical statement is true" but rather in the course of thinking about, and using a "present tense" language "of objects and their properties" for talking about, what such experiences are like. The distinction is crucial; when one carefully examines the experience of proving a mathematical statement S and thereby getting into a state "of seeing that S is true," one finds that the conclusion of an act of proof is indeed an act of recognition, of "seeing" something.[34] However, when one merely reflects in a general way upon what such experiences are like, it is possible to lose sight of what it is that one does "see" and to confuse it with the sign that one uses to signal that one has seen such a thing. And one product of that

---

adequate response. Moreover, he may argue *from* the belief to the conclusion that any such criticism of it must be misguided. See, for example, page 85 of Quine (1970), where Quine talks about what *he* calls "a confusion between knowledge and truth."

[34] For example, if S is the statement "There is a prime number greater than 10," an act of proof might consist in representing 11 in the form $11 = QB + R$, with Q a positive integer, for each positive integer value of B from 2 through 10 and *seeing that* in each case the value of R is positive.

confusion may be a belief that one knows "what it is like" for "a mathematical statement to be true without there being any way of proving it."

What one "sees" or "discovers" at the conclusion of an act of proof is that a certain structure (which is constructed in the course of the proof) displays a certain form: a form of the type that, according to the conventions of mathematical language use that have been established, entitles anyone who observes it to say "S is true."[35] But "S is true" is merely what one *says,* not what one *sees;* the expression itself is merely the "brand name" for *the type* of thing that one sees at the conclusion of the proof. And it is a type of thing that may be seen only by constructing a proof—not because we need to use the proof as "a ladder" to get ourselves into a position to see it but rather because what one sees is "in" the structure that is created by the act "of making the proof."

Evidently, when one views things in this way, the idea of "a statement being true without there being any way of proving it" is a contradiction in terms. However, if one has not made the observations just described, the usual way of talking "about statements being true" makes it all too easy, when thinking in a general way about what acts "of proving that a statement is true" are like, to confuse what one does discover at the conclusion of a proof with the sign, or signal, one uses to announce the discovery: "that S is true." And if one does make this confusion—if one does fail to recognize that the actual discovery is, of necessity, always about the form of structures that are constructed in the course of the proof—and accepts instead that what one discovers is simply "that S is true," then it will indeed appear to be the case that the possibility of constructing a proof is not a necessity for "a statement to be true." And that, in essence, is the belief "about mathematics" that is needed to make excluded middle reasoning seem right.

iii. While the contemporary mathematician certainly is not alone in his belief that he possesses a concept of "truth independent of knowledge," there does not seem to be any other contemporary scientific discipline that requires such an absolute commitment to this belief as does pure mathematics.[36] There are some philosophers of science, such as Karl Popper (1972), who think otherwise and say that physics is such a discipline, whether or not the physicists themselves are aware of it. However, those whom I have read invariably arrive at this conclusion by confusing what it actually is like not to believe that one possesses a concept of "truth independent of knowledge" with what it appears to be like from the standpoint of someone who does believe that he possesses such a concept.[37] Quite predictably, what these authors come up with as an account of what is like for someone not to hold this belief is the well-known picture of a solipsist: a person who says that "the world is my dream." And they consider this to be a damning criticism. However, from the very standpoint they are criticizing, their own

[35] I am ignoring, for the moment, the "predictive" aspect of the knowledge that is provided by an act of proof: knowledge that *were* one to make certain computations they *would* display a certain form. However significant this aspect may be, it has no bearing upon the present discussion.

[36] Furthermore, in contemporary science, a belief in a concept of "truth independent of knowledge" need not consist in anything more than a belief that one knows "what it is like" for an event to occur—a tree to fall in the forest, or Icarus from the sky—without anyone being there to observe it. And in the context of pure mathematics a belief of this sort does not produce anything more than the "modest" one, discussed above, that is too weak to support the "self-evident correctness" of the principle of excluded middle.

[37] Moreover, they sometimes compound this confusion by failing to make a distinction between the "more modest" and "stronger" forms of this belief that were discussed above in the context of pure mathematics. They do this by treating their criticism of what they take to be the position of not holding the more modest belief as if it constitutes an argument in support of the stronger one.

position appears to be that of someone who says "my dream is the world." Is that also a damning criticism? No? Yes? How do we decide? By failing to take into account the standpoint dependent nature of their own view of other views, the so-called "realist" or "objectivist" philosophers end up committing the very error of which they accuse others: namely, that of seeing other sentient beings *only* as projections of one's own self.

CONCLUDING REMARKS

At the beginning of this chapter I asserted that pure mathematics has fallen into a certain intellectual trap. I have attempted to show you something of what this trap is like, why it is so easy to fall into it, and what happens when one does. As I now look back over the account I have presented, I am only too aware of the major respects in which it is incomplete. That no point has been argued even nearly adequately is, I think, too obvious to require further comment. What concerns me more, however, is that I have had to leave out significant portions of the total picture. For example, I have not managed to say anything, until now, about the bizarre situation that has been created by the insistence that even the activity of mathematical construction[38] be carried out *within* the contemporary mathematician's belief system. On the subject of mathematical construction the contemporary literature is so unreliable that when an author asserts that he has constructed an X he may just as well have constructed an X', or nothing at all; and when he asserts that he has *not* constructed an X he may well have constructed one anyway.[39] In my view, the travesty that contemporary mathematics has made of the activity of mathematical construction is, in a practical if not in a legalistic sense, the reductio ad absurdum of the position upon which it is based. However, this is but one of a number of equally important subjects that have not been dealt with here.

Also, no attempt has been made to examine how well the arguments presented in the latter part of the chapter support the claim that the contemporary mathematician's belief system really is a trap according to the precise meaning I gave this term earlier. My own view is that when the whole case is laid out the only point about which there is some doubt is whether the

[38] That activity that the contemporary mathematician would describe as "the activity of finding mathematical objects of a given type or of constructing rules, algorithms, and explicit formulas for so doing."

[39] He may say, in such a case, "I have proved that there exists a such and such, but I don't know any way of finding one," whereas, in fact, his proof does provide a way of "finding" one. A notable instance of this is Littlewood's proof of the existence of a sign change for the function $\pi (x) - \text{Li} (x)$; see Ingham (1932) and also Kreisel (1952).

contemporary mathematician's basic position really is, on its own terms, irrefutable. Certainly it appears to be;[40] moreover, I believe that a good case can be made out that it is. However, if I should be proved to be wrong on this particular score, then so much the better!

The Title Question Answered

The title question of this chapter is: Can an inquiry into the foundations of mathematics tell us anything interesting about mind? There is a tradition of answering this question in the affirmative, usually by constructing an argument that our capacity for obtaining pure mathematical knowledge can be accounted for only by the existence of some special faculty of mind. Anyone who shares the mathematical world-view of the contemporary mathematician is bound to feel at least some temptation to answer the question with an argument of this sort because he does not have any other way of explaining how it is that we are able to know of and to obtain nontrivial knowledge about a domain of nonphysical "objects" whose existence is "independent of us." Nor does he have any other way of explaining how it is that the beginning student of pure mathematics invariably finds the law of excluded middle, as well as the other logical "laws," to be self-evidently correct. It certainly is not knowledge that is acquired in any ordinary way, that is, by observing the world or by having it demonstrated.[41] Therefore—so this particular line of reasoning goes—it must be knowledge that is somehow "given" to us as part of the basic structure of our faculty of understanding.

But, of course, there is another explanation available: Namely, that this purported knowledge does not exist and that the contemporary mathematician's impression that both he and the entering student do possess such knowledge (or, at least, the capacity for possessing it) is merely an illusion—albeit a very powerful one—arising from certain unfounded, and also unarticulated, beliefs "about mathematics" which themselves are the product of certain unwittingly performed acts of acceptance as such in the domain of ordinary language use. Such is the explanation that has been

---

[40] As is evidenced by the traditional response that is given by the contemporary mathematical community to Brouwer's "constructivist" critique, and also to more recent variations on it.

[41] Indeed, if a student were to fail to assent to the "self-evident correctness" of the law of excluded middle—if, say, he were to request a much fuller account of the matter on the grounds that he has never used such terms as "is true" with the kind of exactness that seems to be called for here—there would be nothing that could be done. There is no "fuller" account. Everything depends upon the student's immediate assent.

offered in this chapter and, if it is right, the contemporary mathematician's way of answering the title question in the affirmative is nothing more than a fantasy produced by language.[42]

Furthermore, if one examines the positive part of the account I have presented here—that is, my little sketch of the nature of pure mathematical knowledge and the process by which it is acquired—one will find that, according to it, there is nothing special, nothing peculiarly "nonempirical," about those states of knowledge that we label "mathematical."[43] To put the matter as plainly as I can, in the course of my own investigation into the foundations of mathematics—the one I have reported on here—I have found no evidence to support the view that pure mathematics, or for that matter logic, is in any respect, like language, a "mirror of mind."

And yet I have asserted, at the beginning of this chapter, that I do see the body of my remarks as constituting an affirmative answer to the title question, albeit one of a radically nontraditional kind. I am referring here to the remarkable phenomenon of mind being acted upon by language and producing a "reality," or world view, of the sort that was described in this chapter.

That language can affect us so powerfully is itself nothing new. We do not need to conduct an inquiry into the foundations of mathematics in order to make the observation that people—all of us—are capable of being taken in by talk, of being carried away by it, of reading into what someone says more than is actually there. Indeed, it is just because experiences of this kind are so familiar—so ordinary—that it may be considered illuminating to discover how much of the contemporary mathematician's perception of an "objective" mathematical reality is actually a product of experiences of this kind. But the case itself is not an ordinary one, except for someone who is strictly in the position of an outside observer. To anyone who starts off inside the contemporary mathematician's belief system, the discovery that an entire component of the "reality" of one's experience is produced by acts of acceptance as such in the domain of language use is not merely illuminating. In a literal sense, it is shattering: Once a mathematician has seen that his perception of the "self-evident correctness" of the law of excluded middle is nothing more than the linguistic equivalent of an optical illusion, neither his practice of mathematics nor his understanding of it can ever be the same.

---

[42] Moreover, even as a fantasy it is rather thin.

[43] On the other hand, there does appear to be something peculiarly nonempirical about what I termed before, somewhat inaccurately, the "predictive" aspect of mathematical knowledge. However, that is a subject for another discussion.

It is my view that a general acceptance of the conclusions that are suggested by this account of contemporary pure mathematics would entail a radical but also very desirable change in the way in which contemporary science is practiced. As things now stand, despite a general awareness that language does seem to have the power to make us "see things," it is not taken seriously that language may be a determining influence—and possibly a source of major error—for the contemporary scientist's own "objective reality": the one into which he enters as a student and then shares with a community of fellow practitioners. However, if there is any lesson to be learned from the case of contemporary mathematics it is that language may be acting upon us in precisely such a way; and that, therefore, it is incumbent upon us as scientists to begin to take this possibility very seriously indeed. Whether we shall ever do this I dare not venture to say, but I suspect that if we do, it will be discovered very quickly that there also are other areas of contemporary science besides pure mathematics for which some significant component of what is taken to be "objective reality" actually is produced in the domain of language use by acts of acceptance as such. And I think that if we do find this to be so, we will have learned something important both about ourselves and the world that we did not know before.

REFERENCES

Bishop, E. *Foundations of constructive analysis*. New York: McGraw-Hill, 1967.

Brouwer, L. E. J. Philosophy and foundations of mathematics. In A. Heyting (Ed.), *L. E. J. Brouwer: collected works* (Vol. 1). Amsterdam: North-Holland, 1975.

Dummett, M. The philosophical basis of intuitionistic logic. In H. E. Rose & J. C. Shepherdson (Eds.), *Studies in logic and the foundations of mathematics* (Vol. 60). Amsterdam: North-Holland, 1975.

Ingham, A. E. *The distribution of prime numbers*. Cambridge: Cambridge University Press, 1932.

Kreisel, G. On the interpretation of non-finitist proofs, part II. *Journal of Symbol Logic*, 1952, *17*, 43–58.

Lakatos, I. *Proofs and refutations: The logic of mathematical discovery*. Cambridge: Cambridge University Press, 1976.

Popper, K. *Objective knowledge: an evolutionary approach*. Oxford: Oxford University Press, 1972.

Quine, W. V. *Philosophy of logic*. Englewood Cliffs, N.J.: Prentice-Hall, 1970.

Russell, B. *Introduction to mathematical philosophy*. London: Allen & Unwin, 1919.

chapter 13

Discussion of the Chapters by Stolzenberg and Chomsky

JACK CATLIN

Although my comments will focus on the issues raised by Noam Chomsky (Chapter 11), they are akin, in spirit at least, to Gabriel Stolzenberg's contribution (Chapter 12). All three of us share—as did Eric Lenneberg—a concern for critical assessment of the methodological and theoretical foundations of inquiry, regardless of whether the topic be mathematics or language.

Chomsky addresses himself to aspects of two topics: (a) the psychological status of generative grammar; and (b) the innateness of universal principles of language. I have worked to make my discussion of these issues simple, for the sake of brevity; to my knowledge, however, I have not simplified in such a way as to distort the basic ideas under consideration.

FORMAL GRAMMAR

Let us look first at the question of the psychological status of formal grammar. I have been helped along in my thinking on this topic by interac-

271

PSYCHOLOGY AND BIOLOGY OF LANGUAGE AND THOUGHT
Essays in Honor of Eric Lenneberg

tion with many at Cornell University—especially John Bowers, Susan Kemper, and Dennis Micham—and also by the writings of Chomsky (1965, 1975) and Pylyshyn (1972, 1973).[1] In addition, my views seem to be compatible with Lenneberg's belief, stated in his later writings (1969, 1972), that the proper goal of grammatical inquiry is the description of facts of language structure.

For this discussion, we can distinguish two broad classes of data available to us in our attempts to understand the psychology of language—behavioral, and intuitional. I interpret "behavioral data" broadly; included are, for example, experimental studies of language processing using standard performance measures, observational studies of language acquisition and use in natural settings, and psychobiological studies of development and of brain mechanisms. By "intuitional data," in contrast, I mean native speakers' intuitively based judgments about language structure. This second class of data is of great importance, as linguistic intuition in many cases reveals, or attests to, facts of language that might never have been discovered by behavioral studies alone.

The first thing to be emphasized about facts of language as revealed by linguistic intuition is simply that there are a fair number of them. Let me illustrate with one standard form of example. Consider the following sentences:

(1) *Sincerity frightens John.*
(2) *John frightens sincerity.*
(3) *John is frightened by sincerity.*
(4) *Sincerity is frightened by John.*

Sentences (1) and (3) are fine as sentences of English, whereas (2) and (4) are odd as sentences of English. Further, intuitively given facts of language are not necessarily limited to facts about single sentences. For example, most speakers of English would presumably agree that (2) and (4) are odd for the same reason—specifically, that sincerity is not the sort of thing that can be frightened. And some facts will be more well established than others, in that the consensus of judgment of native speakers will be broader and clearer.

Now, consider the set of facts of language for which the following two conditions hold:

1. There is consensus among native speakers about the structural regularity in question.
2. This consensus of judgment is not contaminated by extraneous factors.

[1] See also Bever (1970) and Watt (1970, 1972).

In such cases, the psychological reality of the facts of language revealed is indisputable. By this, I mean simply that the structure of language is that which we know it to be. Any adequate theory of the psychology of language must include an account of these aspects of our knowledge of language.

Linguists, of course, are not content to rest merely with accumulating intuitively given facts of language. They are concerned to formulate *theoretical generalizations,* within and across languages, generalizations *not* directly revealed by intuition, but rather established by a discursive process of constructing arguments and adducing evidence. A simple example of this sort has been presented by Chomsky. Consider his sentences:

(5)   *Violins are easy to play sonatas on.*
(6)   *What sonatas are violins easy to play on?*
(7)   *We found out who wrote the book.*
(8)   *What book did we find out who wrote?*

Examples (5) and (7) are fine as sentences of English, whereas (6) and (8) are odd as sentences of English. Chomsky's conjecture is that (6) is odd for the same reason that (8) is odd.

Note, however, that unlike sentences (2) and (4) above, the oddness of (6) is not, by *intuition,* obviously of the same type as the oddness of (8). Thus, support for the conjecture must come from a discursive process of constructing arguments and adducing evidence. A critical question for the larger psycholinguistic community is, what is the psychological status of such conjectures, such theoretical generalizations?

Two things must be kept in mind initially. First, it would be premature for the psycholinguistic community to accept such a conjecture as true in the absence of consensus among grammarians that the arguments and evidence are sufficient. Second, in cases where such consensus *is* achieved, it would be perverse for the larger psycholinguistic community not to accept the generalization so established, unless there were evidence of some other sort incompatible with the generalization.

To focus the discussion, consider the following hypothetical situation (see Figure 13.1). Grammarians have reached consensus about the appropriate network of theoretical generalizations for describing the facts of English, and about the appropriate formal grammar for representing this network. (I take the network of theoretical generalizations to constitute the *empirical content* of the formal grammar, on the understanding that there is room for debate about just which aspects of the formal grammar represent actual empirical claims, and which do not.)

In the absence of contrary evidence of some other sort, it would be perfectly appropriate to accept this grammatical analysis as a descriptive

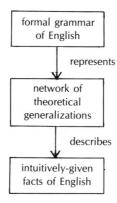

Figure 13.1. The grammatical account of English, at some point in the future.

account of the structure of English, and thus of our adult knowledge of English. To accept the grammatical analysis, so far as I can see, is to accept the network of theoretical generalizations as a characterization of our mental representation of language structure. The empirical content of this idea would be that our mental representation of language structure in some manner *conforms to* the network of theoretical generalizations.[2] This is what I take Chomsky to mean when he says that formal grammar specifies "abstract conditions that unknown mechanisms must meet." And it is consistent with Pylyshyn's (1972) discussion of competence:

> The contribution of the competence formulation is primarily that of providing for the psychologist a systematized body of rather fundamental evidence which a theory of cognition ought to take as a starting point. It is not meant to be a theory of psychological mechanism but rather of an important class of *facts about mental representations* which such mechanisms need to take into account [p. 551].

But I am uncertain if I fully agree with Chomsky's remarks on this topic. Certain of his statements confuse me. One is: "We impute existence to certain mental representations and to the mental computations that apply in a specific way to these mental representations." And another: "We attribute 'psychological reality' to the postulated representations and mental computations."

Perhaps the problem is only one of rhetoric. Perhaps these statements are intended to mean nothing more than what I have just said. If this is so, we

---

[2] This discussion assumes that the notion *mental representation* will prove useful to us in our attempts to understand the nature of language knowledge. Some might question this assumption.

are in agreement. On the other hand, if they are intended to mean something *more*, my problem is that I do not understand, in any clear way, what it *is* they are intended to mean.

There is one further aspect of this topic, the psychological status of formal grammar, that I wish to explore. What might be the consequences for the grammatical account of English portrayed in Figure 13.1 if we went on to try to formulate an integrated psycholinguistic theory? Such a theory would be accountable not only to intuitional data about language structure, but also to behavioral data about language acquisition and language processing.

One thing that might happen is that certain generalizations formulated in the grammatical account of language structure would not survive confrontation with a wider range of data. Chomsky himself (1975) has noted this possibility; for example, in a footnote to *Reflections on Language*, he says:

> Consideration of broader data (in this case, data of performance) might indicate that what appeared to be genuine explanatory principles are spurious and that generalizations discovered are accidental. Investigation of the theory of performance might thus lead to different theories of competence [p. 248].

But what of those theoretical generalizations that *do* survive confrontation with behavioral data, and the formal grammar that represents them? What is their place in an integrated psycholinguistic theory?

In answer, I can do no better than to quote Pylyshyn (1973):

> One must not make too much of the exact form of the competence theory in the related task of building a broader psychological theory.
>
> The form of the grammar (or of any theory of human competence) is settled on for very good reasons—but reasons which do not attempt to take into account any data other than primary linguistic intuitions. Had the model been developed initially to account for this data plus other evidence, the form of the model would very likely have been quite different.
>
> The development of a more general theory of cognition should proceed by attempting to account for the structure which is the output of a competence theory, together with the other kinds of psychological evidence, rather than to incorporate the competence theory as formulated [pp. 45–46].

To close my discussion of this topic, let me note what I believe to be a significant parallel between Stolzenberg's views and my own. The parallel focuses on the question of imputing existence to things. Stolzenberg, a constructivist mathematician, takes issue with the classical mathematical tradition that appears to impute existence, of some Platonic sort, to the objects of mathematical inquiry. I, as a psychologist raised on the notion of converging operations, am rather wary of imputing existence to any hypothesized mental entity or process—be it proposed by a grammarian or by a psychologist—until I see symptoms of the hypothesized entity or process in more than one domain of data.

INNATE KNOWLEDGE

Let us turn now to the innateness of universal principles of language. Lenneberg's thinking on this subject (1967, 1969, 1974), as well as that of others studying the psychology and biology of development,[3] has greatly influenced my own. My primary concern in these remarks will be to clarify the notion *innateness* in relation to the notion *epigenesis*.

What does it mean to say that some principle of language knowledge is innate? I will call a particular principle *"innate"* if it comes to be in the mind by some means other than induction over experience. That is, the principle is innate if it does *not* come to be in the mind through learning. (I interpret the notions *learning of a principle* and *induction over experience* rather broadly. For example, I specifically wish to include, as cases of learning, instances where the organism entertains a restricted set of hypotheses and accepts one over the others on the basis of congruence with the data of experience.)

On the basis of an examination of his writings—especially *Biological Foundations of Language*—I feel that this usage of the term "innate" is consistent with the views held by Lenneberg.[4] As I also believe that this is the most productive usage, my further comments will be predicated on the understanding that some principle of language knowledge is innate insofar as it has been achieved other than by learning, by induction over experience.

If some principle of language knowledge is universal, is it also innate in this sense? To address this issue, I must introduce the notion *epigenesis*, a notion adopted from developmental biology and central to Lenneberg's thinking. Historically, the doctrine of epigenesis is the view that each organism, and each part thereof, is created de novo in the course of individual development. The opposing doctrine of *preformation* is that the organism (or parts thereof) is, in some sense, fully formed at some initial point in development. In accordance with contemporary thinking in developmental biology, Len-

---

[3] For general background, I have found Waddington (1961, 1968) and Piaget (1971) of great value. Also useful are the review articles by Nottebohm (1970) and Gottlieb (1976).

[4] This is also the view of James (1890, Chap. 28), who argues for a basic distinction between front-door knowledge, which the mind acquires on the basis of experience proper, and back-door knowledge, which comes to be in the mind by other means.

neberg (1967, 1969), like Piaget (1971), adheres to the doctrine of epigenesis and rejects that of preformation.

At the most general level, the epigenetic viewpoint commits us to the framework for studying development shown, greatly simplified,[5] in Figure 13.2. In the diagram, development proceeds from left to right as a complex

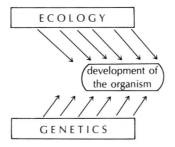

Figure 13.2.   General epigenetic framework for the study of development.

interaction between the organism, genetics, and ecology. By genetics I mean here the totality of genetic influences on the organism; by ecology, the totality of environmental influences on the organism. To understand any particular aspect of an organism's structure or function, we must understand it epigenetically—that is, we must uncover the critical aspects of the complex interaction of organism, genetics, and ecology, over time, that give rise to that which we wish to understand. It is important to note that this epigenetic framework assumes that genetics plays a major role. But it makes no dogmatic assumptions about the exact nature of the respective roles of genetics and ecology in the development of any particular aspect of the organism's structure or function. Those roles remain to be discovered through empirical investigation.

To return to an examination of the question previously posed: If some principle of language knowledge is universal, is it also innate? As I see it, two basic insights underlie the conjecture that universals are innate. On the one hand, it does not appear plausible to consider as innate those things that vary across languages. On the other hand, those things that do *not* vary across languages certainly might have come about by some means other than induction over experience. Thus, universal aspects of language knowledge are, at least, plausible *candidates* for the status of innateness.

[5] At this global level, I have omitted even the portrayal of possible influences of the developing organism on activation of specific genetic material and also influences of the organism on the structuring of its surrounding environment.

There is, however, no general argument that assures the validity of the inference from universality to innateness. There is no reason to rule out the possibility that a universal might come about through learning, on the basis of universal environmental regularities. As Chomsky notes, the conjecture that universals are innate is an empirical one; it stands in need of verification or disconfirmation in each particular case.

How, then, are we to ascertain empirically whether some particular universal of language knowledge is innate? In principle, the answer is clear—within the framework of epigenesis. We will need a fair amount of information about how a particular aspect of language knowledge *is* achieved, before we can reach any firm conclusion about whether induction over relevant experience is critical to that achievement.

It is also worth noting what does and what does not follow simply from the correct classification of an aspect of language knowledge as not learned.[6] To say that a principle of language is innate in this sense is only to state how it did *not* come about. Such a statement in itself constitutes no *positive* characterization of how the mind came to attain that principle; its developmental history remains unexplained. One of Lenneberg's major insights is that to achieve any deep understanding of *any* aspect of language—learned *or* innate—we must inquire into its epigenesis.

I turn now to a comparison of Chomsky's and Lenneberg's views about the innateness of universal grammar. While their views on this matter appear to be quite similar, I feel there may be a subtle, and interesting, difference. Lenneberg (1967) states that "Language potential and the *latent structure* [i.e., universal grammar] . . . are a consequence of human-specific cognitive processes and a human-specific course of maturation [p. 377]." Chomsky's view is that "principles of universal grammar may be regarded as an abstract partial specification of the [child's] genetic program [for language] [p. 201 of this volume]."

Both men make the (empirical) conjecture that universal grammar is innate in the sense that it is unlearned. The difference that I see is that Lenneberg's views about universal grammar are stated in terms of *species specificity*, while Chomsky speaks of *genetic programming*. Lenneberg's discussion of species-specific traits (1967, Chap. 9, Section I) allows that environmental influences, while they do not *shape* species-specific traits, may play a role in their development. In accordance with this, Lenneberg also holds that the relationship between genetics and language is an indirect one: "Genetic transmission is relevant to language facilitation. However, there is no need to assume 'genes for language' [p. 265]." Lenneberg's view of the matter is thus consistent with the framework of epigenesis.

---

[6] Here, and on the question of genetic determination, see Beach (1955).

On the other hand, Chomsky's conjecture about the innateness of universal grammar appears to be of a preformationist type. His usage of the phrase "genetic program" suggests a direct linkage between genetic structure and universal grammar. Also, he specifically states that the *alternative* to his conjecture is that "[the] deeper principles [of universal grammar] might result from some sort of organism–environment interaction [p. 218 of this volume]." Chomsky's conjecture, while acknowledged to be subject to empirical evaluation, appears to categorically rule out the influence of environmental factors on universal grammar.

Insofar as there is a difference, Lenneberg's formulation seems to me to be more useful, as it leaves open (except for effects of learning) the question of exactly what genetics–organism–environment interactions give rise to the emergence of universal grammar in the individual. Lenneberg himself (1969) states quite clearly the nature of the fallacy that his views avoid:

> The nonbiologist frequently and mistakenly thinks of genes as being directly responsible for one property or another; this leads him to the fallacy, especially when behavior is concerned, of dichotomizing everything as being dependent on either genes or environment [p. 638].

In order to circumvent this fallacy, firm adherence to the epigenetic framework, to the goal of understanding the development even of innate traits in terms of the influences of genetics *and* ecology, is necessary.

A second parallel can be drawn between my remarks and Stolzenberg's chapter. Inasmuch as mathematical objects do not preexist in some Platonic Realm of Forms, mathematicians must ask how they come about in the process of inquiry. Inasmuch as language knowledge does not preexist in some genetic program, biologists and psychologists must ask how it comes about in the process of epigenesis.

REFERENCES

Beach, F. A. The descent of instinct. *Psychological Review,* 1955, *62,* 401–410.

Bever, T. G. The cognitive basis for linguistic structures. In J. R. Hayes (Ed.), *Cognition and the development of language.* New York: Wiley, 1970.

Chomsky, N. *Aspects of the theory of syntax.* Cambridge, MIT Press, 1965.

Chomsky, N. *Reflections on language.* New York: Random House, 1975.

Gottlieb, G. Conceptions of prenatal development: Behavioral embryology. *Psychological Review,* 1976, *83,* 215–234.

James, W. *The principles of psychology.* New York: Holt, 1890.

Lenneberg, E. H. *Biological foundations of language.* New York: Wiley, 1967.

Lenneberg, E. H. On explaining language. *Science,* 1969, *164,* 635–643.

Lenneberg, E. H. *Knowledge of grammar—and grammar of knowledge.* Unpublished manuscript. Ithaca, N.Y.: Cornell University, 1972.

Lenneberg, E. H. *Brain and behavior models: Some general comments*. Unpublished manuscript. Ithaca, N.Y.: Cornell University, 1974.

Nottebohm, F. Ontogeny of bird song. *Science,* 1970, *167*, 950–956.

Piaget, J. *Biology and knowledge: An essay on the relations between organic regulations and cognitive processes*. Chicago: University of Chicago Press, 1971.

Pylyshyn, Z. W. Competence and psychological reality. *American Psychologist,* 1972, *27*, 546–552.

Pylyshyn, Z. W. The role of competence theories in cognitive psychology. *Journal of Psycholinguistic Research,* 1973, *2*, 21–50.

Waddington, C. H. *The nature of life*. New York: Atheneum, 1961.

Waddington, C. H. The basic ideas of biology. In C. H. Waddington (Ed.), *Towards a theoretical biology: 1. Prolegomena*. Chicago: Aldine, 1968.

Watt, W. C. On two hypotheses concerning psycholinguistics. In J. R. Hayes (Ed.), *Cognition and the development of language*. New York: Wiley, 1970.

Watt, W. C. Competing economy criteria. *Social Sciences Working Papers, No. 5*. Irvine: School of Social Sciences, University of California, Irvine, 1972.

Bibliography of
Eric Lenneberg

1953 Cognition in ethnolinguistics. *Language, 29*, 463–471.
1954 A study in language and cognition. *The Journal of Abnormal and Social Psychology, 49*, 454–462. (With R. W. Brown.)
Review: *Meaning, Communication, and Value*, by P. Kecskemeti. *Language, 30*, 96–99.
1955 A note on Cassirer's philosophy of language. *Philosophy and Phenomenological Research, 15*, 512–522.
Review: *Psychologie der Sprache*: Vol. 3, *Physiologische Psychologie der Sprachvorgänge*, by F. Kainz. *Language, 31*, 489–492.
1956 The language of experience: A study in methodology. Indiana University Publications in Anthropology and Linguistics, Memoir 13 of the *International Journal of American Linguistics* (Supplement to Volume 22). (With J. M. Roberts.)
1957 A probabilistic approach to language learning. *Behavioral Science, 2*, 1–12.
Review: *Der Mensch und sein Wort*, by A. Schlismann. *Language, 32*, 714–716.
Review: *On Human Communication: A Review, a Survey, and a Criticism*, by C. Cherry. *Language, 33*, 568–575.
Review: *Fundamentals of Language*, by R. Jakobson and M. Halle. *Contemporary Psychology, 2*, 133–134.
1959 *Invitation to join us in research on problems of speech and other skilled bodily movements*. Boston: Speech Research Laboratory, Children's Hospital Medical Center.

281

1960   Language, evolution, and purposive behavior. In S. Diamond (Ed.), *Culture in History: Essays in Honor of Paul Radin*. New York: Columbia University Press.

Review: *Speech and Brain Mechanisms*, by W. Penfield and L. Roberts. *Language, 36*, 97–112.

1961   Color naming, color recognition, color discrimination: A re-appraisal. *Perceptual and Motor Skills, 12*, 375–382.

Review: *The Sounds of Language: An Inquiry into the Role of Genetic Factors in the Development of Sound Systems*, by L. F. Brosnahan. *Contemporary Psychology, 7*, 230–231.

1962   A laboratory for speech research at the Children's Hospital Medical Center. *New England Journal of Medicine, 266*, 385–392.

Understanding language without ability to speak: A case report. *The Journal of Abnormal and Social Psychology, 65*, 419–425.

The relationship of language to the formation of concepts. *Synthese, 14*, 103–109.

Review: *The First Five Minutes: A Sample of Microscopic Interview Analysis*, by R. E. Pittenger, C. F. Hockett, and J. J. Danehy. *Language, 38*, 69–73.

Review: *The Role of Speech in the Regulation of Normal and Abnormal Behavior*, by A. R. Luria. *Psychosomatic Medicine, 24*, 231.

Review: *Speech Disorders*, by Sir Russell Brain. *Pediatrics, 30*, 505–506.

The acquisition of language in a speechless child. Psychological Cinema Register, Pennsylvania State University. (Film)

1963   Review: *Message et Phonétique: Introduction à l'Étude acoustique et physiologique du Phonème*, by Jean-Claude Lafon. *Language, 39*, 246–247.

1964   Language disorders in childhood. *Harvard Educational Review, 34*, 152–177.

A biological perspective of language. In E. H. Lenneberg (Ed.), *New Directions in the Study of Language*. Cambridge, Massachusetts: MIT Press.

The capacity for language acquisition. In J. A. Fodor & J. J. Katz (Eds.), *The Structure of Language: Readings in the Philosophy of Language*. Englewood Cliffs, New Jersey: Prentice-Hall.

How babies learn to talk. *Parents' Magazine*, September.

Primitive stages of language development in mongolism. In D. McK. Rioch, L. C. Kolb, & J. Ruesch (Eds.), *Disorders of Communication*, Research Publications of the Association for Research in Nervous and Mental Disease, Vol. XLII. Baltimore: Williams & Wilkins. (With I. A. Nichols and E. F. Rosenberger.)

Speech as a motor skill with special reference to nonaphasic disorders. In U. Bellugi & R. W. Brown (Eds.), *The Acquisition of Language, Monographs on the Society for Research in Child Development, 29* (1, Serial No. 92).

Apparatus for reducing playback time of tape-recorded, intermittent vocalization. In U. Bellugi & R.W. Brown (Eds.), *The Acquisition of Language, Monographs of the Society for Research in Child Development, 29* (1, Serial No. 92). (With C. H. Chan and F. G. Rebelsky.)

Discussion of Dr. Holzman's paper. American Psychiatric Association, *Psychiatric Research Report, 19*, 93–96.

Review: *Disorders of Language*, Ciba Foundation Symposium, A. V. S. de Reuck and M. O'Connor, eds. *Pediatrics, 34*, 898–899.

1965   The vocalizations of infants born to deaf and to hearing parents. *Human Development, 8*, 23–37. (With F. G. Rebelsky and I. A. Nichols.)

Review: *Signs, Signals and Symbols: A Presentation of a British Approach to Speech Pathology and Therapy*, S. E. Mason, ed. *Language, 41*, 91–94.

1966   Speech development: Its anatomical and physical concomitants. In E. C. Carterette (Ed.), *Brain Function* (Vol. III). Los Angeles: University of California Press.

The natural history of language. In F. Smith & G. A. Miller (Eds.), *The Genesis of Language: A Psycholinguistic Approach*. Cambridge, Massachusetts: MIT Press.

Verbal communication and color memory in the deaf and hearing. *Child Development, 37*, 765–779. (With D. Lantz.)

In search of CNS correlates of reading skills and disabilities. In *Project Literacy Reports*. Ithaca, New York: Cornell University.

1967   *Biological Foundations of Language*. New York: Wiley.

The biological foundations of language. *Hospital Practice, 2*, 59–67.

Discussion of: The general properties of language, by Noam Chomsky. In C. H. Millikan & F. L. Darley (Eds.), *Brain Mechanisms Underlying Speech and Language*. New York: Grune & Stratton.

Reply to: Language and the search for origins (book reviews of *Biological Foundations of Language* by S. Klassen and J. M. Wepman; H. G. Furth; and J. W. Black). *Journal of Communication Disorders, 1*, 320–322.

1968   The effect of age on the outcome of central nervous system disease in children. In R. Isaacson (Ed.), *The Neuropsychology of Development*. New York: Wiley.

1969   Problems in the systematization of communication behavior. In T. A. Sebeok & A. Ramsay (Eds.), *Approaches to Animal Communication*. The Hague and Paris: Mouton.

On explaining language. *Science, 164*, 635–643.

Language in the light of evolution. In T. A. Sebeok (Ed.), *Animal Communication: Techniques of Study and Results of Research*. Bloomington: Indiana University Press.

A word between us. In J. D. Roslansky (Ed.), *Communication*. Amsterdam and London: North-Holland.

1970   What is meant by a biological approach to language? *American Annals of the Deaf, 115*, 67–72.

The neurobiology of language: Practical applications. *Bulletin of the Orton Society, 20*, 7–13.

Fundamentos biológicos da linguagem. *Publicaçoẽs Avulsas do Museu Nacional* (Rio de Janeiro) No. 53.

Brain correlates of language. In F. O. Schmitt (Ed.), *The Neurosciences: Second Study Program*. New York: The Rockefeller University Press.

An acoustic analysis of the Turkish whistling language of Kusköy. *Revue Phonetique Appliqué, 14–15*, 25–40.

1971   The importance of temporal factors in behavior. In D. L. Horton & J. Jenkins (Eds.), *Perception of Language*. Columbus, Ohio: Charles E. Merrill.

Of language knowledge, apes, and brains. *Journal of Psycholinguistic Research, 1*, 1–29.

Developments in biological linguistics. *Georgetown University Monograph Series on Language and Linguistics, 24*, 199–209.

Review: *Language Disturbance and Intellectual Functioning*, by C. K. Lubin. *Linguistics, An International Review, 67*, 113–117.

1972   Prerequisities for language acquisition by the deaf. In T. J. O'Rourke (Ed.), *Psycholinguistics and Total Communication: The State of the Art*. Washington, D.C.: American Annals of the Deaf.

1973   What is meant by knowing a language? In P. Pliner, L. Kranes, & T. Alloway (Eds.), *Communication and Affect: Language and Thought*. New York and London: Academic Press.

The neurology of language. *Daedalus, 102*, 115–133.

Review: *Elizabeth*, by Sharon Ulrich. *Merrill-Palmer Quarterly, 19*, 147–149.

Review: *Phrase and Paraphrase: Some Innovative Uses of Language,* by Lila R. Gleitman
and Henry Gleitman. *Language, 49,* 519–523.

1974   Language development. In J. A. Swetts & L. L. Eliot (Eds.), *Psychology and the Handi-
capped Child.* Washington, D.C.: Department of Health, Education, and Welfare,
U.S. Government Printing Office.

Biological aspects of language. In G. A. Miller (Ed.), *Psychology and Communication*
(Forum Lecture Series). Washington, D.C.: Voice of America.

Language and brain: Development aspects. *Neurosciences Research Program Bulletin,
12,* 513–656. (Edited and with an epilogue by E. H. Lenneberg.)

1975   The concept of language differentiation. In E. H. Lenneberg & E. Lenneberg (Eds.),
Foundations of Language Development: A Multidisciplinary Approach. New York and
Paris: Academic Press and Unesco Press.

In search of a dynamic theory of aphasia. In E. H. Lenneberg & E. Lenneberg (Eds.),
Foundations of Language Development: A Multidisciplinary Approach. New York and
Paris: Academic Press and Unesco Press.

1976   Problems in the comparative study of language. In R. B. Masterson, W. Hodos, &
H. Jerison (Eds.), *Evolution, Brain, and Behavior: Persistent Problems.* Hillsdale, New
Jersey: Lawrence Erlbaum Associates.

1977   Introduction to section on language acquisition. In F. Caplan (General Ed.), *Parenting
Advisor.* New York: Anchor Press/Doubleday.

1978   Some new prospects for neuropsychological research on disorders of perception and
language. In M. H. Appel (Ed.), *Topics in Cognitive Development* (Vol. 2): *Language
and Operational Thought.* New York: Plenum Press. (With L. Chapanis Fox.)

Author Index

Subject Index

A
B
C 8
D 9
E 0
F 1
G 2
H 3
I 4
J 5